BLUE SKY GOD

Blue Sky God is a passionate and inspiring call for us to understand the true message and example of Jesus in the contemporary world. With careful scholarship and flowing prose, Don MacGregor explains the insights of modern science and spirituality, and how they provide a new context for the healing and redemptive heart of Christian spirituality. With today's current interest in Eastern and indigenous religions, it is important that we also appreciate and bring home the true power and love of Jesus. Don MacGregor succeeds in this significant task. The Appendix with its reformulations of the Christian Healing Service and Holy Communion also make *Blue Sky God* a valuable asset. I warmly recommend this book.

William Bloom, author of *The Power of Modern Spirituality*

This is a fascinating and profound exploration of the deep resonances between the discoveries of the Christian Mystics and those of modern science. We are living in an era in which mystical and scientific proof are coming ever closer to open up for the human race a wholly new way of approaching reality and potentially solving the enormous problems that keeping science and religion apart have created. I salute the courage of this book and hope it will attain a large and enthusiastic audience.

Andrew Harvey, author of *The Hope: a Guide to Sacred Activism*, *Son of Man* and others

For many of us, the churches have seemed like the flat earth society, hanging on to old interpretations of institutional faith despite our contemporary knowledge and understanding. Now, from within the ranks of the priesthood, comes a breakthrough book that offers a synthesis of science and spirituality as an opening for orthodoxy to make a quantum shift. Don MacGregor offers scientific explanations of the intuitive knowing so many have had and challenges us to expand our consciousness towards a more comprehensive world view. At last, on our awakening journey and regardless of different sectarian backgrounds, we can know the 'Source' or 'God' as the compassionate consciousness in which we all reside and embrace "love as the evolutionary driver for connection in the universe". *Blue Sky God* is a must for everyone, both in theological colleges and the pews, the science labs and high street centers. We can meet together here in the unity of new understanding.

Janice Dolley, Development Director of the Wrekin Trust

This is a brave and important book, dispelling confusions and misunderstandings, and making clear the relevance of a Christian path today. Don MacGregor integrates modern science, mystical experience, history, philosophy and biblical scholarship in a new synthesis that shows how religious practice is evolving in the twenty-first century. I particularly enjoyed his discussions of the Holy Trinity and the Virgin Birth. As the old dogmas of science and materialism break down, he gives good grounds for hope.

Dr. Rupert Sheldrake, author of *A New Science of Life*, *The Science Delusion* and others

A refreshing and ground-breaking book that opens up new avenues of understanding between spirituality, science and religion by formulating the Divine as the Ground of Being as Compassionate Consciousness and the role of Jesus as an exemplar of one who transcended his Egoic Operating System and replaced it with a fully developed Heart Operating System – thus showing us the transformative way of love and wisdom and thereby changing the morphic field of humanity. Don's new versions of the confession and creed come across as contemporary while remaining authentic to the tradition. The book is a bold and necessary statement.

David Lorimer, Programme Director of The Scientific and Medical Network, President of the Wrekin Trust.

Blue Sky God is an elegant weaving of science, consciousness studies and classic Christian wisdom. It is a necessary breath of fresh air for our times. Allow it to shake you, awaken you and startle you with the realization that Christianity is indeed evolving and Don MacGregor is paving the way. I recommend it highly.

Leslie Hershberger, author of *Coming Home: An Integral Christian Practicum*

This book is testimony to the length of a journey, through teaching physics, the Green Movement, University Chaplaincy, parochial ministry and into contemplative prayer. The interface between religion and science is becoming a creative field in which Don MacGregor offers a way through some of the uncertainties that bewilder people. It is to be hoped that the author will now produce a study guide for the non scientist in the pews to help them see that quantum physics may offer an affirmation of what many have felt for centuries but not been able to articulate since the enlightenment told them to keep their superstitions to themselves. Is this why the Prologue to St John's Gospel still resonates so deeply for so many?

Revd Canon Jeremy Martineau, OBE

Blue Sky God

The Evolution of Science
and Christianity

Blue Sky God

The Evolution of Science
and Christianity

Don MacGregor

Winchester, UK
Washington, USA

First published by Circle Books, 2012
Circle Books is an imprint of John Hunt Publishing Ltd., Laurel House, Station Approach,
Alresford, Hants, SO24 9JH, UK
office1@jhpbooks.net
www.johnhuntpublishing.com
www.circle-books.com

For distributor details and how to order please visit the 'Ordering' section on our website.

Text copyright: Don MacGregor 2011

ISBN: 978 1 84694 937 1

A CIP catalogue record for this book is available from the British Library.

Design: Stuart Davies

The Scripture quotations contained herein are from the New Revised Standard Version Bible, copyright © 1989, by the Division of Christian Education of the National Council of the Churches of Christ in the U.S.A., and are used by permission. All rights reserved.

Printed and bound by CPI Group (UK) Ltd, Croydon, CR0 4YY

We operate a distinctive and ethical publishing philosophy in all areas of our business, from our global network of authors to production and worldwide distribution.

CONTENTS

Preface

Who Am I?

I am a Christian. But what do I mean by that? I mean that I am a follower of the teachings and example of Jesus the Christ. More than that, I am a seeker after truth – things have to make sense to me. Following the teachings of Christ has made sense to me as the best way to live. I sometimes ask myself, in reflection, 'Why am I a Christian?' It is a very healthy thing to do. Before I started following Christ seriously, I had looked into various other religions of the east: Hinduism, Buddhism and more esoteric teaching like Theosophy, plus all the Mind, Body Spirit stuff that you see in the bookshops. I was drawn, fascinated and inspired throughout the late 1970s. So if I've looked into all that, why am I a Christian? Because I believe and have come to experience that, in the teachings of Christ, there is a spiritual path worth following for growth and transformation. I am a questioner, I don't take things for granted, I don't have 'heroes,' and I'm open-minded about a lot of what the Church has tied down as Christian doctrine, or Christian 'truth'. It has been worked out over the years by all sorts of theologians, many of whom have had their own axe to grind at times. I suppose we all have our own axe to grind and this book is my offering.

For instance, Thomas Cranmer, Archbishop of Canterbury, almost single-handedly put together the Book of Common Prayer in the mid 1500s. Those writings have influenced our view of Christianity for four centuries. Beautifully polished phraseology it may be, but it contains views of Christianity that many would not agree with nowadays. The confession during Holy Communion contains *"We acknowledge and bewail our manifold sins and wickedness, which we, from time to time have most grievously committed...The remembrance of them is grievous unto us, the burden of them is intolerable."* At Morning and Evening prayer,

1

the plea to God is to *"have mercy on us miserable offenders,"* and more in the same vein. It has always seemed to me that either people were much more sinful and guilty in those days, or Cranmer was rather overzealous about it. Whilst it is true to say that there is 'manifold wickedness' in the world, it is a very negative viewpoint to be starting at every time we come to worship. That kind of 'woe is me' mentality, constantly whipping ourselves into paroxysms of guilt is not healthy for us, nor does it seem to be in line with belief in the God of love revealed by Jesus. 'Woe-is-me' Christianity held the Anglican Church in its thrall for four centuries, and we are only just beginning to escape from it through revision of the liturgies we use. I seek the truth, and in the teachings of Jesus, I find a God of love and a way of being, the kingdom way, that is the best way to live and grow. So I am a follower of Christ for that reason, and find freedom in casting off some of the expressions of Christianity that have arisen over the millennia that I do not find helpful.

How did I get there? I grew up in a middle-class household, secure and loving, with a Christian background, going to Sunday school until I was nine, but then not entering a church again until I was thirty. In secondary education, I took the scientific route, with an agnostic view of the world – there might be some force behind the universe, but it had nothing to do with me. I eventually became a science teacher in a secondary school in the Midlands, UK. Whilst teaching, personal circumstances brought me to the end of my self-reliance. My wife suffered a severe depressive episode over a period of four years, which faced me up with my own limited resources. Descended as I am from a line of stoic Scots, it took me a while to face the fact that this situation was beyond my ability to solve. I had tried everything I knew to help, in both medical and complementary therapies, all to no avail. This was new territory for me, taking me out of my reliable self into uncharted land. In this situation of desperation, I cried out "If there is a God, help!" And that was the awakening of my spirit.

Around that time, I read a book called *"The Secret Life of Plants,"*[1] which was all about how plants responded to their owners in measurable ways. Then I read *"The Findhorn Garden"*[2] about the founders of the Findhorn Community in Scotland, who grew enormous vegetables from next to nothing by loving their plants and communing with the plant spirits or 'devas'. This connected with my scientific mindset and led me to a broader interest in spiritual writings. Along with my wife, I spent a number of years searching and exploring various aspects of Hinduism, Buddhism, Theosophy and the teachings of Alice Bailey, which included daily meditation and praying the 'Great Invocation'[3]. I was a 'New Ager' in the late 1970s and early 80s. Through these teachings and meditation and numerous experiences, I came to a belief in God, although still in a very cerebral way. Something else had to happen to join my head to my heart, which I found in the experience of Christ.

I turned to Christianity aged thirty, and we joined a large, loving and active church in Leicester in 1983. I was still searching for something. Later that year, whilst on holiday in Pembrokeshire, Wales, I had a profound conversion experience of God's love, my heart was opened, and my path became that of a 'born-again' charismatic evangelical. During the following 7 years, I had numerous profound experiences of what was termed 'baptism in the Holy Spirit', but what I would now prefer to call 'an experience of oneness with the divine or unitive consciousness.' Evangelical terminology can be a help or a hindrance. The central spiritual reality of what occurred was what mattered. Although a recognizable Christian, I always knew, somewhere in my being, that my previous experience in and understanding of the New Age sphere was not wasted and would need to be integrated at some stage.

I felt the call to full-time ministry in the late eighties, trained as an Anglican priest in Nottingham from 1991-1993, and was a priest in a large evangelical middle-class church, then a small mid-Anglican Church. Following that, I was chaplain to a major UK university, and am now a priest in the Church in Wales for three traditional churches in Pembrokeshire. In the last fifteen years, I have been drawn to the silence of contemplative prayer and meditation, the wisdom of the mystics, and a more liberal and radical theology. During this time, I have been walking joyfully into a deeper understanding of the spiritual path, reading all sorts of other teachings outside of the church, ranging from quantum physics to metaphysics and the spiritual realms, and perceiving many connections between the two. My faith has become deeper, richer and wider in its embrace. This book is about those connections. Some of the mystics recognized this long ago:

> Everything that is in the heavens, in the earth, and under the earth is penetrated with connectedness, penetrated with relatedness.
>
> Hildegarde of Bingen (12th century mystic)

Lately, I have begun to recognize a movement in human consciousness taking place over the last fifty years. I am not alone in this perception – many traditions are currently aware of a global shift. It appears to be another evolutionary stage in the story of humanity, a quickening, beginning to move us from tribal behavior between peoples and nations to a place of compassion and recognition of our common humanity and unity. *Blue Sky God* is an attempt to join up some of the dots between Science and Christianity, both of which are evolving to a new understanding in their respective spheres.

My thanks go to Janice Dolley of the Wrekin Trust for her encouragement to get on with writing, to Revd Canon Jeremy Martineau, Revd John Henson and Elizabeth Daniels for their insightful comments on the text, to Nuri Wyeth for editorial assistance, and to my wife, Jayne, for her constant encouragement and patience, and her invaluable assistance in shaping the concepts and ideas in the text.

Don MacGregor

Introduction

Why does Christianity need to Evolve?

Our highest truths are but half truths;
Think not to settle down in any truth.
Make use of it as a tent in which to pass a summer's night,
But build no house of it, or it will be your tomb.
When you first have an inkling of its insufficiency
And begin to descry a dim counter-truth looming up beyond,
Then weep not, but give thanks:
It is the Lord's voice whispering,
'Take up thy bed and walk'.
　　　Earl Balfour[2]

Our contemporary theological task can win itself a new credibility and social relevance only through an intellectually responsible account of the Christian faith which meets the demands of the gospel and of the third millennium. We need this account for the journey into a period of world history that has been characterized as post-modern.
　　　Hans Kung[1]

Blue Sky God

I live in Pembrokeshire on the West Coast of Wales, surrounded by sea, where the color of the sky is an intense blue that can take my breath away at times. And it is huge – a vast vista of sky stretching out to Ireland and then across the Atlantic to North America. The enormous sky can neither be described adequately, nor confined. 'Blue Sky Thinking' is a term used to describe ideas from 'outside the box', ideas that are not limited by current thinking or beliefs. Blue Sky God is about that divine presence that can neither be defined nor confined. Humanity always comes up with some new thinking, some Blue Sky thinking about God when attempts at definition and containment seem to be breaking down. Now is such a time.

All things evolve in this world. It is a principle of life. Cultures and societies evolve as well, and the expressions of all religions change as societies change. There are many questions in today's society that are not addressed within traditional Christianity, and many issues that need to be looked at again in the light of discoveries and realizations within the last 150 years. In the Western world, huge numbers of people have walked away from the traditional, doctrinal, overarching story offered by the institutional Christian Church – and that is very sad as it actually has so much to offer if only it can escape from its straightjacket of doctrine and liturgy. A straightjacket holds a person rigidly, so that they cannot move, cannot harm themselves and can do no damage to others. That is exactly the rationale behind the institutional churches in their use of language, hymns and doctrine to define, limit and keep in order the belief of the people. It has, for the most part, not been intentional, but has arisen out of theological questions that were answered in the understanding prevalent in the early days of the Church. It has resulted in some creative and spiritually inspiring hymnody and liturgy.

However, much of the doctrine and liturgy has come from a worldview that has been superseded. We now know far more about the universe and its workings than we did when the New Testament was put together, or when the doctrine of the Church was worked out. Scientists have seen how the universe is still evolving, and has been for nearly 14 billion years, at the current estimate. Our understanding of the faith surely has to evolve as well, or we risk becoming another version of the Flat Earth Society, who state, *"Why do we say the Earth is flat, when the vast majority says otherwise? Because we know the truth."*[3] The Church

7

sometimes defends its doctrine like the Flat Earth Society, to the ridicule of those outside it.

Science and Christianity

Christianity has been shaken up and moved on many times by the revelations of scientific enquiry and discovery. The spherical nature of the earth was one of the first problems posed by scientific theory for Christian theology. The idea that there might be other human beings on a landmass, the antipodes, on the other side of the sphere upset the Pope. It was 'obvious' that there could not have been any form of transport from Europe to those regions, and therefore any people in the supposed 'antipodes' did not descend from Adam, and such belief denied the 'truth' of the story of creation. This revelation caused some consternation and threats of excommunication within the Church at the time – Bishop Vergilius of Salzburg (c. AD 700-784) was threatened in such a way by Pope Zachary at one stage. Vergilius was accused of teaching a doctrine of the 'rotundity of the earth', which was 'contrary to the Scriptures'. Pope Zachary's decision in this case was that

> If it shall be clearly established that he professes belief in another world and other people existing beneath the earth, or in *(another)* sun and moon there, thou art to hold a council, and deprive him of his sacerdotal rank, and expel him from the Church.[4]

But soon exploration of the earth overcame that and a new understanding of the continents moved theology on, with little real difficulty in adapting to the new world view.

Another major challenge came with the scientific insights of Nicolas Copernicus. In 1530 AD, he completed his treatise *De Revolutionibus*, which claimed that the sun was the center of the universe, and that the earth revolved around the sun. Fortunately for him, it was published shortly before his death in 1543[5], or his demise might have been of an altogether more painful form. The Roman Catholic Church placed it on their list of proscribed books, and he would probably have been tried for heresy and burnt had he still been alive. Giordano Bruno, an Italian Dominican friar, was not so fortunate. He was burnt at the stake in 1600 AD for similar beliefs, after a trial lasting seven years.[6] Soon, Galileo Galilei made his claim that the recent scientific invention, the telescope, proved Copernicus's theory to be correct. He was tried by the Inquisition, forced to recant his belief and put under house arrest for years until his death in 1642. The Church does not have a very good track record of coping with new scientific insights.

Later came Darwin and his theory of evolution, and there is a struggle that still continues for much Christian theology and liturgy to catch up with that, let alone the more recent discoveries and theories of relativity, quantum mechanics, and fields of energy. As our understanding of the nature of creation grows and evolves, so our understanding of theology and the nature of God has to change. Christianity has to evolve to be credible for every new generation as the worldview evolves.

Four Angles of Approach

I have approached this from four main angles. Firstly, science is also evolving. Recent emerging scientific theories about the nature of reality have challenged established theories of the cosmos and existing medical knowledge. Some of these discoveries and theories can be integrated with an updated and evolved Christian understanding. A major new paradigm emerging in physics is the Primacy of Consciousness. This assumes that consciousness is the ground of being, which has huge implications for our understanding of God, the role of humanity and prayer. This and other theories are introduced and reflected upon in Chapters 1-4, and lead to some radical views on the nature of God and Jesus the Christ.

Secondly, I believe our human-shaped, anthropomorphic view of God has to change. I have lived with the certainties of an evangelical faith and literalist Christianity and found it rigid and lacking in credibility. To my mind, it fails to take on board that we have moved on from a medieval, anthropomorphic mind-set where an all-powerful God intervenes. This interventionist God makes everything better for some, while others seem to be punished by a remorseless tyrant-God. I understand the arguments about God being with us in the suffering, but the main problem seems to be that we continue to hold to the idea that God intervenes in a very human way. One wit said, *"God created us in his own image – and then we returned the compliment!"* We need to move on from this way of thinking about the human-like God that we have created. As we have evolved in society and grown in awareness and understanding of the nature of the universe we live in, so we need to evolve in our understanding of religion, faith, and the nature of God. God may be unchanging, but our understanding of the nature of God is not – it is constantly evolving, maturing and growing.

Thirdly, as a result of some of the new science that is emerging, there are all sorts of possibilities for the individual human being that give hope for the human race. New generations are asking both old and new questions. Young people are often keen to know more about scientific views of reality, and how we can make this world a better place to be. They have searching questions about life – what's it about, what's it for, what am I for? Many are fascinated by the idea of the supernatural, or the undeveloped abilities they might have. A new world is coming, tantalizing and bursting with possibilities. We all seek to make sense of our existence, which is now so interconnected, so global, that a radical vision of reality is called for. What is life really about? How should I live mine? What possibilities are there if human beings were to attain their full potential? One of the particular questions for me has been "Was Jesus divine or just a human being who achieved his full potential? Is that what being divine is?"

Fourthly, I have long thought that healing is an area in which Christianity needs to listen to those involved in complementary therapies and the new science of more subtle energies, now often termed 'energy medicine'. Many of these therapies arose in a specific culture and context, but can now be released for the benefit of all humanity. Scientific theories are now emerging which place the power of intention at the center of any healing process, linked to an understanding of quantum physics and the nature of reality. Can we escape from skepticism, cynicism, suspicion and fear enough to embrace these, or at least to investigate them with open minds? Can a step be taken outside existing Christian doctrine and dogma to evaluate these theories and reshape some theology to fit the observed world around us?

Scientific Evolution
The scientific worldview is also changing, and the change is as huge as the one that flat earth believers had to make to adjust to the idea of a globe. It is as enormous as Copernicus's idea that the sun does not revolve around the earth, despite the seeming evidence of our eyes to the contrary. It started slowly with Darwin's theory of evolution, and then in the early twentieth century came Einstein and relativity, leaving Newtonian mechanics in its wake. It became more complicated but gradually picked up momentum with quantum physics and the realization that observations cause things to happen. It has hit 'warp speed' with the new science of epigenetics, which says that our thoughts, emotions and energy fields affect which of our genes are 'switched on' or not, and hence our behavior, our health and our spiritual life. Add to that the investigations into the nature of consciousness and the power of intention, and you have a heady brew.

But I am getting way ahead of myself. Part One of this book is not going to be a closely argued thesis, but an overview of some current theories that have an immediate bearing on our understanding of Christian theology. We have nearly all been taught some science at school, but for most of us, that science is probably out of date. Many basic scientific theories have moved on and give us a new, deeper view of reality. This new view is a challenge to be faced not just by the religious community, but by many in the the scientific community as well, and one that some find difficult to come to terms with. New scientific concepts challenge the worldview of the scientists as well as those holding religious views. Part Two of the book seeks to integrate the new science with theology, ending with some suggestions for the way ahead for Christianity.

The Guru's Cat

New scientific insights have much to say to Christianity, but there is also much resistance within the Church to anything that threatens to change the doctrine of the centuries, as enshrined in much liturgy and hymnody. There is a story about the Guru's cat that has something to say here:

When the guru sat down to worship each evening, the ashram cat would get in the way and distract the worshipers. So he ordered that the cat be tied up during evening worship. After the guru died, the cat continued to be tied up during every evening worship. And when the cat expired, another cat was brought to the ashram so that it could be duly tied up during evening worship.

Centuries later, learned treatises were written by the guru's scholarly disciples on the liturgical significance of tying up a cat while worship is performed.[7]

In the following chapters, the guru's cat will be addressed in various guises as new insights are considered in the light of existing Christian theology. All these considerations give us new ways of looking at the spiritual journey and evolving understandings of the physical reality. This is largely a book of possibilities, a book of questions and suggestions, a book in which I am trying to join things up. If I am trying to join things up, then there must be many others seeking to do the same. This book is an offering to them. Some of the suggested answers go beyond the accepted doctrine of the Church and may be seen by some as bordering on heresy, but it is essential to suggest new ways forward for a new world. This is not a fully worked out thesis, and I'm sure there will be many cries of "But what about...?" as it is read and challenges existing traditions, but we are in a time of change, a time to formulate new concepts of the Blue Sky God. The fine detail can come later – for now, these are some broad brushstrokes.

Christianity can only become the living truth for successive generations if thinkers constantly arise within it who, in the spirit of Jesus, make belief in him capable of intellectual apprehension in the thought-forms of the worldview proper to their time.
Albert Schweitzer[8]

Behold the turtle. He only makes progress when he sticks his neck out.
James Bryant Conant[9]

Part One

From Science to Sacred

The intuitive mind is a sacred gift and the rational mind is a faithful servant. We have created a society that honours the servant and has forgotten the gift.
Albert Einstein

Chapter 1

Quantum Reality and God as Consciousness

~

This first chapter sets out a central tenet of the book, that God is the consciousness, the Ground of Being, that sustains the material reality in which we live, stemming from the concept of consciousness in quantum physics. It goes on to outline some of the implications for the Christian understanding of God and humanity.

~

Frontier research into the nature of human consciousness has upended everything that we have hitherto considered scientific certainty about our world. These discoveries offer convincing evidence that all matter in the universe exists in a web of connection and constant influence, which often overrides many of the laws of the universe that we used to believe held absolute sovereignty.

Lynne McTaggart, The Intention Experiment[1]

Quantum Science and Consciousness

Science has cracked the atom, gone deep into the nature of reality at quantum levels, developed huge technological prowess, and has now come around to pondering on why we are able to ponder. Human beings are conscious, but just what is consciousness? In recent years, there has been a huge flowering of research into what consciousness really *is*, much of it stemming from the theory that it is consciousness, and not matter, which should be the starting point of an understanding of the universe. Fifty years ago, school pupils were told that the atom consisted of electrons whizzing like little planets around a central nucleus, made up of protons and neutrons, and that everything is made up of atoms. I taught exactly that as a science teacher in the 1980s, and I realized from listening to a radio program recently that this is still being taught. Conventional science takes the perspective that matter is the building block of all things and that life, mind and consciousness arise from these building blocks of matter as it becomes ever more complex. In the beginning, the conventional view says, atoms combined to form molecules, which reacted in ever more intricate ways until eventually organic life emerged, and gradually, over the eons, became increasingly complex. The brain developed to coordinate the living matter, and consciousness gradually emerged within that evolved brain. We are all very familiar with this conventional view; it is part of the backdrop to Western society.

However, a new way of looking at things has emerged in scientific thought – a new paradigm that has been around since the 1920s, but has taken a while to percolate down into everyday understanding. It has come from the world of quantum physics, a strange, unpredictable world where sub-atomic particles behave in ways that defy conventional science and thought. This new paradigm suggests that the prime mover in the universe is not matter, but consciousness. We are all a part of that consciousness, all interconnected at some level. Consciousness is what holds everything in being, and this consciousness works through energy fields. Everything actually consists of energy fields, not matter. However, we see it and feel it as matter – a table is hard, the ground is solid, my body is real to me. So what is meant by this new approach? The world of matter, substance, hard, solid 'stuff', arises from the collapse of quantum energy waves into quantum particles, brought about by the effect of *consciousness* on them. To get an idea of this, imagine walking into a room that is full of smoke that came originally from a piece of smouldering wood, now burnt up. The instant you see the smoke, it collapses back to recreate the piece of wood, like a film on rewind. This collapse of the smoke back into the wood is caused by you actually observing it. The smoke is like a quantum wave, filling all space, but as soon as we observe it, the wave collapses to become a particle. We *observe* things into being. This is a staggering theory, which has tremendous implications for our understanding of the metaphysical and spiritual world as well as the physical.

To delve a little deeper into this world of quantum mechanics, consider an electron, a tiny sub-atomic particle. Quantum theory says that this electron does not exist in one location, but only as an energy wave of possibilities, *until it is observed*. This is known as wave-particle duality, the realization that sub-atomic particles sometimes behave as if they are waves, and sometimes as if they are particles. A wave is a movement of energy within the medium that conducts it. Think of a wave in the ocean – the wave energy moves along whilst the ocean, the medium, only moves up and down. Electrons behave like a wave of energy in an ocean, describable by a mathematical model called a wave function. What brings about the hard reality of an electron particle from all the potential, possible locations as a wave function is *being observed*. To give another analogy, it is a little like rain forming from water vapor in the air. Water vapor is invisible and is everywhere, but when the conditions are right, it condenses into visible, individual droplets, which we see as clouds. Similarly, when the conditions are right, energy waves become individual particles that we could see and feel if we could experience that tiny level of reality. To quote from physics professor, Amit Goswami:

Before observation, the electron does spread all over space, but only as a wave of possibility. Observation brings about the collapse of the possibility wave into an actual event.[2]

Put very basically, we see things into material existence! Physicists say that sub-atomic particles are *observed* into material existence. In order for an energy wave to collapse and become a particle, it has to be observed, it has to be perceived by some form of consciousness. This theory that consciousness brings things into being has brought about a turn-around in some scientific thought, although it has taken about eighty years to percolate down from academia. Previously, what is called 'upward causation' was the way things were understood – elementary particles make atoms, atoms make molecules, molecules make cells, cells specialize to make the brain, and the brain gives rise to consciousness. However, a basic question arises from this, which was avoided for years: how can conscious observation cause the collapse of these possibility waves into actual particles, if consciousness only arises *after* the material world has evolved to the stage of conscious beings? It is putting the cart before the horse! Basically, the quantum insight says that if there is no consciousness in the beginning, then particles would never have come into existence and the material world that we live in and are part of would not exist. We could express this as thought bringing things into being, or even "mind makes matter." This gives an immediate resonance with the first chapter of Genesis: *"Then God said, "Let there be light"; and there was light."* (Genesis 1:3) God visualized and creation came into being; we exist because of the creative mind of God, operating according to quantum mechanics.

The Primacy of Consciousness

In this new understanding, consciousness is the starting point, the primal state, and 'downward causation' happens as consciousness brings about material reality by 'choosing' from the range of possibilities offered in the energy wave. Put simply, the universe does not seem to exist without a perceiver of that universe. As an analogy, consider a laptop computer. It contains immense possibilities and potential; it can show beautiful pictures, play gorgeous music, display the most elegant prose, perform enormous calculations, but until the consciousness of a person acts on it, nothing appears at all. In the same way, energetic possibility waves exist in the universe, with all the potential to form material particles – electrons, protons, atoms, molecules – but until consciousness acts on them, nothing will come into material being. Consciousness is the underlying reality of everything, the matrix in which everything is held. Nobel Award winning physicist, Max Planck, said as much on accepting the award for his study of the atom:

> As a man who has devoted his whole life to the most clear-headed science, to the study of matter, I can tell you, as the result of my research about atoms, this much: "There is no matter as such!" All matter originates and exists only by virtue of a force that brings the particles of an atom to vibration and holds the most minute solar system of the atom together.... We must assume behind this force the existence of a conscious and intelligent mind. This mind is the matrix of all matter.[3]

Consciousness is then no longer seen as a phenomenon of the brain, but as a divine matrix, the ground of being, in which all material possibilities are held in potential, as Amit Goswami states:

> Consciousness can collapse material possibilities because it transcends the material universe; it is beyond the jurisdiction of quantum mechanics. All possibilities are within consciousness.[4]

Ground of Being and Consciousness

The 'Ground of Being' is a term that has been used for many years as a description of the divine. The theologian Paul Tillich was the first to coin the phrase, and it was later popularized by Bishop John Robinson in his controversial book *"Honest to God."* As individuals, we all think and feel as separate entities, we all seem to have our own separate consciousness, our self-consciousness. This immediately gives us a problem in understanding the notion that consciousness brings material reality into being. Surely we each possess an individual consciousness – I am me and you are you. At a very basic level, the obvious question arises, how can two separate 'consciousnesses' bring about material reality without conflict? If two individuals are simultaneously observing the same situation, surely there will be some difference in the way they perceive it or want it to be, and there will be some conflict between their 'consciousnesses'? So what decides how the world will look? The answer to that from the physicists is that there are actually no individual, separate consciousnesses; there is only one consciousness, of which we are all a part. There is only one vast field of consciousness in which the universe exists, which holds it, and us, in being. Consciousness is all one.

Another analogy may help – a glass of water is but a part of the water present on the planet. It has been part of the oceans, it has been vapor in the air, clouds in the sky, rainfall to the ground, water in the streams and rivers. It is part of the water of the earth. It is only a glassful of water, contained and still, but of the same essence as all the water of the planet. Released from the glass, it will again become part of the ocean or the air, or the clouds. It is all one water, there is no such thing as *a* water. So it is with consciousness – there is only one, as Goswami indicates:

> You and I have individual thoughts, feelings, dreams, etc., but we don't have consciousness, let alone separate ones; we are consciousness. And it is the same consciousness for all of us… Consciousness is the ground of being; we cannot turn it off.[5]

This theory of downward causation, that all things stem from consciousness, is still disputed amongst scientists, yet it is gaining ground as it gives explanations for all sorts of paranormal and psychological phenomena which have been observed and recorded, but which do not fit with the traditional notions of the material universe. An attempt to bring it to media attention was made in the film *"What the Bleep do we Know,"*[6] which has gained almost a cult following with its own website, newsletter and worldwide media attention, despite much criticism. Ervin Laszlo, systems theorist and Nobel prize nominee, has written of his optimism for the future based on the idea that human consciousness is evolving:

> Consciousness evolution is from the ego-bound to the transpersonal form. If this is so, it is a source of great hope. Transpersonal consciousness is open to more of the infor-mation that reaches our brains than the consciousness still dominant today. This could have momentous consequences. It could produce greater empathy among people, and greater sensitivity to animals, plants and the whole biosphere. It could create a subtle contact with the rest of the cosmos. When a critical mass of humans evolve to the transpersonal level of consciousness a higher civilization is likely to emerge, with deeper solidarity and a higher sense of justice and responsi-bility.[7]

We can see the seeds of this higher level of transpersonal consciousness in our world today. Globalization has brought an awareness of the problems faced by humanity all around the world. Ecological issues facing the whole world have come to the forefront of the political agendas. No longer are we simply caught up in the problems of our own nation. Many people today are still stuck in the tribal mentality that says 'These are my people, this is my club, this is my country, we are in and you are out'. Tribal mentality defines borders and barriers to say who is in and who is out. It is the root of all war. For thousands of years, wars have been fought because of tribal mentality, because we cannot find a way to live in harmony with each other – or maybe because we have chosen to ignore the way to live in harmony and peace with each other. The evolution of consciousness to a transpersonal level is beginning to plant seeds of hope for a new way. We have gone global, and we know what it is like for people living in all sorts of places in the world. It opens our hearts and awareness to other people in places that we knew nothing about in previous generations. It paves the way for our 'tribe' to grow to be not just our town, not just our nation, not just our part of the world, but to embrace the whole world and work towards ways of achieving lasting peace, ways of bringing justice to the oppressed, and ways of making this world sustainable for the future. I believe that tribalism is slowly becoming globalism as we become more aware of our oneness in consciousness – and that is our hope for the future. If human awareness can come from a compassionate center that sees all humanity as one, then the human race can move from tribal competitiveness to global cooperation and begin to live in harmony and peace with one another and all of creation. A dream it may be, but some dreams become reality – "mind makes matter."

Consciousness & Christianity

The concept of God as the Ground of Being speaks into the whole realm of spirituality, across all religions. The mystical experience of oneness, or unitive consciousness, is common to all faiths. Jesus used his own shorthand for this, talking about the kingdom of God, a new way of being. This was the good news he came to proclaim, that the kingdom of God was near.

Jesus came to Galilee, proclaiming the good news of God, and saying, "The time is fulfilled, and the kingdom of God has come near; repent, and believe in the good news." (Mark 1:14-15)

A more evolved civilization, living in transpersonal consciousness with greater empathy, understanding and compassion, sounds like Jesus' vision of the kingdom of God (more on this in Chapter 6). Consciousness as the 'Ground of Being' is effectively another way of talking about God. The Christian understanding is that God holds everything in being, is infinitely creative, and sustains all. We can read of this in the New Testament, referring to the Christ, or Logos (word) of God

In the beginning was the Word, and the Word was with God, and the Word was God. He was in the beginning with God. All things came into being through him, and without him not one thing came into being. (John 1:1-3a)

All things were created by him and for him. He is before all things, and in him all things hold together. (Colossians 1:16-17)

The Son is the radiance of God's glory and the exact representation of his being, sustaining all things by his powerful word. (Hebrews 1:3)

This theological concept that God sustains all things in being dovetails neatly with the idea emerging from physics that consciousness is the ground of being. (Most physicists would not see that ground of being as deity or sentient, hence I do not capitalize it here.) We can think of God as the immense consciousness which holds the universe in being, which is called the Godhead in Christianity, or Yahweh in Judaism (the "I AM" – see Chapter 5 for further comment on this name for God), or the Tao in Taoism. This is God as the creative principle, bringing the universe into existence and sustaining it by the Word, which is God's energy poured out through his consciousness.

Where does that leave us as individuals? As the Bible puts it, we are the temple of the Holy Spirit, or the Holy Breath. God breathes us into existence, through, of course, a process of evolution. In every human being there is a spark or awareness of God's consciousness, the God within that *is* us, because we only exist within that consciousness – it sustains us in being. Without the Ground of Being, there is no being to be had! It could be said, and has been said by many, that we are part of God. However, we as individuals cannot fathom the limitlessness of the consciousness that sustains the whole of creation in being, that works through all sentient beings, and even all matter, throughout the universe. In that sense, we are not God. So we have a paradox – we are both God and not God. Like the individual quantum particles that seem to also exist as a wave throughout spacel, we are both part of the wave field of God-consciousness, yet we are also individual beings – a quantum paradox!

The paradox can be approached in this way: as conscious beings, our consciousness is a part of the divine consciousness of the universe. Opening ourselves up to the realm of God-consciousness happens through religious experience, meditation, contemplative prayer, mystical experience, and at moments of heightened reality. In these experiences, our own individual ego-selves fall away and we become aware of the sea of God-consciousness of which we are a miniscule drop. It is the mystical experience is of being one with all, being united, an interconnected whole, the "I am" within the "I AM." Anyone who has read mystical spiritual literature of all faiths, or has personally had a mystical experience of union with God will see all this as already known and accepted. However, the difference in the 21st century is that science is now beginning to come to agreement with the viewpoint that has been held by the mystics for millennia, in the theory of the primacy of consciousness.

Recent well-founded scientific experiments have gone even further to show that it is not just sub-atomic particles that can be influenced by focused consciousness, but that atoms and molecules, the building blocks of matter, actually behave in the same way – they don't exist as matter until consciousness impinges on them. In the famous 'double-slit' experiment[8], it has been shown that not just tiny electrons, but large molecules behave as if they are waves of possibility, not particles.[9] This is an enormous jump from the subatomic level, far too small to be seen, to matter large enough to show up on an electron micro-scope – still tiny, but visible with electronic help. All scientific theories are just that, theories, until experimental evidence either proves or disproves them. It was considered that quantum particles might behave in these strange ways, but not anything larger. But now the quantum world is shown to exist in real, measurable ways and cannot just be dismissed as a 'quantum quirk' in the realm of the subatomic.

Other experiments have shown how the power of focused consciousness can influence random event generators. These are the computerized equivalent of tossing a coin – the result can be 'heads', or 'tails'. Statistically, it should work out at fifty percent of each. The studies ask people to try to influence the outcome so that, for example, more 'heads' come up. Over two and a half million trials have shown that human intention can influence these electronic devices, and results have been replicated independently by 68 investigators[10]. Other experiments have involved attempts to influence the throwing of dice. Numbers on the dice should normally come up an equal number of times, but it was found that human intention could affect the normal result that would be expected by chance alone. In 73 studies, involving 2500 people and more than two and a half million throws, the odds of the results occurring by chance were calculated to be 10^{76} to one (10^{76} is 1 followed by 76 zeroes)[11]. Consciousness and conscious intent seems to be an active, powerful thing – now proven scientifically[12].

Another aspect of this quirky quantum world is the discovery that quantum particles have a strange connection with each other. Once they have interacted with each other, they are then able to influence one another instantaneously across vast distances, in a way that is outside our current understanding of space and time. Experiments have shown that this happens, but without a full understanding of how it can happen, leading to the conclusion that these 'correlated', or 'entangled' quantum particles must be interconnected in some domain that transcends space and time, maybe the domain of consciousness. These are called "non-local connections." What this really says is that the nature of reality is only beginning to be understood, and there is a long way for science to go to reach anything like a full picture. The idea of non-local connections, outside of accepted understanding of space-time, opens up all sorts of possibilities for explanation of recognized human phenomena. Whilst the experiments are talking about tiny quantum particles, we should not lose sight of the fact that this is what we are made of. The quantum particles interact with each other when we form relationships with each other – maybe non-local connections could be the explanation for phenomena such as awareness of things happening to loved ones in other places, premonitions, telepathy, etc.

Consciousness and the Holy Trinity

The potential overlap between this theory of downward causality from consciousness and our spiritual understanding is immense. One of the difficulties for many people with the Christian tradition is its anthropomorphic or *person-like* view of God. Gregory of Nyssa (circa AD335 – after 384), one of the early Church Fathers, appreciated how impossible it is for our minds to understand the nature of God.

Every concept formed by the intellect in an attempt to comprehend and circumscribe the divine nature can succeed only in fashioning an idol, not in making God known.[13]

God is talked about as the Father, Son and Holy Spirit, and the Holy Trinity is seen as the three persons of the one God. The early theologian responsible for the development of the Trinitarian terminology is Tertullian. He invented many new Latin words in his writing, one of which was *Trinitas*, the Trinity, formed of three *persona*, which has invariably been translated into English as 'person'. In the Latin, it literally means 'a mask', as worn by actors in a Roman drama. The actors wore different masks so that the audience knew which character they were playing, as one actor may have played more than one character. So the term *persona* came to mean 'the role that someone is playing'. Professor Alister McGrath, author of *Christian Theology: An Introduction* and many other books, explains what this means for the Holy Trinity:

It is quite possible that Tertullian wanted his readers to understand the idea of "one substance, three persons" to mean that the one God played three distinct yet related roles in the great drama of human redemption. Behind the plurality of roles lay a single actor. The complexity of the process of creation and redemption did not imply that there were many gods; simply that there was one God, who acted in a multiplicity of manners... Substance is what the three persons of the Trinity have in common.[14]

So Father, Son and Holy Spirit are of the *substance* of God, aspects of the one substance, metaphors which are very helpful to many in their understanding of God, but which can evolve into a deeper understanding. Unfortunately, they are often taken as literal truth. We do not take other metaphors as literal. 'The Lord is my rock' is a metaphor often used in the Old Testament of the

Bible. It tells us that God is solid, unmovable, a solid base for life. It does not say that God is grey, with sparkly bits in, sticking out of the ground. We know which aspects of the metaphor are truth, which qualities of rock are being referred to. God as the Holy Trinity is also a metaphor that has been very helpful as Christianity has evolved and grown in its theology. We should know which bits of the metaphor are truth, but the Church has had a tendency to become more and more literal in its interpretation of this metaphor, to the extent that it has become a stumbling block for many, with God literally seen as a father, existing in that human form in 'heaven', even sitting on a white cloud with his flowing beard.

However, if we take the model of consciousness as the ultimate reality of God, then we can expand the traditional model of the Holy Trinity, without denying it as a metaphor. Professor John Macquarrie, in his *Principles of Christian Theology*, describes the Trinity in terms of his understanding of God as 'Being', which is a similar concept to thinking of God as consciousness, as in this book. The Father is understood to be *Primordial Being*, the source of all that is and all that has the potential to be. The Son is *Expressive Being*, the way in which the Primordial Being expresses itself in the world. The energy of Primordial Being pours itself out through Expressive Being. The Holy Spirit is *Unitive Being*, which seeks to restore and strengthen unity between the Primordial Being and the world of 'beings', leading back to a richer unity with Being. We can translate this into the terms used in this book:

- The Father is the compassionate consciousness that holds everything in being, like Macquarrie's Primordial Being.
- The Son is the Christ expression, manifesting in the human being who has awakened to the stage of unitive consciousness. Jesus was the prime example of the Expressive Being worked out in human form

- The Holy Spirit is the driving evolutionary force of love that draws everything back into relationship with the Father, the Unitive Being.

The doctrine of the Trinity shows how we struggle greatly with words and language to describe the divine. No words can really do justice to the Source of all. An early Church father, John Climacus (7th century), put it like this:

God is love. Whoever sought to define him would be like a blind man trying to count the grains of sand on the sea shore.[15]

Using words like compassion and feelings imply personhood, but it is not that God is person-like, it is that we are God-like, in that we are part of the consciousness of God and therefore have some of the attributes of God. We are held in being by the presence of God's consciousness within us, which has compassion as the motivating force. We are brought into being by that consciousness, and are therefore, in our deepest nature, God-like, with an impulse towards compassion, because we are conscious beings. The story of humanity is one of slow progress towards a compassionate way of living, growing slowly in compassionate consciousness. God is the total consciousness, awareness, and reality, in which everything has its being. This Ground of Being is creative, compassionate consciousness, willing everything into being and holding it there.

Many authors have dealt with this sort of subject matter. I am reminded of the film, 'The Never-Ending Story', based on Michael Ende's book, in which 'Fantasia' is willed into existence by the reader. But the fantasy world is falling apart because the young reader holds it all together by his thoughts, and he does not believe he has the power to create the story. Eventually, the plaintive cry of the princess is heard as she clings to the last vestiges of the world, "Bastian, what is my name?" The young reader, Bastian, realizes in amazement that he is part of the story, gives her a new name and then starts recreating Fantasia by his thoughts. There are similar ideas in the 'The Matrix' film trilogy. In this case, reality as experienced by humans is the Matrix, generated by a computer mind, and the people in the generated world have the capacity to see through the illusion to the real state of things. The first person to do this is called 'the One', with allusions to Christ Jesus as the first to break through from our own world to the real nature of reality. Unfortunately, in 'The Matrix' the real state of things is not very pleasant, a battlefield between man and machine!

Evolving Christianity

Bishop John Spong of the Episcopal Church in the USA has summarized his view of the God who holds all and is Being, which ties in well with the idea of God as compassionate consciousness:

> This God is not a supernatural entity who rides into time and space to rescue the distressed. This God is the source of life, the source of love, the Ground of Being. The theistic God of yesterday is a symbol for the essence, the being of life which we share.[16]

So an evolving, emerging view within Christianity is that God is ultimate, unitive compassionate consciousness, in which we and the whole universe exist. As we have seen, quantum physics now tells us that we only exist as matter because of consciousness. Our physical beings are made, formed, and developed in God's image, not in physical resemblance but to be *conscious* beings. More than that, we have evolved to be self-conscious and thereby have the capacity to become aware of God-consciousness. Maybe that is really what the story of Adam and Eve and the Fall[17] is all about. The Garden of Eden is the Ground of Being in which we all exist, and in its center is the Tree of Life and the Tree of the Knowledge of Good and Evil. Eating the fruit of the Tree of Knowledge of Good and Evil can be seen as a metaphor for becoming self-conscious beings. Prior to being self-conscious, we were like the animals and all other life, held in God-consciousness in a state of innocence. Adam and Eve existed in this blissful state with God, until they ate of the Tree of Knowledge of Good and Evil – then they became aware that they were naked, put on the fig leaves and hid from God, and were cast out of the garden of Eden.

One way to view this is that it is the story of every person as we leave childhood behind and go through adolescence, becoming aware of the damage we can inflict through our powers and choices and freedoms, and as we move into adulthood, hopefully becoming self-aware and responsible beings. However, we can also think of it as a time in human evolution when our brains developed to the stage where we became self-aware, we began to see ourselves in a different light, we became self-conscious. At that stage in our evolution, we became aware of ourselves as individuals, separate from God, no longer held in a blissful state of innocence. Becoming self-aware changes us. As individuality took hold, so our egos started to develop, and we began to lose our awareness of God's presence in us. We perceive ourselves as being individual entities. We have then lost our awareness of being *in* God. The growth of ego has given rise to wanting things for ourselves, to greed, to envy, and the roots of all that is wrong with our world. The spiritual journey is about finding our way back into the presence of God, back to Eden. But it only happens as we let go of our ego and surrender to God. Our spiritual journey is to come back to identity with the consciousness of God. The journey is common to all religions, to come back to oneness with God. Olivier Clément sees a similar strand in the writings of the early Church Fathers:

The account of the 'fall' in Genesis is given by several (early Church) Fathers a very profound interpretation... The 'tree of life' was the tree of contemplation, the possibility of knowing the world in God. Adam and Eve would not have been able to approach it except after a long preparation; if they had gone there in a state of childish innocence, or in an attitude of egocentric greed, wanting to plunder the world instead of reverencing it and offering it to God, they would have been burnt by the brilliance of the godhead. They needed to mature, to grow to awareness by willing detachment and by faith, a loving trust in a personal God. ... They wish to 'take possession of the things of God without God'. And God keeps them away from the tree of life to avoid their being defiled whilst in a state of falsehood and 'self-idolatry'.[18]

We see the same story retold in the parable of the prodigal son.[19] We can take the son to represent humanity, and the father to represent the God-consciousness in which we are held. The son takes the father's riches and goes off on his own, which is the evolution of the state of self-awareness and ego and the separation out from God. Eventually, as everything goes wrong, he realizes that he cannot survive without the father – and then he is welcomed back into the father's home with loving arms. We let go of, or move beyond our ego, our separateness, and we are welcomed back into God-consciousness. In traditional Christian terms it would be called surrendering to the grace of God. This is the meaning of some of the enigmatic phrases Jesus used. Here we consider two of them:

> Then Jesus told his disciples, "If any want to become my followers, let them deny themselves and take up their cross and follow me." (Matthew 16:24)

Denying ourselves in this context is not psychological

suppression or repression but it means not giving attention to the ego, the part of self that is simply our experience of separateness from God. Denying the ego, or transcending the selfish nature, is hard, it is a cross to bear, to be picked up. So the meaning becomes "let go of your ego and pick up the cross of surrender – let go and follow the Christ."

Those who find their life will lose it, and those who lose their life for my sake will find it. (Matthew 10:39)

On the surface, this is very difficult to understand. However, we can paraphrase it to "Those who find life in their ego alone will lose the divine, but those who let go of their ego life will find divine life." It now begins to make much sense.

Consciousness, by its very godly nature, leads to a capacity for compassion and caring, and has different levels of awareness or vibration. At an instinctive level, compassion and caring is expressed between parents and offspring in the bonding within families. This enables the next generation to be nurtured, but, as mentioned earlier, the higher the consciousness, the more compassion spreads out to include others. At an animal level, the compassionate consciousness includes the family group, the pack, but then in humanity, greater awareness includes the neighborhood, the village and tribe, then the nation – until at higher levels of consciousness, compassion embraces all that there is; universal love wants the best for everything and cares deeply about the interconnectedness of everything. Consciousness is the presence of God among us, and in us. We cannot define it but we, by definition, are aware of it – we are conscious beings.

We might then ask where evil comes from in the world if all is held in divine compassionate consciousness. How is it that some humans appear to be deliberately evil and commit what can only be called evil acts? Without getting too diverted into the problem of good and evil, we can see that this bears on the whole issue of sin, or human beings expressing their free will and going their own way. One of the risks of having free will is that the individualized, self-conscious being can take decisions independently of the divine consciousness that sustains it. Until that individualized consciousness comes back to the state of oneness, of unitive consciousness, there is always the risk of evil, but the evolutionary driving force of love is gradually moving the human race on to more developed stages of consciousness.

To take this even further, it means that all matter exists in God's consciousness, and hence has some elementary consciousness. Experiments have shown that plants share in consciousness to some degree and will react to other plants being mistreated.[20] On a larger scale, in recent years we have realized the intricate and complicated nature of the biosphere in which we live and the interconnectedness of everything on earth. This leads to theories that maybe even planets share in consciousness, of a different order from humanity, presumably accessing a different aspect of the immense consciousness of God. Much has been written about James Lovelock's Gaia hypothesis, which says that the biosphere acts like a living organism, in that it has self-regulating mechanisms similar to those in organic, living beings. What if there is more to it than that and the earth itself has a form of consciousness? Its consciousness would not be of the same order as ours but, in order for it to exist, it must still be part of the consciousness of God.

There are many esoteric writings putting forward the view that every material thing shares in consciousness of sorts, and that even planets have particular beings in the spiritual realms that are the spiritual counterpart to their physical existence. This is the cosmic view held by Theosophists such as Helena Blavatsky and Alice Bailey, and more recently William Meader. This has been very influential in the formation of some of the philosophies and beliefs in the melting pot of what was known as 'New Age' teachings, but now come under the banner of contemporary or holistic spirituality. There are complicated cosmologies containing hierarchies of spiritual beings, ascended masters and levels of the ascension of the spirit. Whilst it is a natural progression from realizing that the compassionate consciousness of God holds all material existence in being, to saying that everything has some degree of consciousness, which sustains its existence, it can be a diversion from the real process of transformation in our realm of existence to get caught up in too much speculation about other realms. God's consciousness pervades all, is in all, sustains all in being. It is the Ground of Being, and all manifest reality shines forth from the divine Source. The Wisdom tradition of Christianity, upheld by many of the mystics through the ages, takes this path, and Cynthia Bourgeault, an Episcopalian priest and Wisdom teacher, encapsulates it.

> As we begin orienting ourselves on the Wisdom road map, it is with the recognition that our manifest universe is not simply an "object" created by a wholly other God out of the effluence of his love, but *is that love itself*, made manifest in the only possible way it can, in the dimensions of energy and form. The created realm is not an artifact but an instrument through which the divine life becomes perceptible to itself. It's the way the score gets transformed into the music.[21]

Co-Creators

The understanding that humanity exists as part of God's consciousness can be applied in other areas of theology and practice as well. Prayer can be seen as the power of focused consciousness, or intention, in which we raise our level of awareness to the consciousness of God and hence influence what is to become from all the potential possibilities. We become co-creators with God by helping to bring material possibilities into existence (more on this in Chapter 2). We create because we have consciousness, which is spiritual energy, God-stuff. We create by a process of awareness, focusing this spiritual energy through the images that we allow our conscious attention to dwell upon. St Paul seemed to recognize this, and wrote to the Philippian Church urging them to focus their attention on healthy virtues:

> Finally, beloved, whatever is true, whatever is honorable, whatever is just, whatever is pure, whatever is pleasing, whatever is commendable, if there is any excellence and if there is anything worthy of praise, think about these things. (Philippians 4:8)

In other words, if we think pure and noble thoughts, wanting the best for others, then the pure spiritual energy, the consciousness of God, builds the form of the images that we hold in our minds, collectively. Therefore, we are constantly co-creating. The other side of the coin is that we create in negative terms as well. If our thoughts are hateful, or self-loathing, then we are building negative energy into creation. However, if we are becoming God-conscious, then we will be building in line with the compassionate consciousness of God, contributing to the outworking of God's intent for his creation. Our prayers will be focused intention that contributes to the spiritual and physical whole. As our God-consciousness grows, so we become more able to contribute to change by that prayer and focused intention. An evolved understanding of the nature of Jesus is that he reached the ultimate stage of the merging of human and divine, able to heal, to change the world of form and matter, so that his individual life affected everyone around him, through his oneness with God. He fulfilled the full potential of a human being to be one with God. (What this did for humanity is discussed in Chapter 3 in a section on *morphic resonance*.) The exciting thing is that this is the potential for every one of us! Dawson Church, in his book *'The Genie in Your Genes'*, sums it up:

We now realize that consciousness underlies and organizes matter, and not the other way around. We have discovered that changes in consciousness precipitate changes in matter. We have realized that consciousness is primary, and matter secondary. The changes in our bodies produced by consciousness reveal the most potent tool for healing we have ever discovered. To a culture accustomed to looking for solutions 'out there', it seems inconceivable that the answers might lie within.

An ancient Sufi story tells of the angels convening at the dawn of time to discuss where to bury the meaning of life, a secret so sacred that only the most worthy of initiates should be allowed to access it.

"We should put it at the bottom of the ocean," one exclaims.

"No, the highest mountain peak," argues another.

Eventually the wisest angel speaks up: "There is one place no-one will look. We can hide it in plain sight: in the center of the human heart."[22]

From the Christian tradition, we have the story of the expulsion of Adam and Eve from the Garden of Eden, because they have eaten from the tree of knowledge of good and evil, and have become self-aware. But there is another secret in the garden – the fruit of the tree of life at the center of the garden.

Then the LORD God said, "See, the man has become like one of us, knowing good and evil; and now, he might reach out his hand and take also from the tree of life, and eat, and live forever" – therefore the LORD God sent him forth from the garden of Eden, to till the ground from which he was taken. (Genesis 3:22-23)

Continuing the interpretation of the story as an allegory of human consciousness, the tree of life is to be found when we return to the garden of the consciousness of God within us, in surrender of our individual ego-nature. When we let go of the ego and enter the state of unitive consciousness, of oneness with the divine, we become aware of the true interconnected nature of life and reality. We discover the tree of life. As the Sufi story said, the meaning of life is hidden in the center of the human heart.

The key to the relationship between science and spirituality lies in an understanding of consciousness from both a scientific and spiritual perspective, not as opposites, but as different lenses into the nature of the same ultimate reality. This theme of God as compassionate consciousness runs through the rest of this book as its implications are worked out in various areas of Christian thought and theology.

Chapter 2

Epigenetics, Healing and Prayer

~

In this chapter, we consider the way in which energy fields affect our body processes and the new area of epigenetics, which is to do with how our minds affect the genetics of our body cells. This opens many insights into the healing process and the way in which prayer and intention works.

~

"The cure of many diseases is unknown to the physicians of Hellas, because they are ignorant of the whole which ought to be studied also: for the part can never be whole unless the whole is well."
Plato, 2500 yrs ago

"Miracles do not happen in contradiction to nature, but only in contradiction to that which is known in nature."
St Augustine, 1600 years ago

Biology and Energy Fields

It is not just physics and quantum theory that have something to say to religious thought. In the biological sciences, there are also fascinating new insights, which have radical implications for the healing of mind, body and emotions. Certain areas of scientific exploration are beginning to draw conclusions about energy that biological science is only just beginning to take on board. Each of us emits energy at a certain wavelength, and different parts of our body emit different levels of energy. It has been shown that healthy tissue emits energy differently from diseased tissue[1]. When you go for an MRI (Magnetic Resonance Imaging) scan, it is this energy that these machines pick up. Medics find them a tremendous new diagnostic tool.

> Though conventional medicine has not focused on the role energy plays as 'information' in biological systems, ironically, it has embraced non-invasive scanning technologies, which read such energy fields... Physicians are able to diagnose internal problems by differentiating the spectral energy character of healthy and diseased tissue in the scanned images.[2]

However, the medical world is only just beginning to make the link between this energy that can now be detected with the new technology, and how we can be healed. Energy has been linked with healing for eons in a whole variety of psycho-spiritual practices to be found in most ancient societies. The assertion I make is that Jesus intuitively knew the link 2000 years ago, and was able to raise his vibrational energy levels to bring healing to those around him. Biologists are beginning to see that our bodily functioning is determined by information fields of energy that govern the workings of the different parts of our bodies. Basic questions, such as how do the simple cells of an embryo know to start to differentiate into a muscle, skin or liver cell, can be resolved by the theory that there are information fields that guide those cells to develop into the shape of the body. Fields are the formative principle behind the material reality. If those energy fields can be affected, then maybe healing can come from another person having a higher level of energy, a more wholesome vibration. We can affect each other by the energetic field that we generate. The way in which this works is thought to harness the power of human intention, i.e., thought patterns

directed with strong feeling. This has the capacity to revolutionize medical practice in future years.

In 1997, two researchers, William Braud and Marilyn Schlitz,
did an analysis of all the experiments they could find that had
investigated the effect of intention on other living things. Their
study revealed that research had taken place all over the world
into the way that human intention could affect bacteria, yeast,
plants, ants, chicks, mice, rats, cats, dogs, human cellular prepa-
rations and enzyme activity. In addition, they found evidence to
show that humans could successfully affect various physiological
functions of other human beings, such as eye and motor
movements, breathing and even brain rhythms. Furthermore,
these small but consistent results were not obtained from trained
subjects but from ordinary people doing this for the first time.
Schlitz and Braud showed, by statistical analysis of all the results,
that these experiments had a success rate of 37 percent, far
exceeding any chance effect, estimated at 5 percent.[3] It was
becoming apparent that intentional thought had the ability to
influence other living things at all sorts of levels.

Another possibility was suggested by these studies – that the
expectations of people involved affected the results. If people
believed that everything was interconnected and that there was a
way their thoughts could affect other living things, then they
were more likely to succeed. The more it mattered to the person,
the greater likelihood that their thoughts would be of effect, and
the greatest effects were observed when it was another person to
be influenced, and the person really needed it. The flip side to
that was that if good thoughts could affect living things, then
what about bad thoughts? Can negative thoughts bring physical
effects? There are many stories about the effect of voodoo and
curses. Braud did some preliminary studies that showed that it
was possible to visualize a protective shield that would prevent
the penetration of a malign influence.[4] This type of research has
immediate implications for the Christian practice of calling on

God or the name of Christ for protection from evil, and indicates that it is the visualization process and the effect of trusting belief that have the ability to create some form of energetic, protective shield for minds and bodies. This sort of visualization is exactly what is suggested in the Bible in Paul's exhortation to put on the whole armor of God, albeit in the forms of understanding of the first century AD:

> Put on the whole armour of God, so that you may be able to stand against the wiles of the devil. For our struggle is not against enemies of blood and flesh, but against the rulers, against the authorities, against the cosmic powers of this present darkness, against the spiritual forces of evil in the heavenly places. Therefore take up the whole armour of God, so that you may be able to withstand on that evil day, and having done everything, to stand firm. Stand therefore, and fasten the belt of truth around your waist, and put on the breastplate of righteousness. As shoes for your feet put on whatever will make you ready to proclaim the gospel of peace. With all of these, take the shield of faith, with which you will be able to quench all the flaming arrows of the evil one. Take the helmet of salvation, and the sword of the Spirit, which is the word of God. Pray in the Spirit at all times in every prayer and supplication. (Ephesians 6:11-18)

Epigenetics – what goes on around the gene

Other areas of biological research yield much food for spiritual thought. One of the big discoveries of the last century was deoxyribonucleic acid – the DNA helix. Since then, the genetic code or sequence has been broken, in that we understand the process by which genetics works, and we are now in the stage of genetic manipulation to create plant and animal species with certain advantageous characteristics. The morality of it is open to debate. Our genes rule, or so it would seem, as there is a widespread belief that genes control all of our traits – physical, behavioral and emotional. It is the reason why we look for traits that run in families and why scientists keeps searching our genes for this or that particular characteristic. The rhetoric says that our fates are locked in our genes and, because we cannot change our genes, we are victims of our own genetic heredity. It leads to a rather fatalistic view of life – if my genes say I'm going to get cancer, then I can do nothing about it. Yet, as in everything to do with the amazing human body, it is not as simple as that.

Developments are happening in biology with the growth of a whole new area of *epigenetics* (the study of the way in which the environment around the cell affects the way in which genes work inside the cell). Much of this stems from the research of Bruce Lipton. His 'Big Idea' is that DNA is not the brain of the cell. This turns years of biological thinking on its head as genetic theory says that the DNA helix determines everything that a cell does. However, it is apparently far more complex than that. The DNA helix is surrounded by a sheath of protein molecules that act like switches. These protein switches can switch on and off different parts of the DNA gene structure, which then changes the behavior of the cell. But these proteins are themselves switched by other protein chains that eventually permeate the cell membrane and are receptors of external influences. So genes are ultimately switched on and off by protein receptors on the surface membrane of cells. These protein receptors are influenced by electrical and chemical signals in the environment *around* the cell. It is these signals that switch the protein receptors and, further down the chain, switch the proteins surrounding the DNA and hence turn genes on and off. Therefore the controlling factor is the cell environment, not the DNA. Obviously, we can only utilize the DNA that we have inherited, but which doors are open in the library of DNA is determined by the cell environment.

The environment around the cells is influenced in two ways.

Firstly, our thought processes produce electrical and chemical signals, and release chemicals into the bloodstream that find their way to the cells. Secondly, some of these protein receptors are also influenced by electromagnetic radiation, the fields of energy that are generated by all manner of living beings, including ourselves. It is these more subtle energies that are suspected to be the way in which one person can influence the health of another and of oneself. Bruce Lipton highlights the many research studies that have shown the effect of electromagnetic radiation on genetic function.

> Specific frequencies and patterns of electromagnetic radiation regulate DNA, RNA and protein syntheses, alter protein shape and function, and control gene regulation, cell division, cell differentiation, morphogenesis (the process by which cells assemble into organs and tissues), hormone secretion, nerve growth and function. Each one of these cellular activities is a fundamental behavior that contributes to the unfolding of life. Though these research studies have been published in some of the most respected mainstream biomedical journals, their revolutionary findings have not been incorporated into the medical school curriculum. [5]

This says that our basic biological processes are influenced and can be altered by the energetic environment in which we exist. The implications of all this research are profound. We actually have far more influence over the ways in which our bodies function than we have ever thought. Our thoughts and emotions, and the prayers and intentions of others, affect us at a biological level. When we walk into a room, we engage with the energetic field of other people in the room, and that conveys information. When we smile at another human being, whether they see it or not, we send good will towards them. Dawson Church has brought much of this research into focus in his book "The Genie in your Genes."

> Science is discovering that while we may have a fixed set of genes in our chromosomes, which of these genes is active has a great deal to do with our subjective experiences, and how we process them.... We are discovering that our genes dance with our awareness. Thoughts and feelings turn sets of genes on and off in complex relationships.[6]

It all starts with a signal coming from outside the cell – from the hormones, electrochemical and electromagnetic signals that we produce by thinking and feeling as we react to external or internal circumstances. This means that what we think and feel and also what others are thinking and feeling towards us can affect our health and well-being. For instance, lack of self-esteem can be a significant factor in causing ill health. The way in which we think about ourselves and the way in which we process our thoughts is very important. Negativity about ourselves has physiological consequences. Very often we have subtle, psychological 'loops' running in our subconscious, maybe from childhood, that tell us we are useless, or unworthy, or cannot take risks, or should not try to achieve because we will fail. These subtle programs affect the cell function in our bodies.

> When you understand that with every feeling and thought, in every instant, you are performing epigenetic engineering upon your own cells, you suddenly have a degree of leverage over your health and happiness that makes all the difference.[7]

We have always known that our consciousness, our emotional thought processes, and our feelings have the ability to affect our health for better or worse, but now science is beginning to understand how that works, and hence to develop ways to harness that latent power. It places the responsibility for our health firmly back with each of us – it begins with us. Positive thinking or intention, optimism, prayer, and meditation have all been shown to have positive effects on health and length of life. Subtle energy or bio-energetic medicine is the name of a range of therapies from hands-on healing to wearing a magnet or copper bangle. It goes under a panoply of different names, and is becoming more and more accepted, even though its effects are still mostly denied or ignored by mainstream medicine. But then, it has the name 'subtle' for a reason – it is sensitive, and some experiments have shown that if the researcher who carries out the experiment is full of skepticism and negative energy, then this will affect the experimental results. So it comes as no surprise that much research by medical skeptics finds no evidence for the effectiveness of various subtle energy treatments. This is one of the difficulties of experimental technique in assessing the result of subtle energy experiments – the energy and intention of the healer, the person receiving the healing and the experimenter can all affect the outcome.

In another series of studies, it was shown that both the energy and intention of the healers, and the patients belief that he or she had received healing, promoted the actual healing. Belief that it works helps it to work![8] As Jesus said, after many of his healings, "Your faith has made you well." (Mark 5:34, 10:52, Luke 17:19) Both the healing energy of Jesus and the belief of the person that they can be healed affected the cell function of the body. The placebo effect has long been recognized as contributing to healing. It has also been shown by the Center for Advanced Wound Care in Reading, Pennsylvania, that patients with slow-healing wounds often have negative thought patterns and behavioral or emotional wounds, such as guilt, anger, and lack of self-worth which affect their ability to self-heal.[9] So we see that there are incredibly complex and subtle interactions between our thoughts and emotions, and our immune system and self-regulatory mechanisms. This is the ideology behind most complementary and alternative therapies, but is not recognized by most mainstream medical practitioners.

Complementary Therapies and Epigenetics

Some of the more 'respectable' forms of alternative medicine, such as acupuncture and homeopathy, have some credence amongst medical practitioners, but are still pilloried by many. The House of Lords Select Committee issued a report on Complementary and Alternative Medicine (CAM) in the year 2000[10] in which they classified them into three groups. The first group contained *'Professionally organized alternative therapies with an individual diagnostic approach'*. This covered osteopathy, chiropractice, acupuncture, herbal medicine, and homeopathy. The second category was *"Therapies which are used to complement conventional medicine and do not 'diagnose'"*, and included the following:

- aromatherapy
- the Alexander Technique
- Bach and other flower remedies
- body work therapies, including massage
- counseling stress therapy
- hypnotherapy
- meditation
- reflexology
- shiatsu
- healing
- Maharishi Ayurvedic Medicine
- nutritional medicine
- yoga

The third group of CAM classified by the Select Committee was divided into two subgroups as follows:

Other disciplines which 'diagnose' as well as 'treat', and which embrace different frameworks of belief and disease causation to conventional medicine.

Group 3a

Long-established and traditional systems of health care

Anthroposophical medicine

Ayurvedic medicine (from Hindu tradition)

Chinese herbal medicine

Middle Eastern medicine (Tibb)

Naturopathy

Traditional Chinese medicine

Group 3b

– other disciplines which *"lack any credible evidence base"*

crystal therapy

dowsing

iridology

kinesiology

radionics

There are many, many other therapies that were not referred to by the House of Lords, such as: Reiki healing, Color therapy, Light therapy, Sound healing, Emotional Freedom Therapy, various bio-magnetic and energetic therapies, Aura healing, FengShui, Neuro-Linguistic Programming, Tachyon Energy, Cranio-sacral therapy, Sekhem healing, Healing voice, etc., etc. The development of this huge variety of techniques is confusing, but does indicate a real shift in the way in which many people are considering their own health, and are looking for additional treatment outside the conventional health system.

One of the problems that Dawson Church articulates is the hold that conventional medical thought, allopathic medicine, has on the way we think about health (allopathic is evidence-based medicine involving the practice of using prescription drugs or operations to treat or suppress symptoms of disease, rather than getting to the root cause):

> What is frightfully wrong is to presume that conventional allopathic medicine is the whole of medicine. This is like the drum thinking that it's the whole orchestra: while it might be a fantastic drum, providing exactly the right drama and exactly the right effects during its assigned parts of the symphony, when it starts to sound continuously, the result is a cacophony that masks subtler sounds. Just as you wouldn't try to treat appendicitis with the laying on of hands, there are a great many medical complaints for which the first response might be a consciousness-based intervention – even before visiting your physician to rule out a medically treatable organic cause.[11]

The emerging story is that genes are activated by signals from the environment that surrounds them, not from within the cell. The way in which a cell functions is not determined by the DNA, but by the signals that can activate parts of the DNA from outside the cell. That exterior environment is affected by many things, not least our own thoughts and feelings. DNA and the genes are like a huge reference library for the cell, but one in which certain areas are behind closed doors. The keys to unlock the doors to different parts of the library are held outside the library. We might enter the library and only be allowed in to the cookery book section, and our reading could only be about cookery. But then we might be given the key to the gardening section and it would open up a whole new world of possibilities for us to find out about, which would also inform our cooking. The library contains vast amounts of information, but if we do not have access to some parts, they cannot help us. The keys are not in the library, they are held outside. DNA contains immense amounts of information and instructions for the body's cells, but which parts of it have been opened is determined by 'keys' in the environment outside the cells. These keys in the environment are directly available to us. Dawson Church laments the lack of acknowledgement of the medical potential of these discoveries.

> When you start to put all the pieces together; the scientific studies of Energy Psychology, the thousands of case histories reported on the websites of practitioners, and the research on the effect of belief and faith on healing, it is apparent that a huge arsenal of treatments is emerging that is safe, swift and effective. We are no longer limited to a repertoire of drugs and surgery for our wellbeing. The new medicine also offers each of us a degree of control over our wellness, down to the very level of our cells – one that science never even dreamed of a generation ago.[12]

However, to some extent this seems to fly in the face of common sense. Surely we do not have control over our health? We are invaded by bacteria, viruses, protozoa and suffer from all sorts of strange conditions such as M.E. and post-viral fatigue syndrome, and there are the killer conditions such as cancer, motor-neurone disease, Parkinson's disease, Alzheimer's and so on. How can we say that the mind has any control over these? Yet this is the conclusion that is being reached. There are many cases of what is called in the medical profession 'spontaneous remission', where a patient with a terminal illness has defied all understanding of the way the illness normally progresses. The Institute of Noetic Sciences has gathered together numerous recorded cases, showing that there are instances of virtually all types of illness in which vital organs or body parts that are supposedly irretrievably damaged have spontaneously healed.[13] The hardest problem is to know what is going on subconsciously in our emotions and deepest self, and the barriers to self-healing that these subconscious feelings are causing. We all have hidden, repeating loops of emotional thought stemming from damaging experiences and early traumas, that can seriously block our body's function, and it is often these that need to be brought into our awareness before any healing progress can be made.

It is possible to imagine a time in the near future when *paying attention* will be the first thing we do when we get sick. Spiritual and emotional remedies will be the first line of defense, not the last. Sufferers will seek metaphysical solutions, not when they've exhausted all conventional means, but instead before they submit to the drugs and the surgery of allopathic medicine. Allopathic medicine might become a medicine of last resort, rather than of first.[14]

The Power of Prayer

The Christian approach has always acknowledged the spiritual element to healing, because of the belief in a God of love, the God who is love (1 John 4:8) As set out in Chapter 1, the understanding being put forward is that God is the compassionate consciousness, the divine energy that holds and sustains the universe in being. Our energy fields exist in a greater field of compassionate consciousness, which is God, the Source, the Ground of Being. God's energy is a healing energy, wanting wholeness, seeking to bring everything to maturity. Following this through, prayer for healing is focusing God's divine energy, joining with that compassionate consciousness, trusting that the energy will bring a degree of wholeness, hoping it will restore things to the state in which they were meant to be. This view of prayer applies on a wider basis as well, praying for God's healing love to be active in the wider world, bringing harmony and peace, seeking the good in all situations, restoring relationships, and working for the best. Prayer is for the healing of the individual and the healing of the world, in accordance with the divine energies of God – the all-loving, life-sustaining breath of

God, breathed into each one of us and into all creation.

If positive intention can have the effect of switching genes on or off, then we begin to have a mechanism for how prayer works. And it does work – the Office of Prayer Research has investigated over 227 studies, deducing that 75 per cent show that prayer has a positive impact.[15] I use the word 'prayer' because that is the terminology I am used to. I could equally say that I am holding a healing intention for someone. Recent research has shown that the central issue in this focused intention is the emotion and power of love. Over 60 scientific studies have provided evidence to show that prayer has a measurable impact on healing. These studies collectively reveal that, regardless of which religion or form the prayer takes, without love and compassion, the prayer has little or no effect. One researcher asked a Buddhist abbot to explain why the monks chanted for hours every day, asking, "When we see your prayers, what are you doing?" The abbot replied, "You've never seen our prayers, because a prayer cannot be seen. What you've seen is what we do to create the feeling in our bodies. Feeling is the prayer." The abbot realized that thought alone is not enough, there has to be a corresponding emotion to give power to the thought.

It seems that research is also telling us that the power of focused healing intention is not in the thought, but in the feeling that is generated. This is found in the Bible as well. The biblical injunction to *"ask and you shall receive"*, when looked at in the original Aramaic that Jesus spoke (by translating the biblical Greek back into Aramaic), has far more shades of meaning, and could be expanded to *"Ask without hidden motive and be surrounded by your answer – be enveloped in what you desire that your gladness may be full."* This is because there are fewer words in the Aramaic language, so each word has a greater range of meaning. Expanding the meaning shows us that the asking is to be done in an envisioning way, with real desire for it to happen. *"Be surrounded by your answer"* is to create a vision of the way you want things to be. This also says that if there are hidden motives getting in the way, they can prevent the intention from being effective. There is so much more meaning than just *"ask and you shall receive."* We lose so much in translation. (More on this in chapter 9)

In the Christian tradition, at the end of every prayer, 'Amen' is said. The Amen means 'So be it', or 'Let it be like that'. Intentional prayer is internally creating the experience of what we desire, as if it already exists, with the emotion and power of compassion. Let it be like that! Effective prayer is to imagine a person or situation well or resolved, with a feeling of compassion. Hidden motives and subconscious programs, in us or the person we are praying for, can interfere and hinder this process. For instance, we may pray for a work colleague who is off sick to be healed, but subconsciously we like it when they are not at work because the colleague is rather critical. The hidden motive is there within us, and will prevent an effective prayer unless we deal with it. In prayers for healing, as in many healing therapies, hands are often laid on or over a person. Praying for an individual by the laying on of hands is doubly effective if it is entered into with compassion, integrity and imagination – and self-knowledge.

Subtle Energy Medicine and Christianity

Words are tricky and there are so many terminology problems when we start looking at any of the alternative therapies in the area of subtle energy medicine. What is this subtle energy that is bandied about? Sometimes it is referred to as electromagnetic energy but other times it seems to be something more than that, reaching into what has always been seen as the spiritual realm. We cannot assume that no other forms of energy exist simply because they have not yet been proven or discovered by science. Yet even with existing science, some new explanations for old therapies are offered. Take acupuncture, for instance. Some fundamental or conservative evangelical Christians would denounce acupuncture because it is from another religion, or even on the supposed grounds that it is connected with the occult. However 'the occult' is not any definite thing. The word occult can be used to describe things that are simply beyond human understanding; they are hidden from view, not as yet explicable in Western scientific terms. The word does not actually occur in the Bible at all. My view is that in past times many people, through a compassionate desire to heal and make better, have discovered ways of healing that worked, and then have sought ways to understand how they work. In doing so, they have interpreted these methods of healing in the terms of the faith and belief system of the time.

For instance, the theory and practice of acupuncture go back to at least 540 BC in China, and their explanation for it was that life was thought to be dependent on balancing two energies, the yin and yang, sun and the earth, and sickness resulted from an imbalance. Health is thought to be maintained by movement of the vital force in channels between the vital organs, these channels in the body being called 'meridians'. It was thought possible to influence the movement of this vital force and restore normal flow by stimulating these meridians at various points with needles. A traditional acupuncturist will work on that basis and will have undertaken extensive training to locate the relevant meridians and diagnose the patient in the complex system of Traditional Chinese Medicine.

A Western acupuncturist may not see it quite like that, and may try to explain it in Western medical terms. Acupuncture was discovered in a different culture and time, and an explanation for it was developed within the worldview of that culture. But just because something *works*, it does not necessarily mean that the culture's explanation for the *way* in which it works is universally appropriate. The traditional description of how acupuncture works is being reinterpreted because we now have some knowledge of how it may work in physiological terms – we can use the technique and reject or adapt the traditional working explanation in favor of our own. Traditional acupuncture uses a terminology that is alien to most Western ears, but can be reinterpreted. There is much evidence that acupuncture can be helpful, and many doctors seem to be accepting it in that way as an additional tool. However, to practice acupuncture well requires years of training, and a sensitivity to the subtle energies and an observation of the workings of the body, which does imply a difference in training from the Western medical viewpoint. Acupuncture does not have to be practiced within the culture and worldview that came from traditional Chinese society. There is now an understanding of how it works through the connective tissue in the body, as Dawson Church explains:

> Connective tissue is what holds all the body parts together – a series of 'wires' and 'bags' that encase all the organs and join everything together as ligaments and tendons. Taken as a whole, it is the largest organ of the body. Connective tissue is made of collagen fibers, arranged in highly regular parallel arrays of molecules. They function as a huge liquid crystalline structure, a semiconductor able to conduct electrical energy very quickly from one place to another, hence passing information around the body. This explains how tapping or putting a needle in one part of the body, which creates a piezoelectric signal, can then affect a distant part of the body, or in the entire body.[16]

Traditional Chinese medicine stimulates the 'meridian points' on the skin, which are connected, by connective tissue, to all parts of the body and influence the energy flow around the body. The meridian points used in traditional acupuncture and acupressure have been shown to have a much lower electrical resistance than the surrounding skin.

When these points are stimulated with a low frequency current, the body responds by producing endorphins and cortisol. When they are stimulated with a high frequency current, the body produces serotonin and norepinephrine. When the surrounding skin receives the same current, these neurochemicals are not produced.[17]

Endorphins are the natural painkiller in the body, cortisol is a steroid that helps tissue repair, and serotonin and norepinephrine are mood-regulating neurotransmitters. With this knowledge, the first glimmerings of how acupuncture works can be seen. Studies by Dr Robert Becker with a rolling recording device have shown that there are electrical charges in the same places on everyone tested, and these correspond to the Chinese meridian points.[18] Other studies have shown that depressed people were helped by this meridian stimulation, and 64% reported a complete remission.[19] Hopefully such scientific studies can begin to break down some of the prejudice that exists both within the medical profession and the conservative Christian towards complementary medicine in general. Indeed, some of the medical profession have had their eyes opened in dramatic fashion:

Isador Rosenfeld, M.D., recounts the following story: "In 1978 I was invited to China to witness an open heart procedure on a young woman. She remained wide awake and smiling throughout the operation even though the only anesthesia administered was an acupuncture needle placed in her ear."[20]

Power of the Mind

There are many examples of the power of the mind over the body. In the BBC series, "Your Life in Their Hands," Dr Angel Escudero, of Valencia is said to have performed more than 900 cases of complex surgery without anesthesia. The BBC filmed a woman having an operation whose only anesthesia was repeating to herself *'My leg is anesthetized'*, while keeping her mouth full of saliva. Physiologically, a dry mouth is one of the mind's first signs of danger. The reasoning was that when the mouth is kept lubricated, the brain assumes all is well and turns off its pain receptors.[21] Another fascinating study, although rather ethically dubious, was carried out by Dr Bruce Moseley, a specialist in orthopedics. He took 150 patients suffering from severe osteoarthritis of the knee, who were expecting a cleaning operation on their knee joint. All expected the operation, two thirds received it, but a third did not, although they were surgically prepared, given anesthesia and an incision in the knee. Over the next two years they were monitored, all reported some improvement and the remarkable result is that the placebo group had better results than some who had received the actual operation. It seems that the mental expectation of healing kick-started the body's own healing mechanisms. The intention, created by the expectation of a successful operation, produced a physical change.[22]

This may also give an explanation for the phenomenon of stigmata, where the wounds of Christ are manifested on a devout Christian. The Association for the Scientific Study of Anomalous Phenomena has documented at least 350 cases of this. It would seem that the strength of intentional prayer and identification with the crucifixion can actually result in physical change.[23]

Other studies have been carried out into the occurrence of spontaneous cures from terminal illnesses, that is, without any medical intervention. These have shown that 1 in 8 skin cancers spontaneously heal, and nearly 1 in 5 cancers of the genitourinary system do as well. There is evidence that all sorts of other long-term diseases can also spontaneously heal. It often seems that if some big positive psychological shift can take place in the patient, which brings renewed purpose to life, then the mind's intention can bring about healing.[24]

Energy Psychology

A whole range of therapies has recently become established which center around intentions combined with the practice of 'tapping', that is, stimulating the meridian points by tapping them with the fingertips. One of the best known is the 'Emotional Freedom Technique', or EFT. It claims that tapping some of the meridian points at the same time as repeating a phrase, an intention, can release psychological tensions and traumas that have been held for years. This whole area is known as 'Energy Psychology', and again it is thought to work through the connective tissue system. This is the piezoelectric effect, which is that when a crystal is compressed, it can cause a discharge of static electricity, a spark. Devices based on this principle are used by many of us to light the gas fire or cooker. Because of the crystalline structure of connective tissue, tapping at the meridian points creates a tiny piezoelectric charge that travels along the connective tissue, and can affect the environment around cells, and thus, via the protein receptors, can also affect the genes of the DNA.

The probability is that tapping creates a piezoelectric charge that travels through the connective tissue along the path of least electrical resistance. When coupled with the conscious memory of a trauma and awareness of the site in the body that holds the primary memory of the trauma, the IEGs (immediate early genes) that are implicit in healing are activated, and the intensity of physical feeling at the site is discharged, taking with it the intensity of emotion related to the trauma.[25]

There are many other areas of research to do with energy and energy fields: how water is able to hold information in a vibrational energy, a kind of memory of what it has contained, to which the body reacts, as in homeopathy; how a healer's hands change in the balance of their ions, altering the electromagnetic energy field around them; how one person's energy field can create a resonance in another person's to stabilize it; and how the so-called placebo effect, seen as an annoying factor in drug research, actually reveals the power of our mind and emotions in healing. Without going into these in detail, it has become obvious that the human body is repeatedly proving to be capable of far more than was previously thought, as Lynne McTaggart makes clear:

Dozens of scientists have produced thousands of papers in the scientific literature offering sound evidence that thoughts are capable of profoundly affecting all aspects of our lives. As observers and creators, we are constantly remaking our world at every instant. Every thought we have, every judgment we hold, however unconscious, is having an effect. With every moment that it notices, the conscious mind is sending an intention.[26]

To express a Christian perspective again, I believe that healing, or an urge to wholeness, is a godly potential of the human race, a divine energy flowing through all creation. The problem is we do not know how to harness it properly yet. Complementary medical techniques are, on the whole, still rather hit-and-miss approaches, because of the subtlety of their interaction with the mind and body. What we do know is that healing is not just about our physical bodies, but about our mental and spiritual state as well. It is all one. It is ultimately about the wholeness that is the potential in a relationship with the divine consciousness within us. Christianity is, or should be about restoring that relationship in following the way and teaching of Christ. He was a healer; he was able use healing energy to influence others in a way that enabled their bodies to 'sort themselves out'. He was a fully developed human being, fulfilling all the potential that the human person has for healing, being able to direct the healing energy of God to where it was needed most. The essential message and declaration of Jesus has been distorted in translation and tradition to 'turn and be saved'. It should be more like 'Come into God and be made whole'. This may not always mean full *physical* health, but a greater fullness of spirit, of inner oneness and peace, transcending physical disability, disease and ultimately, death. (This will be followed up in Chapter 7).

Chapter 3

Morphic Fields and the Works of Christ

~

In this chapter, we consider the information fields that govern the way the world works, and take a look at Rupert Sheldrake's theory of morphic fields and morphic resonance. We then consider the implications of the effect of the life and death of Jesus of Nazareth on the morphic field of humanity.

~

Fields and Forms

Another area of new scientific thought that casts light on spirituality is to do with fields and forms, so here is given a brief explanation. Modern physics understands that we all exist in a whole variety of energy fields, containing information that determines the form of our physical existence. All forces and energy have to have a medium through which they travel. Water waves are energy traveling through water, sound waves travel through air. Water and air could be called the '*fields*' through which water or sound waves travel. We exist in a gravitational field that fills the whole universe. It causes a force of attraction between any two bodies, and the bigger the body, the bigger the force. The earth, being a large body, has a large gravitational force that holds us on its surface; otherwise we would simply fly off into space. The moon's gravitational pull creates our tidal system. The gravitational pull is transmitted through the universal gravitational field. We also exist in an electromagnetic field, which is the medium through which all electro-magnetic radiation passes:

micro-waves, radio waves, infrared, light, X-rays and gamma rays. The only difference between these forms of electromagnetic energy is the level of vibration, the frequency. Electromagnetism is intimately involved in all the interactions of our in daily lives. It is the force between electrically charged particles of the atoms from which all matter is made, it is the energy by which oxygen is created by green plants to enable us to live, and it is the energy by which radio, television and mobile phone signals are conveyed. The electromagnetic and gravitational forces are two of the four known fundamental forces. The other known fundamental forces are the strong nuclear force (which holds tiny energy bundles called quarks and atomic nuclei together), and the weak nuclear force (which causes certain forms of radioactive decay). All other known forces (e.g. friction) are ultimately derived from these fundamental forces. (Note the stress on *known*. We cannot assume there are no other fundamental forces, only that we know these ones.)

You may, at school have done an experiment with a magnet and iron filings, which illustrates the presence of a magnetic field. Iron filings are sprinkled on a piece of paper, making no discernable pattern. A magnet is brought up under the paper, and the paper is tapped gently. Lo and behold, the iron filings rearrange themselves into a clear pattern of concentric curves coming out of the poles of the magnet. The iron filings are influenced and rearranged to conform to the invisible magnetic field. Fields are influencing us all the time.

If we consider the electromagnetic field, our bodies are not exempt from the forces generated in this field, for it is all-pervading, indeed it is thought to be a means of communication within the body. We emit electromagnetism ourselves, which can be detected by sensitive modern medical instrumentation, such as brain and heart monitors, MRI scans, etc. We are surrounded and immersed in a sea of vibratory energy, of which we can only see or feel a tiny part – heat and light. We also exist within the magnetic field of the earth, which various animal species use for guidance in ways not yet fully understood, but thought to be because of tiny crystals of iron ore (magnetite) that exist in the brain. There are also various kinds of fields at the level of particles of matter, such as the electron field and the neutron field. All matter exists within them as quanta (plural of quantum) of vibrational energy. Fields are all around us and within us. It does not take much of a leap of imagination to suggest that there are other fields that we cannot detect because we have not yet devised the instrumentation to detect them. These may have a profound effect on us and be an explanation of many of the puzzles of life. There are fields, within fields, within fields, determining and governing the reactions and phenomena that we see and can measure in the physical world.

Rupert Sheldrake and Morphic Resonance

This understanding is helpful not only to the physicists, but to the biologists as well. For many years, biologist Rupert Sheldrake puzzled over what it is that determines the form of a body. The DNA in every cell in the body is the same, so what is it that makes some liver cells, some skin cells and some brain cells? What is it that draws the cells into a particular 'form', a particular body, be that of plant, animal or human being? Sheldrake has developed the understanding of morphogenetic fields (form-shaping fields), which he calls 'morphic field.' His work includes the idea of , that is, one field influencing another. Resonance happens when one source of vibrational energy sets off another. For instance, playing a piano in a room in which a guitar is standing will set some guitar strings vibrating in resonance, the ones that are on the same frequency. Sheldrake applies this to his understanding of morphic fields. He proposes that there are fields within fields within fields, so that the growth and form of each part of a body is determined by its own morphic field. Thus a cutting from the branch of a plant will conform to its field, will be shaped by it and start growing roots, and a flatworm can be chopped into small pieces and each piece will grow into a new flatworm, determined by its morphic field.

Furthermore, he proposes that each species has a field for the whole species, which has a kind of in-built memory that stores information relevant to that species. Thus there is a species memory, which is contributed to by all members of the species. Every species of being has a species-specific morphic field that determines not just its form, but also its behaviors, its social and cultural systems and mental activity.[1] This field memory is cumulative; it is based on what has happened to the species in the past, shaped by the experiences and behavior of all the previous generations. These can be considered as fields of information, based on the biological evolution of the species. This is similar to the idea of 'collective unconscious' put forward by Carl Jung.[2]

Morphic resonance is the concept that an individual organism can be influenced by the behavior of another organism of the same species, despite having no physical contact with it, because there is a connection through the morphic field of the species. Any new development or behavior by one individual becomes a part of the morphic field and the expectation is that it will be easier for any member of that species to acquire the new skill or habit that has been learnt elsewhere in the species. This idea applies not only to living organisms but also to protein molecules, crystals, even to atoms. Sheldrake puts it like this:

> For example, if rats learn a new trick in London, then rats everywhere should be able to learn the same trick more quickly than they could before because the rats have learnt it in London. The more rats that learn it, the easier it should become to learn it everywhere. Likewise, if a new chemical compound is crystallized in New York for the first time, the more this is done, the easier it should become for these

crystals to form all around the world. If children learn to play a new video game in Japan, it should be easier for children to learn the same thing in other countries. These effects should happen without any normal means of communication.[3]

This effect has indeed been experimentally observed with a variety of species. Sheldrake cites a number of cases.[4] For example, Pavlov did an experiment with white mice, training them to run to their feeding place when a bell was rung. The first generation of mice took an average of 300 trials to learn this new behavior, but by the fourth generation, it was down to 10 trials before they learnt it. William McDougall did a comprehensive experiment with rats in a maze in which they had to learn which exit to come out of – the illuminated one gave an electric shock if they exited that way, but which one was illuminated kept changing. The first generation of rats made an average of 165 errors before learning which exit to take. By the thirtieth generation, only 25 errors were being made before they learnt the new behavior. Following the publication of this, another biologist in Edinburgh, F.A.E. Crew, decided to repeat McDougall's experiments, but found that his first generation of rats learnt very quickly, with an average of only 25 errors, as if they had continued where McDougall's rats had left off. In Melbourne, the experiment was again repeated with fifty generations of rats over twenty years, and showed the same pattern. But they also did the experiments with rats whose parents were totally untrained, and found a similar improvement. These results are all what would be expected in order to conform to the theory of morphic resonance.

One of the best-documented and most interesting examples of the spread of a new habit is to do with blue tits and their ability to open the tops of milk-bottles as they stand on the doorstep. In 1921, this was first observed in Southampton, along with several cases of blue tits actually falling head-first into the bottle and drowning in the cream! From there, the habit spread, often jumping 50 or a 100 miles to a new location. Blue tits are territorial and rarely travel more than four of five miles. By 1947, it was widespread across Britain. In Scandinavia and Holland, the habit showed up in the 1930s and spread similarly. But the most interesting thing is that from 1940, during the war, there were no milk deliveries to doorsteps in Holland. Milk deliveries did not resume until 1948. Since blue tits usually live only two to three years, there probably were no blue tits alive in 1948 that had been alive when milk was last delivered. Yet when milk deliveries resumed in 1948, the opening of milk bottles by blue tits sprang up rapidly in quite separate places in Holland and spread extremely rapidly until, within a year or two, it was once again universal. The behavior spread much more rapidly and cropped up independently much more frequently the second time round than the first time. This example demonstrates the evolutionary spread of a new habit that, in Sheldrake's opinion, is not genetic but rather depends on a kind of collective memory due to morphic resonance. Sheldrake gives a helpful analogy, which I quote in full:

> The differences and connections between these two forms of heredity become easier to understand if we consider an analogy to television. Think of the pictures on the screen as the form that we are interested in. If you did not know how the form arose, the most obvious explanation would be that there were little people inside the set whose shadows you were seeing on the screen. Children sometimes think in this manner. If you take the back off the set, however, and look inside, you find that there are no little people. Then you might get more subtle and speculate that the little people are microscopic and are actually inside the wires of the TV set. But if you look at the wires through a microscope, you can't find any little people there either.

You might get still more subtle and propose that the little people on the screen actually arise through "complex interactions among the parts of the set which are not yet fully understood." You might think this theory was proved if you chopped out a few transistors from the set. The people would disappear. If you put the transistors back, they would reappear. This might provide convincing evidence that they arose from within the set entirely on the basis of internal interaction.

Suppose that someone suggested that the pictures of little people come from outside the set, and the set picks up the pictures as a result of invisible vibrations to which the set is attuned. This would probably sound like a very occult and mystical explanation. You might deny that anything is coming into the set. You could even "prove it" by weighing the set switched off and switched on; it would weigh the same. Therefore, you could conclude that nothing is coming into the set.

I think that is the position of modern biology, trying to explain everything in terms of what happens inside. The more explanations for form are looked for inside, the more elusive the explanations prove to be, and the more they are ascribed to ever more subtle and complex interactions, which always elude investigation. As I am suggesting, the forms and patterns of behavior are actually being tuned into by invisible connections arising outside the organism. The development of form is a result of both the internal organization of the organism and the interaction of the morphic fields to which it is tuned.[5]

Applying this theory to human beings means that whenever a human being does something which goes further than anyone has gone before, it effects changes in the morphic field for the whole human race, making that act more possible for everyone to do. This effect can be seen in various human achievements. Since Hillary and Tensing climbed Mount Everest, many are doing it every year. Since Bannister broke the four-minute mile, it is consistently broken regularly. Since the English Channel was first swum, it has been accomplished time after time. However, all these are affected by other factors as well – improved nutrition and fitness levels, better training, an increased field of selection, and technological advances. Another example is the constant cry of the examination boards in Britain that the exams are no easier than they were years ago, yet the pass rate is much higher. Is that solely due to better teaching, or does morphic resonance have an effect as well? It is very difficult with human beings to filter out the effects of all sorts of other factors and isolate what could be put down to morphic resonance.

Morphic Resonance and the Works of Christ
The theory of morphic resonance has been considered pseudo-science by some, because it is seen as unverifiable, but is gradually gaining support from many corners. If we assume for the moment that this actually is the way the world works, then the theory of morphic resonance has profound implications for the death and resurrection of Jesus and the theology of atonement. Christian theology tells us that Jesus was fully human. Therefore what he did and how he behaved will affect the morphic field of humanity, and enable others to do the same. In the gospel of John, Jesus says:

> Very truly, I tell you, the one who believes in me will also do the works that I do and, in fact, will do greater works than these, because I am going to the Father. (John 14:12)

Consider what Jesus is reported to have done in his life and death. He demonstrated the ability to heal the human body, and he lived a life given in dedication to God. Jesus' path was one of 'kenosis', or self-emptying. In Philippians 2, Paul first applies this word to Jesus, for it is precisely the path Jesus took.

> Let the same mind be in you that was in Christ Jesus, who, though he was in the form of God, did not regard equality with God as something to be exploited, but emptied himself, taking the form of a slave, being born in human likeness. (Philippians 2:5-7)

Jesus was able to surrender his ego, his lower self, to God, and awaken fully into God's consciousness. And yet he was fully human, the same as us, so he did have an ego-nature. The story of his years of ministry shows him repeatedly going beyond that ego, that lower self, and becoming one with God, fully divine. He repeatedly emptied himself and surrendered to the process.

We see this in the temptation narratives in Matthew chapter 4. Jesus was tempted three times. Firstly, to change rocks to bread – to use his powers selfishly and for his own ends. Secondly, to throw himself from the pinnacle of the temple – the temptation to use sensationalism to gain a selfish, ego-boosting following. Lastly, he was tempted to worship Satan in exchange for selfish power and prestige. In each case, Jesus responds by simply letting go of the bait being dangled, content to follow the path of surrender and emptying himself of egoic desires for more. Jesus was not concerned about power, adulation or prestige – he had gone beyond the need for them. He had let go of his ego and was full of the compassionate consciousness of God.

We see this egoic surrender again in the garden of Gethsemane[6] – as Jesus faces what he has to go through, he is tempted to turn aside – but *"not my will but yours"* he said to God. He surrendered to the process and put his own ego aside. This self-emptying continued in his reactions to the process of the trial, the torture and the crucifixion. Surrender and kenosis was his way, to act out of the love and compassion that became his as he put aside his ego-self and awakened into the immense field of God's compassionate consciousness. He acted and was energized from the deep well of love, the Ground of our Being that is God. The implication in the Bible is that this is possible for all humanity.

In John's gospel, this awakening into unitive consciousness is expressed as "oneness with the Father."

The Father and I are one. (John 10.30)

Holy Father, protect them in your name that you have given me, so that they may be one, as we are one. (John 17:11)

As you, Father, are in me and I am in you, may they also be in us, so that the world may believe that you have sent me. (John 17:21)

These quotes, whether the actual words of Jesus or not, imply that Jesus knew a level of oneness with God that is a possibility for all humanity to achieve. He was the first to follow fully the way of transformative love and therefore forged the path and changed the morphic field for all humanity, making it more possible for all to rise beyond the ego and have this mystical experience of connection with the compassionate consciousness of God. Other great teachers and masters within both Christianity and other religions will have contributed their parts to the change in the morphic field of humanity as well, so the Buddha and other teachers take their place in the picture. If morphic resonance is a reality, then we all contribute to the range of possible achievements for human beings. The other side to the coin is that negative contributions have an effect as well. Atrocities committed by human beings will affect the morphic field, and it then depends on what sort of energies we align ourselves with as to what deeds we accomplish. The whole focus of Christianity, and most other world religions, is towards love. As Jesus expressed it, we are to love God, love our neighbor, love ourselves and even love our enemies.

Atonement – Death and Resurrection

The atonement in Christian theology is the doctrine concerning the reconciliation of God and humankind, especially as accomplished through the life, suffering, and death of Christ. One of the traditional views of the atonement centers very much on the idea of sacrifice. The prophets in the Old Testament were constantly calling people back to God, and the people came back with animal sacrifices to appease their God. Cynthia Bourgeault makes her unease with this theology very clear:

> Atonement theology presents Christ as the spotless and unsinning "great high priest," whose death on the cross would take away the sin of the world. The theology is laid out chapter and verse in the New Testament book of Hebrews; it pictures Jesus' sacrifice as an expiation for human sinfulness, an idea deeply rooted in Old Testament cultic traditions. And what I am describing here is only atonement theology at its most blind and affirmative version; in the darker version that dominates so much of fundamentalist theology, we hear it said that God was "angry" and demanded the sacrifice of his son to appease his anger. This primitive, monstrous interpretation does no justice to the depths of love in either Old or New Testament. But for many Christians, it's what they've grown up with. The whole notion of atonement presented in this fashion makes a complete mockery of kenosis and cancels out Jesus' own understanding of what he was about.[7]

One of the strands of the Old Testament is that God, through the prophets, pointed out that sacrifice was not what he wanted.

For you have no delight in sacrifice; if I were to give a burnt offering, you would not be pleased. The sacrifice acceptable to God is a broken spirit; a broken and contrite heart, O God, you will not despise. (Psalm 51:16-17)
"The multitude of your sacrifices – what are they to me?" says the LORD. "I have more than enough of burnt offerings, of rams and the fat of fattened animals; I have no pleasure in the blood of bulls and lambs and goats." (Isaiah 1:11)

For I desire steadfast love and not sacrifice, the knowledge of God rather than burnt offerings. (Hosea 6:6)

Initially, animal sacrifices were understood by the Israelites to be what God required in order to be appeased, but later insights went beyond that primitive notion. God did not want the death of animals, their blood or their life. What he wanted, the prophets said, was a changed heart and mind, bringing justice, mercy and compassion.

A new heart I will give you, and a new spirit I will put within you; and I will remove from your body the heart of stone and give you a heart of flesh. (Ezekiel 36:26)

He has told you, O mortal, what is good; and what does the LORD require of you but to do justice, and to love kindness, and to walk humbly with your God? (Micah 6:8)

The call of Jesus was for the same thing, a changed heart and mind, to live the kingdom way, to be born again into God's way. Paul, whose letters are the earliest Christian scriptures, written before any of the gospels (with the possible exception of the gospel of Thomas, rediscovered in Egypt in 1945), took the idea of sacrifice and applied it differently. Paul spoke of the *'eyes of our hearts being enlightened'*[8] and of being *'transformed by the renewing of our minds, so that our own bodies can be presented as the living sacrifice'.*[9] This is a spiritualizing of the idea of sacrifice. Paul was deeply embedded in Jewish culture and history, an educated man. The Jews were so steeped in the idea that God required sacrifice that they found it virtually impossible to conceive of a God who did not require it in some way. But it was not the message of Jesus at all. The call of Jesus was to a changed heart and mind, expressed by the gospel writers in different ways as they tried to voice a mystical reality that goes beyond words. Mark, the earliest of the gospel writers, quotes Jesus as saying:

> The time is fulfilled, and the kingdom of God has come near; repent, and believe in the good news. (Mark 1:15)

"Repent" is the Greek word *metanoia*, and is often expressed as "turning around." But its more literal meaning is 'going beyond the mind' or 'changing the mind' (*meta* means around or beyond, and *noia* means mind). This carries the meaning of embracing thoughts beyond present limitations, or thinking outside your current box, and this gives a very different sense to the word. In business parlance, *metanoia* is "blue sky thinking," the metaphor used for the title of this book. The kingdom of God was, I believe, Jesus' shorthand way of speaking of what it is like to enter the compassionate consciousness of God and live a God-filled life. This is the main message he was trying to teach. (More on this in Chapter 6.) When Jesus was put to death, the people soon reverted to the sacrificial viewpoint, understanding Jesus death as a sacrifice once for all. In trying to work out why he died, they went back to their old understanding. Sadly, this has remained the predominant view of Jesus' death. The most extreme understanding, mentioned by Bourgeault above, is called penal substitution and says that we all fall far short of God's standards, and therefore deserve eternal damnation. The wrath of God is then expressed through the death of his one and only Son on the cross.

God gets the sacrifice he demands in killing his own Son, and we are put right with God. To imagine a more barbaric view would be hard. This was not what was intended by Jesus. This idea of substitionary punishment is, in many Christian eyes, sub-Christian in the way it thinks about God and reconciliation. Theologian John Macquarrie speaks out against it:

This view of atonement... is an example of the kind of doctrine which, even if it could claim support from the Bible or the history of theology, would still have to be rejected because of the affront which it offers to reason and conscience.[10]

The classic view of atonement is that the work of Christ, his life, death and resurrection, was a victory over all the powers that enslave humanity, and so a deliverance from them. This is *redemption*, being bought back from slavery and then set free. Salvation is freedom from enslavement and healing of the inner demons, or being set free into wholeness and healing. One's own self, one's own ego, is the last power to be transcended, which Jesus did in the utter surrender to his passion and death. But in doing so, if Sheldrake's theory of morphic resonance is correct, Jesus effected a change in the morphic field for all humanity, opening up a new way of being in relationship with God. Macquarrie talks of this in terms of his explanation of God as Being.

At the same time, this work opens up a new possibility of existence, an existence orientated towards Being, sustained by the grace of Being, and made capable of self-giving love.[11]

This is the opening of the heart that theologian Marcus Borg speaks of, an opening of the self at the deepest level, affecting our thought, feelings and will.[12] It is the way of the kingdom that

Jesus spoke so much about, living in the awareness of the compassionate consciousness of God. In his life and death, Jesus modeled this way of being and thus, by the theory of morphic resonance, made it easier for us all to live in the same way, as the morphic field of humanity was altered to enable this new way for us all. Jesus established a breakthrough in consciousness and potential for all humanity. It was not just his death that accomplished it, but his life, his depth of conscious awareness of unity with God. The death of Jesus on the cross was the end result of his life of surrender to the way of forgiveness and compassion, creating a breakthrough for all humanity. So the idea of morphic resonance can give us a radical new insight into the atonement, based in scientific theory. We can even push this further to consider 'the body of Christ', which theologically is the Church, but could be taken to mean the whole of humanity, as Olivier Clément says.

> The whole of humanity 'forms, so to speak, a single living being'. In Christ we form a single body, we are all 'members of one another'.[13]

Can we go so far as to associate the morphic field of humanity with the body of Christ? All humanity has the potential to be 'Christed', to walk the path that Jesus took, and come back to a state of oneness with God. This is what I am suggesting Jesus established for all humanity in his life and death – the kenotic path of surrender to God that enables the human and divine consciousness to come together. He changed the morphic field so that all humanity is enabled to follow that path more easily. Is this the same as entering the body of Christ? It was done for us by Jesus as an act of compassionate grace, and when we awaken to this good news and follow his way, we are enabled to access the consciousness of God.

Here we begin to tie together a modern scientific concept with the atonement theology. A traditional summary, which has worked for the pre-scientific worldview, is that we are separated from God because we fall short of perfection and are therefore sinners, and fall under his judgment for sinning. It then follows that Jesus, in his death, bought us back, paid the price and died for our sins. We are thus redeemed. In the context of this book, we could rephrase that. The separation from God is not caused by sin, but by the ego-self that has individualized out from the God-consciousness at the core of our being. We have become so self-aware that we have lost our God-awareness and are suffering the consequences of the self turned in on itself. Jesus bought us back, not merely by his self-offering of love at the point of his death, but by his whole life. The way in which he led a life of compassion and kenotic self-surrender meant that he changed the morphic field of humanity, thus enabling us all to follow the same path. It is not so much that he *bought* us back, more that he *brought* us back – he showed us the way. So we move the emphasis of theology of atonement from being the redeemed to awakening and becoming followers of the Way of Christ.

Chapter 4

The Quantum Sea of Light

~

A new area of investigation has opened up in the last 30 years, to do with electromagnetic waves, of which light is one part. Here we attempt to explain the Zero Point Field of electromagnetism and some of its implications for the nature of reality.

(This chapter is the last area of new science we shall consider and contains rather more scientific background than others. For the non-scientist reader, there may be some difficult passages, but it gets easier from here on!)

~

Zero Point Field

The term field is used to describe any information or content that is of the same form, so we can have a field of a crop such as wheat, a field of science such as physics, a field of energy such as the electromagnetic field. The term 'field' simply denotes that everything in it has some common property. Quantum physicists have always known about one particular field called the Zero Point Field. Absolute zero is a measurement in degrees Kelvin, equivalent to minus 273 degrees Celsius, and is the temperature at which everything is supposed to be still, the point where all motion ceases, but this is not the case in the Zero Point Field. Even at absolute zero in degrees Kelvin, quantum mechanics shows that there is a residual field of electromagnetic energy in constant motion, a basic substructure of the universe that cannot be eliminated by any known law of physics. Electromagnetic energy is what we know as radio waves, microwaves, infrared, visible light, ultraviolet, X-rays and gamma rays. These are all part of the electromagnetic spectrum, differing in their frequency and wavelength. They can all be considered as different forms of light – our eyes only perceive the central part of the spectrum of light. Astrophysicist Dr. Bernard Haisch refers to the Zero Point Field as a 'quantum sea of light'.[1] This zero-point energy appeared as a constant in quantum calculations, and did not seem to affect anything, so the majority of quantum physicists subtracted it away in their calculations, effectively ignoring it, a mathematical process called 'renormalization'. Because it was ever-present, it did not change anything, and therefore it did not count. However, some scientists have been quietly investigating this field and its implications for many years, but, up until a few years ago, no one had tried to draw together all the strands of these investigations. It took an investigative journalist, Lynne McTaggart, to eventually piece together all the research, from which she wrote *"The Field – The Quest for the Secret Force of the Universe"* (2001). Her conclusions are staggering.

> If you add up all the movement of all the particles of all varieties in the universe, you come up with a vast inexhaustible energy source all sitting there unobtrusively in the background of the empty space around us, like one all-pervasive, supercharged backdrop. To give you some idea of the magnitude of that power, the energy in a single cubic yard of 'empty' space is enough to boil all the oceans of the world. The Field connects everything in the universe to everything else, like some vast invisible web.[2]

There are several published studies in top-level physics journals that point to the possibility that some amount of this unlimited energy supply may be converted to usable energy. Several scientists[3] are trying to find ways to tap into this field, and if they do, we will have inexhaustible supplies of energy that would transform society as we know it. Imagine a world with no more competition for oil, gas and coal, no more raping of the earth's resources and biosphere to feed the human demand for power. However, as one can imagine, there would be a lot of vested interest from the current energy producers to maintain the status quo of energy production, which may explain why there has been little funded research into the whole area.

As well as the possibility of free energy, these discoveries tell us that we are all connected, and more than that, we are all interacting with this quantum field constantly. As living beings, we radiate levels of energy ourselves – all our biological processes result in energy exchange at very small levels, but now detectable by modern instruments like the MRI (Magnetic Resonance Imaging) scanner. Theoretical mathematics says that energy we give out interacts with the energy of the Zero Point Field, and produces patterns of interference within the field. These patterns of interference act like a recording of all the energy interactions, a sort of memory of everything.

> If all sub-atomic matter in the world is interacting constantly with this ambient ground-state energy field, the sub-atomic waves of the field are constantly imprinting a record of the shape of everything... The Zero Point Field is a kind of shadow of the universe for all time, a mirror image and record of everything that ever was.[4]

This is a difficult concept to imagine, but Ervin Lazlo, systems philosopher and twice nominated for the Nobel Peace Prize, gives a helpful analogy:

> When a ship travels on the sea's surface, waves spread in its wake. These affect the motion of all the other ships in that part of the sea. Every ship – and every fish, whale or object in that

part of the sea – is exposed to these waves and its path is in a sense "informed" by them. All vessels and objects "make waves," and their wave fronts intersect and create interference patterns. If many things move simultaneously in a waving medium, that medium becomes modulated: full of waves that intersect and interfere. This is what happens when several ships ply the sea's surface. When we view the sea from a height – a coastal hill or an airplane – we can see the traces of all the ships that passed over that stretch of water. We can also see the traces intersect and create complex patterns. The modulation of the sea's surface by the ships that ply it carries information on the ships themselves. It is possible to deduce the location, speed and even tonnage of the vessels by analyzing the interference patterns of the waves they have created.

As fresh waves superimpose on those already present, the sea becomes more and more modulated; it carries more and more information. On calm days, we can see that it remains modulated for hours, and sometimes for days. The wave patterns that persist are the memories of the ships that traveled on that stretch of water. If wind, gravity and shorelines did not cancel these patterns, the wave-memory of the sea would persist indefinitely.[5]

So patterns of interference caused by two or more waves interacting can hold huge amounts of information about the source of the initial waves. This is how holograms work. A hologram is a three-dimensional image formed by the interference of light beams from a coherent light source, such as a laser. To produce a simple hologram, a beam of coherent, monochromatic light is split into two beams. One beam is directed onto the object and reflected onto a high-resolution photographic plate. The other beam is directed straight onto the photographic plate, which then records the interference pattern of the two light beams.

When the holographic plate is developed and illuminated from behind by a beam of coherent light, it projects a three-dimensional image of the original object in space, shifting in perspective when viewed from different angles. If a hologram is cut into pieces, each piece projects the entire image. Holographic wave interference patterns can store huge amounts of information. It has been said that with holographic wave interference patterns, all of the US Library of Congress, which contains virtually every book published in English, would fit into a large sugar cube.

Memory

Waves, whether traveling through the sea or through the electromagnetic field, are an extremely efficient way of storing and passing on information. Electromagnetic waves are the means by which mobile phone, television and radio signals are broadcast. They carry information by means of modulation. A musician can modulate the sound wave produced by an instrument by varying the volume, the timing and the pitch. The sound produced then carries information – the tune. Similarly, an electromagnetic waveform can be modulated in amplitude ("volume"), phase ("timing") and frequency ("pitch") and so become a carrier wave, carrying, for instance, the radio or television signal. The interference patterns formed when these modulated waves overlap and interact with the electromagnetic Zero Point Field can store vast amounts of data.

Investigation into the Zero Point Field has led to many speculations. Lynne McTaggart introduces the idea that this form of storage, occurring in the Zero Point Field, could be an explanation for memory.

Storing memory in wave interference patterns is remarkably efficient, and would account for the vastness of human memory.[6]

The speculative concept is that memory does not reside in the brain, but is recorded in the quantum fluctuations of the field and that our brains are receptors and retrieval mechanisms for our own particular vibration within the ultimate storage medium of the field.[7] I use my diary in just this way. I can't remember everything I have to do and arrange, so I write it down in my diary – my brain interacts via pen and paper with the diary, which is the storage medium. When I want to find out what I am supposed to be doing today, my brain accesses the diary, which has it all recorded for me. Imagine if I kept my diary in a world diary library along with everyone else in the world. My memory for what I have to do that day would reside in the pages of the diary. I would need some precise code or key to find my diary in amongst everyone else's.

The idea that the Zero Point Field is our memory store has emerged from the theoretical and experimental work of a number of scientists coming together with their different perspectives. It is interesting to trace some of the history, as described by Lynne McTaggart,[8] because it illustrates the importance of interdisciplinary communication in developing new theories. (What follows is quite technical and some readers may wish to skip to the next sub-heading, "Light.")

Karl Pribram has spent decades investigating the functioning of the brain, its organization and the nature of perception and consciousness. In working with monkeys, he was able to locate the areas of the brain in which cognitive processes, emotions and motivation took place, but was still puzzled as to how this actually happened. The old theories of the supposed correspondence between images in the world and the electrical firing of the brain cells did not seem to make sense. More illumination came when he read about the concept of wave fronts and holography, just being developed in the 1960's.

Pribram now thought that the brain must somehow 'read'

information by transforming ordinary images into wave interference patterns, and then transform them back into virtual images, just as a laser hologram is able to. The other mystery solved by the holographic metaphor would be memory. Rather than being precisely located anywhere, memory would be distributed everywhere, so that each part contained the whole.[9]

Pribram then met up with Dennis Gabor, Nobel Prize winner for his work on holography, and they worked together on the mathematics of interference patterns using a mathematical technique called Fourier transforms. They managed to work out a theory for how the brain may be able to respond to wave interference patterns and then convert the information into thought images. The theory was left hanging for a number of years before Walter Schemp, a German mathematics professor, who had got involved with the mathematics of the fledgling MRI (Magnetic Resonance Imaging) machines in an effort to improve them. Without getting into the detail here of how these complex machines work, Schemp used Fourier transforms to develop his theory of 'quantum holography', showing that information is carried in the quantum fluctuations of the Zero Point Field, and that this information can be converted into a three-dimensional image. Schemp then met up with Peter Marcer, a British physicist, and they collaborated on using the way an MRI scan works to help understand how the brain functions, by reading natural radiation and emissions from the Zero Point Field. Drawn into their work was Edgar Mitchell, the Apollo 14 astronaut and astrophysicist, who had been working on his own theory of human perception.

Next came a collaboration with Stuart Hammerhof, an anesthesiologist, researching how anesthetic gases turn off consciousness. In his work, he found that living tissue emitted photons of light, and that there were connections between and within cells called 'microtubules' that could be the 'light pipes' connecting cells via light energy. Other scientists were taking up Karl Pribram's ideas that the brain made use of quantum processes. It was only through the collaboration of these different scientists, each with their own specialized knowledge, that some light began to dawn. Eventually, many of these scientists came together to formulate a collective theory about the nature of human consciousness.

According to their theory, microtubules and the membranes of dendrites [part of the nerve cell, the neuron] represented the Internet of the body. Every neuron of the brain could log on at the same time and speak to every other neuron simultaneously via the quantum processes within. Microtubules create global coherence of the [light] waves in the body – a process called 'superradiance' – then allowed these coherent signals to pulse though the rest of the body.[10]

We have sketched only the very bare bones of the complicated story in McTaggart's book, *"The Field,"*[11] a story that stretches from the 1960s to the 1990s. The Zero Point Field was central to all this, and out of it came the idea that both short and long-term memory reside not in the brain, but in the quantum interactions of the Zero Point Field. It has thus been argued that the brain is the retrieval and read-out mechanism for the storage repository of the Zero Point Field.

This leads to a possible explanation for bursts of intuitive insight that can suddenly come when someone is relaxed or 'attuned' in some way and other portions of the field memory are accessed. It could also give a possible explanation for the memory of past lives, a phenomena that has been recorded particularly in children. Studies of young children have shown that their brains work in alpha rhythms rather than the normal beta rhythms of adulthood. Adults only display alpha rhythms in states of altered consciousness, meditation and relaxation.

If a small child claims to remember a past life, the child might not be able to distinguish his own experiences from someone else's information, as stored in the Zero Point Field. Some common trait – a disability or a special gift, say – might trigger an association, and the child would pick up this information as if it were his own past-life 'memory'. It is not reincarnation, but just accidentally tuning in to somebody else's radio station by someone who has the capacity to receive a large number of stations at any one time.[12]

This is not denying that reincarnation may be a reality, just that the phenomenon of recall of what seem like past lives may be memory 'leakage' from another part of the Zero Point Field.

Light

Light is one of the most enduring and widely used symbols in religion and spirituality. The very term 'enlightenment' means being filled with light. Jesus is reported to have described himself as *'the light of the world'*, and Christians are encouraged to *'walk in the light'*. We have already touched on the interesting fact to emerge in recent years, that all living things produce light, which may be one of the most crucial aspects of the biological interactions. Lynne McTaggart tells the story of the German researcher, Fritz-Albert Popp, who made the first discoveries in this area in the 1970s.[13] He had an extremely sensitive machine built called a photomultiplier, which could measure light, photon by photon (a photon being the tiniest bundle of light energy measurable). They tested this machine on seedlings and found that they gave out very small amounts of very coherent light. Coherence in the quantum world is when all the particles or energy waves start to show a form of communication with each other in that they get 'in phase', synchronized with each other and begin to behave together – what is done to one will affect all the others. It is a bit like the instruments in an orchestra – they are all playing their individual part, but communicate together to make a greater whole.

Having discovered this, Popp went on to show with his photomultiplier that all living cells emit photons of light – displaying *'biophoton emission'*. This varies from a few photons to hundreds per square centimeter per second. Cells also absorb and store these photons – they store light. Further experimentation showed that this storage and emission happened via the DNA in the cell, which may mean that the DNA uses coherent light as its means of communication within the cell. Coherent light means light waves that are "in phase" with one another. For example, two waves are coherent if the crests of one wave are aligned with the crests of the other and the troughs of one wave are aligned with the troughs of the other. Otherwise, these light waves are considered incoherent. Light produced by a laser is coherent, its waves are all aligned and in phase, so a laser beam travels without spreading out. Light from a light bulb is incoherent, it spreads out in all directions.

Popp went on to show that the biophoton emission from healthy subjects is ordered and coherent, but from cancer patients it was not. It was as if the lines of internal communication were scrambled and their light was going out. With multiple sclerosis patients he found the opposite effect – there was too much light emission and their cells were drowning in light. He also conjectured about the relationship of biophoton emission and the Zero Point Field fluctuations, suggesting that the emission of photons was also a kind of compensatory mechanism to try to maintain the right balance of energy. Health is maintained when the emission of coherent light photons keeps everything in balance in a state of perfect subatomic communication, and ill health was a state where communication breaks down. We are ill when our waves are out of synchronization. We are 'out of sorts'.

Spiritual Light

This discovery of the central role that light has to play in the body's processes begins to make the bridge between the spiritual metaphor of light and the reality of the workings of the human body. The Bible is full of light analogies and metaphors. Amongst the first words of the Bible is the command from God "Let there be light"; and there was light. It is as if the first energy to arise from the divine compassionate consciousness is the Zero Point Field, the quantum sea of light, from which all else emerges. There are many other ways in which the metaphor of light is used in the Bible to indicate the presence of God, both within us and around us. Here is a short selection:

For with you is the fountain of life; in your light we see light. (Psalm 36:9)

O house of Jacob, come, let us walk in the light of the LORD! (Isaiah 2:5)

Then your light shall break forth like the dawn, and your healing shall spring up quickly (Isaiah 58:8)

You are the light of the world. (Matthew 5:14)

Let your light shine before others, so that they may see your good works and give glory to your Father in heaven. (Matthew 5:16)

If then your whole body is full of light, with no part of it in darkness, it will be as full of light as when a lamp gives you light with its rays. (Luke 11:36)

The true light, which enlightens everyone, was coming into the world. (John 1:9)

Jesus spoke to them, saying, "I am the light of the world. Whoever follows me will never walk in darkness but will have the light of life." (John 8:12)

For once you were darkness, but now in the Lord you are light. Live as children of light – for the fruit of the light is found in all that is good and right and true. (Ephesians 5:8-9)

This is the message we have heard from him and proclaim to you, that God is light and in him there is no darkness at all. (1John 1:5)

Incarnation and Photosynthesis

Light is a very useful metaphor for the spiritual illumination. Every religious tradition uses the metaphor of light. If we were to join up the spiritual metaphor with the recently discovered scientific reality, we could get a powerful fusion of ideas. Judy Cannato, in *"Radical Amazement: Contemplative Lessons from Black Holes, Supernova and Other Wonders of the Universe,"*[14] takes this to a deeper level in using the metaphor of photosynthesis to 'shed light' on the incarnation of Jesus. Earth came into being 4.45 billion years ago as stardust coalesced into solid matter. It was another billion years before any living matter appeared, which then evolved to ever-greater complexity. Then, about half a billion years later, a mutation occurred and a single cell began to be able to capture the energy of light from the sun in the process we call photosynthesis. This is the process by which green plants convert energy from the sun by combining it with carbon dioxide and water to make sugar, the nutrient for the plant, and oxygen, on which animal life depends. Cannato recognizes this as a major breakthrough in evolution, a new interaction upon which virtually all life on earth now depends, an amazing break-through over 3 billion years ago. The link she makes is that before this breakthrough, the sun had been radiating its light energy, but until the evolution of this new cell function, light was incapable of being the *nourishing* source that it is now. The relationship between the sun and the earth was restricted because the earth could not receive, not because the sun was not giving. For billions of years the sun has been radiating light energy towards the earth, but it had been 'lost' as there was no receptor for it until photosynthesis came along. From there, she uses photosynthesis as a metaphor to consider the incarnation of Jesus.

> As I reflect on photosynthesis, I am drawn to reflect on the Incarnation – that definitive event in Christianity in which divine life spilled over into human life in the person of Jesus of Nazareth. Looking at the Incarnation through the dual lenses of evolution and the interaction of photosynthesis can give us insights into who Jesus is and his meaning for all creation.[15]

Cannato traces the evolutionary journey of the human race, the development of self-consciousness, the gradual understanding of the nature of God in the Hebrew Scriptures, and then comes to the moment when Jesus came into the world. He is the Incarnation, which means "God-in-flesh," the definitive revelation upon which Christianity rests. Here is a fully human being who embodies the next major evolutionary step in human consciousness. He becomes a receptor for the love of God.

> Just like sunlight, God's grace has always been radiating toward Earth, ceaselessly self-communicating, ceaselessly pushing for life from within and without. With Jesus comes the breakthrough moment. After eons of preparation, humankind is finally able to receive grace in a more *conscious* way. Through Jesus and his interaction with the Holy One, light breaks through into life in a way never before experi-

enced. Jesus is able to absorb the gracious radiance of God in a fashion that transforms those in his midst who are ready to receive the breakthrough event... The universe, developing in and through the love of the Creator in space and time over billions of years, has finally evolved to that place from which it can respond fully to the Creator, in the person of Jesus. His radical acceptance of Creative Love completes the circle that began with the Big Bang, when God's self-communication of love and grace started, continuing through the birth of Earth and the development of life, leaping forward with the dawn of consciousness and emerging with the awareness, embodied in Jesus, that all life is accepted and included in God's love and grace.[16]

This is a lovely use of a scientific concept to give insight into Christian theology. If this sort of language can be embraced by the Church liturgists, we can begin to move to a place of acceptance that science and religion can be complementary, not competitive. Cannato goes on to express how Jesus brought that light into the world and lived it out:

What Jesus began to teach about the divine energy is that it is inclusive, that in its radiant presence it embraces all that is. It is the power of transformative love. The connectedness of all life is not merely a physical phenomenon but an essential expression of that divine presence. Love is not just a feeling, but a force for evolution, bringing everything into relationship. Like the Sun, which pours out its own life to nourish and support life on Earth, the Holy One pours out its own life to nourish and support us. And the nature of this outpouring is love, a love that knows no boundaries to its sacrifice and no limits to its profusion.[17]

We could almost express this as the spiritual energy of light being the carrier wave for love. The divine emanation of light carries with it the evolutionary force of love from the compassionate consciousness of God, and Jesus was the first human being to have a consciousness evolved to the stage that he could fully embody this love. He was both enlightened and 'enlovened', if we can invent a word for a moment. The spiritual carrier wave of light is modulated to carry the information, the 'tune' of love. Jesus embodied love, living out what was later expressed in John's letters in the Bible.

> Dear friends, let us love one another, because love comes from God. Whoever loves is a child of God and knows God... No one has ever seen God, but if we love one another, God lives in union with us, and his love is made perfect in us.
> (1 John 4:7, 12)

The reality is that we exist in a sea of light energy, the Zero Point Field. Light is thought to be the organizing principle in the cells of the body, and light is the central motif in the spiritual journey, stemming from God, who is light and love. It does seem more than a coincidence! It would be misleading to identify the compassionate consciousness of God with the Zero Point Field, as some imply, but to view this 'sea of light' as the first creative ray to have emanated from the divine consciousness is an inspiring way of seeing the link between quantum physics and the theology of creation. There is also an immediate link with God's bountiful nature, as provision may be there for a limitless supply of free energy – that would be just like the abundant God that Jesus revealed, giving the provision that all may have life in abundance. As we approach an energy crisis in the world, it would be a divine coincidence if, at this stage of human development, we stumbled on a limitless supply of free, safe electromagnetic energy!

Eternal Timeless Life

The astrophysicist, Bernard Haisch, suggests a further insight stemming from his research into the Zero Point Field:

If some underlying realm of light is the fundamental reality propping up our physical universe, how does the universe of space and time appear from the perspective of a beam of light? In other words, how would things look if you were moving at the speed of light? The laws of relativity are clear on this point. If you could move at the speed of light, you would see all of space shrink to a single point, and all of time collapse to an instant. In the reference frame of light, there is no space and time.[18]

If we consider a photon of light, the little bundle of energy that light comes in, from the moment of its creation, it zooms off at the speed of light until it contacts some object that absorbs it – or that is how we see it. We calculate the distance to stars by light years – the distance light will travel in a year. Given that it is moving at 186,000 miles per *second*, a light year is a long way (5,865,696,000,000 miles). But for a photon of light, moving at that immense speed, if it could be rational about its own existence, things would seem totally different. To our perception, light from a distant star might take a million years to get to us. From the perception of a photon, there is no space – it is created and instantaneously reaches our eyes in one single, timeless jump, according to the theory of special relativity. This all sounds rather mysterious and mystical, but from the religious perspective, it can give us an insight into what is referred to in the Bible as "eternal or everlasting life." Being with God could mean being in a "realm of light," a timeless and spaceless existence outside the laws of physics, outside the created order, where all things collapse to oneness. Eternal life would be better termed "timeless" life, taking a scientific viewpoint into consideration.

Bernard Haisch came across a passage from the *Haggadah*, a collection of writing within the Jewish Kabbalah, which stunned him, because it distinguished between the light created at the very beginning and the light emitted by the sun, moon and stars, and seemed to imply a knowing of the nature of reality:

> "The light of the first day was of the sort that would have enabled man to see the world at a glance from one end to the other. Anticipating the wickedness of the sinful generations of the deluge and the Tower of Babel, who were unworthy to enjoy the blessing of such light, God concealed it, but in the world to come it will appear to the pious in all its pristine glory."[19]

Here are hints not only of light as a key to creation, but also possible as a hidden and potentially useful power. Is this the same as the Zero Point Field? There are all sorts of insights from the scientific world that can provide nutritious food for theological speculation.

Akashic Field

The Zero Point Field concept is taken a step further by Ervin Laszlo, a systems philosopher, and integral theorist (i.e. one who tries to join up theories to make a bigger whole). Twice nominated for the Nobel Peace Prize, he has written a fascinating theory in *"Science and the Akashic Field."* Many scientists have established that there is a connection, a coherence between all material things, which defies established scientific views. (Coherence, in scientific terms, is a logical, orderly, and consistent relationship of parts. They are 'in phase' with and react to each other.) In everyday terms, we think of space as a vacuum – nothing exists in it. Nothing 'material' may exist, nothing we can see with our eyes or with microscopes, but at an energy level, as we have established, space is buzzing. Electromagnetic waves pass readily through space, light from the sun and stars being one aspect of that. Gravity acts through that vacuum. Energy in various forms can travel through the vacuum of space. But energy must be conveyed by something, and hence the development of universal field theories – that the vacuum of space contains a universal electromagnetic field, a universal gravitational field, a universal Higgs field (to do with the 'mass' of an object), and also the universal Zero Point Field that contains those unimaginable amounts of information and energy. Lazlo also proposes that there is another universal field that conveys the effect of 'non-local coherence', i.e. things having virtually instantaneous connections across space and time. This he terms the 'Akashic' field, a term from Hindu thought.

In the Sanskrit and Indian cultures, Akasha is an all-encompassing medium that underlies all things and becomes all things. It is real, but so subtle that it cannot be perceived until it becomes the many things that populate the manifest world. Our bodily senses do not register Akasha, but we can reach it through spiritual practice. The ancient Rishis reached it through a disciplined, spiritual way of life, and through yoga. They described their experience and made Akasha an essential element of the philosophy and mythology of India.[20]

What is the essence of this world? ...It is the Akasha, out of which all these creatures proceed, and into which they are again received, the Akasha is older than them all, the Akasha is the ultimate end."[21]

This Akashic field is, he proposes, the means by which instantaneous communication happens between particles. Experimental evidence the 1980's by Alain Aspect showed that the speed of communication between particles was at least 20 times faster than the speed of light. Further experiments by Nicolas Gisin in 1997, with particles 10 km apart, showed that these particles appeared to be in communication at least 20,000 times faster than the speed of light, relativity theory's supposedly unbreakable barrier. These particles had become what is known as "entangled," they somehow communicate with each other outside of space and time. It is action-at-a-distance that occurs faster than the speed of light.[22] Extrapolating this into everyday life, people become "entangled" through interaction with each other. Laszlo gives details of a number of experiments by reputable scientists. Two physicists, Russell Targ and Hal Puthoff, showed that a person, the sender, exposed to rhythmic flashes of light in a sealed and electrically shielded room developed a rhythmic pattern in the brainwaves measured on an electro-encephalograph (EEG) machine. A second person, the receiver, was in a different room, but produced the same wave patterns in the brain. Targ and Puthoff also conducted experiments with remote viewing, where one person views an object and another person a long way off tries to receive what the sender saw.

> Independent judges found the descriptions of the sketches matched the characteristics of the sight that was actually seen by the sender 66 per cent of the time.[23]

At the National University of Mexico, several experiments were carried out by Jacobo Grinberg-Zylberbaum. He used two separate "Faraday Cages," which totally block both sound and electromagnetic radiation. Subjects were placed together in one cage and asked to meditate together for twenty minutes, and then they were placed in separate cages. One subject was given all manner of stimuli at random intervals – flashes of light, sounds and even electric shocks – whilst the other subject in another cage was told to relax. Analysis of the EEG traces showed a correlation between the brainwaves of the two subjects in about 25 per cent of cases. If the subjects were not put together at first, there was no correlation, implying that a connection is established going beyond any physical proximity. Two young people taking part in the experiment were deeply in love, and their EEG patterns remained closely synchronized throughout the experiment. Maybe the feeling of oneness experienced as part of a loving relationship is more than an illusion and love is actually the evolutionary driver for connection in the universe.

The phenomenon of "twin pain" is well documented – when one twin senses the pain or trauma that is happening to the other twin who is elsewhere. A television program in 1997 tested four pairs of identical twins, monitoring their brain waves, blood pressure and skin conductivity. One of each pair of twins was subjected to a loud alarm. In three out of four pairs the other twin, in another separate soundproofed room, registered the shock that the first twin received.[24] Laszlo is proposing that this form of telepathic transference between two entangled people occurs through the Akashic Field, outside of the physical time and space, in a nonlocal way. He later quotes the Indian Yogi Swami Vivekananda:

According to the philosophers of India, the whole universe is composed of two materials, one of which they call Akasha. It is the omnipresent, all-penetrating existence. Everything that has form, everything that is the result of combination, is evolved out of this Akasha. It is the Akasha that becomes the air, that becomes the liquids, that becomes the solids; it is the Akasha that becomes the sun, the earth, the moon, the stars, the comets; it is the Akasha that becomes the human body, the animal body, the plants, every form that we see, everything that can be sensed, everything that exists. It cannot be perceived; it is so subtle that it is beyond all ordinary perception; it can only be seen when it has become gross, has taken form. At the beginning of creation there is only this Akasha. At the end of the cycle the solids, the liquids, and the gases all melt into the Akasha again, and the next creation similarly proceeds out of this Akasha.[25]

Connecting with Hindu spirituality in this way, Laszlo brings the whole idea that information and memory is stored in energy fields, to which our brains have access, into the sphere of religion and spirituality. The experience of oneness with the Source, Being, or God that all religions have in some form can be hinted at in scientific terms. The Zero Point Field and the Akashic field provide a theory of connectedness that takes us into new realms of understanding of the nature of humanity and the spiritual life, previously only touched on in ancient spiritualities. Laszlo encapsulates the way in which this view is changing the view of the physical world.

The view that space is empty and passive... is diametrically opposed to the view we get at the leading edge of science. What the new physics describes as the unified vacuum – the seat of all the fields and forces of the physical world – is in fact the most fundamentally real element in the universe. Out of it have sprung the particles that make up our universe, and when black holes "evaporate," it is into that the particles fall back again. What we think of as matter is but the quantized, semi-stable bundling of the energies that spring from the vacuum. In the last count, matter is but a waveform disturbance in the quasi-infinite energy-and-information-sea that is the connecting field, and enduring memory, of the universe.[26]

When this is tied together with the notion that God is the compassionate consciousness in which we all exist, we have the beginnings of a radical theology that concurs with scientific viewpoints rather than competes. God 'thought', and radiated the 'word' of creation, bringing energetic fields into being that have led to the development of matter, life, and self-awareness –and ultimately the ability to perceive the God who started the whole process and sustains it all. The journey for the human being is then back to the consciousness of God, and the circle is completed. Religious insight has been there for eons, but we are now beginning to develop a language and understanding that can join up the dots between religion and scientific thought.

The connections and ideas that are being put together in this book are based on the reading of various scientific theories, and it has to be noted the scientific theories often change and become either superseded or cast aside in the search for the true nature of physical reality. But we can only work with what we have. In the rest of this book, we consider more deeply how the insights outlined in the first four chapters can be worked into Christian theology and practice.

Part Two

Christianity's Evolution

In the second part of the book, the new scientific concepts previously outlined are interwoven into Christian theology and terminology, which is challenging for some areas and illuminating for others.

> In our time we have come to the stage where the real work of humanity begins. It is the time where we partner Creation in the creation of ourselves, in the restoration of the biosphere, the regenesis of society, and in the assuming of a new type of culture; the culture of Kindness. Herein, we live daily life reconnected and recharged by the Source, so as to become liberated and engaged in the world and in our tasks.
> Jean Houston

Chapter 5

Re-Thinking Jesus

~

We now begin the task of relating the scientific insights in the previous four chapters to the person of Jesus the Christ, and the implications for an evolved understanding of his relationship to God. We consider the true meaning of some of the terms used in connection with Jesus and we attempt to penetrate some of the weight of tradition that has built up around Jesus in order to see him afresh.

~

"It takes a gambler's heart to do the spiritual journey"
Brother Raphael Robin[1]

Joining up Science and Religion

In the previous four chapters, we have touched on new and challenging scientific concepts which give real insight into the spiritual journey. The theory that there is a unifying field of consciousness at the ground of being leads to an understanding of God as the compassionate consciousness that holds everything in being, and from which all energy fields and matter emerge. We are all part of that consciousness. This raises all sorts of theological issues to do with the doctrines of the Incarnation, the Trinity, salvation and other major areas of Christian theology. This book does not attempt to answer them all in detail, but is presenting some thinking that can lead to further analysis.

In this chapter we shall explore the implications for the person of Jesus of Nazareth. The idea being put forward is that he became totally one with that compassionate consciousness. In doing so, he fulfilled the human potential, and therefore changed the morphic field of all humanity, making it more possible for the level of spiritual maturity he reached to be gained by others. Epigenetics shows that we have far more control over the health and functioning our own bodies than previously thought, by subtly affecting the environment of the cells in our bodies. This happens by the manner in which we think and feel, which affects the energy fields that hold the pattern of our physical being. Jesus may have gained the ability to use his thoughts and emotions to affect the material world, such that he was able to bring healing to others by the power of his intention, his focussed emotional thought patterns and energies. All these insights stem from new scientific realizations and challenge the assumption that Jesus was more divine than is the potential for humanity – i.e. that he was God in a way that none of us can be. For a traditional Christian believer, this is probably the most challenging notion in this book. In this chapter, we shall explore that idea in more depth.

The Potential of Jesus

To start at the beginning, I believe Jesus was a real, living, fully human being – Jesus of Nazareth, born of Mary. He was not God disguising himself as human. (Concerning the virgin birth, see Appendix 1). Neither was Jesus a country bumpkin. In our Western tradition, there has been a strong tendency to see Jesus as an uneducated carpenter who grew up in a remote region of Galilee. But that does not hold any water when we look more carefully. Jesus was from Nazareth, a small peasant village in Galilee, but only four miles south of Sepphoris, the largest city in Galilee and the center of Herod's administration during Jesus' youth. Flavius Josephus described Sepphoris as the "ornament of all Galilee." Joseph and Jesus may have worked there, as it was rebuilt from about AD 4 onwards. It would have provided regular work for carpenters and stonemasons, and the word translated from the Greek as "carpenter" is actually broader than that and could include stonemasonry. Sepphoris was also built on a hill and was visible for miles. This may be the city that Jesus spoke of when he said, "A city set on a hill cannot be hidden." Jesus may have spent much of his time working in Sepphoris, where donkey-caravans came from all over the region to sell their wares, telling of other places and discussing other philosophies and beliefs.

We tend to think of Jerusalem as the cultural center of the region, and that going to Jerusalem from the Galilean lands was like going up to the big city from a rural backwater. Actually, it was almost the other way around. Galilee was not a backwater, it was a fairly cosmopolitan environment because it lay on the Silk Road, the great viaduct of human commerce that connected the lands of the Mediterranean and Egypt with Central Asia and China, which was already developing in the time of Julius Caesar (100BC – 44BC)[2] and was well established by the first century AD.[3]

Galilee was not just on the Silk Road, but also on the Incense trade route.

The Incense trade route or the Incense Road of Antiquity comprised a network of major ancient trading routes linking the Mediterranean world with Eastern sources of incense (and spices), stretching from Mediterranean ports across the Levant and Egypt through Arabia to India. The incense trade flourished from South Arabia to the Mediterranean between roughly the third century BCE to the second century CE. The Incense Route served as a channel for trading of goods such as Arabian frankincense and myrrh; spices, ebony, silk and fine textiles; and East African rare woods, feathers, animal skins and gold.[4]

These routes passed through Capernaum, where Jesus spent much of his time preaching and teaching – and learning.[5] It was not just goods that were conveyed along these routes, but human culture as well, including other religious understandings. Jesus would have easily picked up ideas and concepts from Hindu and Buddhist teachings of the East and the mystery religions of Egypt and Persia. He would have heard the teaching of the Greek philosophers. He lived in an area rich in spiritual wisdom. We know he could read, as we see him in Luke 4:16 picking up the scroll in the synagogue and reading from it in Hebrew. He probably spoke several languages – he certainly spoke Aramaic and Hebrew, and in the light of his exchange with Pilate, he probably understood Greek and possibly some Latin as well. From the records of the gospels, he was obviously steeped in the Jewish scriptures. This man was no ignorant peasant, but a well-educated, learned wisdom teacher. But, for a Christian, the big question is, in what sense was he the Son of God?

Son of God

> Then Nathanael declared, "Rabbi, you are the Son of God; you are the King of Israel." (John 1:49)

What did the people of Jesus' time mean when they said, like Nathanael, "You are the Son of God"? This may well be the title most used for Jesus but least understood today. It was central to the first Christians in stating their belief in Jesus and expressing their worship of him. However, when the contemporaries of Jesus said it – before his death on the cross, before the resurrection, before the writings of Paul, and before the gospels were written – they meant something very different from the common understanding today. In the Hebrew of the Old Testament, angels could be called God's sons.[6] So could the historical king of Israel,[7] and also all Jews were called sons of God, and at times the whole nation was referred to as the Son of God.[8] In the Old

Testament, God speaks to Moses:

> Then say to Pharaoh, 'This is what the LORD says: Israel is my firstborn son, and I told you, "Let my son go, so that he may worship me."' (Exodus 4:22)

So when Nathanael said, "Rabbi, you are the Son of God; you are the King of Israel," he was not meaning it in the same literal way as we would take it now, a man whose male genes came from God. Son of God was more synonymous with the king, the leader, than anything else. Nathanael, being a faithful Jew, was not saying to Jesus, "You are the eternal God in human form." He was effectively saying, "Teacher, you are the lifeblood of Israel, you are the anointed one, the rightful leader." There may well have been recognition in that of his godly wisdom, his developed intuition and giftedness, but not that he was divine in a way that no-one else could be.

If people were spreading the word, implying that Jesus was to be the new leader of Israel, the Jewish authorities would soon have started getting worried, saying things like, "What right has he to speak like that? Who is he, this upstart from Nazareth of all places? He's getting popular, the Romans will clamp down on us if he gets much more support. We'd better get him out of the way..." The Jews were expecting a Messiah, which means "the anointed one," and it was primarily kings that were anointed. Israel was a puppet state, part of the Roman Empire, brutally repressed. They had been their own free nation once, with their own king – and they longed for another anointed one who would lead them to overthrow the Romans. That is probably what Nathanael was talking about in recognizing Jesus as the Son of God – he was identifying him as the next king or leader who was going to rescue them from Roman domination, which was revolutionary talk. Either that or he was recognizing him as the true inheritor of the spiritual tradition, the one who was going to overthrow the Jewish leaders. Either way, he would be viewed as a troublemaker by the authorities.

Subsequently, Jesus was arrested, crucified, and then resurrected (which can be understood in many different ways – see later in this chapter), and the early Christians had to start making sense of all that. The first early theology of who Jesus was arose out of their worship of him, the post-Easter experience. After Easter, Jesus' followers experienced him as a spiritual reality, not limited to time and space as Jesus of Nazareth was. After the Ascension, he could be everywhere, and his Spirit was available within. Increasingly, he was spoken of as having all the qualities of God. As time went on, phrases like Nathanael's "Son of God" came to be seen as recognition of Jesus as the "only begotten" Son, the one who "sits at God's right hand," etc. Many try to justify that by referring back to Nathanael and others in the gospels, but that is not a valid argument because it is not what Nathanael would have meant by the words attributed to him. Arguments about the nature of Jesus went on for 500 years until the great creeds of the Church were all decided. Everything then became set in stone, challenged only by a few brave theologians who risked their lives and were often labeled heretics and instructed to recant. Those who did not were sometimes executed. By this means, one form of Christianity won out over numerous others. The history of the development of the theology of the Church in the first 500 years is full of alternative forms of Christianity, many of which might have ended up as being the mainstream, had things worked out differently. Professor Bart D. Ehrman, in *"Lost Christianities,"* makes the point clearly that there were Christians who held diametrically opposed views about Jesus.

In the second and third centuries, there were Christians who believed that Jesus was both divine and human, God and man. There were other Christians who argued that he was completely divine and not human at all.... There were others who insisted that Jesus was a full flesh-and-blood human, adopted by God to be his son but not himself divine. There were yet other Christians who claimed that Jesus was two things: a full flesh-and-blood human, Jesus, and a fully divine being, Christ, who had temporarily inhabited Jesus' body during his ministry and left him prior to his death, inspiring his teachings and miracles but avoiding the suffering and its aftermath.... There were Christians who believed that Jesus' death brought about the salvation of the world. There were other Christians who thought that Jesus' death had nothing to do with the salvation of the world. There were yet other Christians who said that Jesus never died.[9]

The question this leaves us with is 'How can all these views have been considered Christian?' Ehrman points out that they did not have the New Testament as we have it – the canon (which books were in and which were out) had not yet been decided, and there were all sorts of other gospels and letters around, with different parts of the Christian world holding fast to "their" scriptures. Ehrman calls the winning side the "proto-orthodox" i.e. those who became the orthodox, traditional Church, and it was this view that eventually swung the day in the debates and councils that happened, but he makes the point that was often a close-run thing – we could easily have ended up with a very different doctrine if others had tipped the balance. Once the proto-orthodox group got the upper hand, they classed all those who had argued with them as heretics, with dire consequences for many of them.

Jesus and Human Potential

The Jesus in the gospels we have is someone who lived a human life, but one in whom the full potential of the human – body, mind and spirit – had been developed, as he awakened into the compassionate consciousness of God. Consider all the skills that we see developed in the full range of humanity. People exist with photographic memories, or incredible mathematical skills, or amazing knowledge of languages or music, or enormous empathy and compassion, and many more unusual talents. They are usually referred to as geniuses or savants. Imagine many of these gifts combined in one person, someone who has the ability and wisdom to know how to use them for the benefit of humanity (which is an essential requisite, the sign of true wisdom). This person may be aware at some level of the subtleties of energy fields and their effects and has some control of the environment by his developed awareness of these quantum energetic fields that underlie everything. He can seemingly manipulate reality, cause "miracles" to happen, maybe even, after the resurrection, control the particles of his own body to appear and disappear at will. This person would seem divine, God-like, yet was still fully human.

However, what if this is the evolutionary direction in which humanity is heading? Science is now beginning to grasp how some of these gifts could potentially be there in the fully evolved human being. Christian theology recognizes Jesus to be a fully divine human being, as fully divine as a human being can be. If we start to say he is *more* fully divine than a human being can be, we stray away from the idea that he is fully human and fully divine. If he is fully human, he cannot be more divine than any other fully evolved human being. What made him fully divine was that his consciousness was one with God's consciousness – he was at-one with God. This makes perfect sense of some of the words attributed to him in John's gospel (the word "attributed" is used deliberately, as the Gospel of John is not only the latest of the gospels, but is very different from the others, containing long discourses of Jesus written some 60-70 years after the events. There is much debate as to whether they are the words of Jesus or John's long and mystically-inspired contemplation on the real

meaning of the Christ event – a developed, insightful understanding of esoteric truth.)

> I ask not only on behalf of these, but also on behalf of those
> who will believe in me through their word, that they may all
> be one. As you, Father, are in me and I am in you, may they
> also be in us, so that the world may believe that you have sent
> me. The glory that you have given me I have given them, so
> that they may be one, as we are one, I in them and you in me,
> that they may become completely one. (John 17:20-23)

Joel S. Goldsmith, founder of *The Infinite Way* movement, has an
interesting view that the unveiled truth of Jesus' teachings was
known by some for about three hundred years after Jesus'
ministry on earth, but that around 300AD, as the creeds were
beginning to be developed, the truth was veiled again and has
remained veiled until recent times.

> Every time truth has been revealed, those to whom it was
> revealed have identified the truth with the name of the
> revelatory and worshiped him. The revelatory never did this,
> because anyone who is high enough in consciousness to
> receive such a revelation would never personalize it. In fact,
> no person could be an open channel to receive such a
> revelation if he were tempted to use it for personal gain or
> aggrandizement. But there are others possibly who, either
> through ignorance or evil intent, decide to build a statue to
> Moses, Elijah, Jesus, or some other revelatory, and then the
> veil is on again. Jesus removed the veil, and he did it so that
> the truth would be perfectly clear throughout all ages.[10]

The truth that Goldsmith talks of is the understanding that we
have the same nature as Jesus, who spoke of himself saying,

I can do nothing on my own... If I testify about myself, my testimony is not true. (John 5:30-31),

My teaching is not mine but his who sent me. (John 7:16).

Goldsmith makes the point that human identity of Jesus was the same as yours and mine – fully human. Yet, in John's gospel particularly, Jesus made what sounds like claims to be God, particularly in the 'I am' statements:

I am the bread of life. (John 6:35)

I am the light of the world. (John 8:12)

I am the gate. (John 10:9)

I am the good shepherd. (John 10:11)

I am the resurrection and the life. (John 11:25)

I am the way, the truth and the life. (John 14:6)

I am the vine, you are the branches. (John 15:5)

The "I AM"

The "I AM" in mystical theology is the part of us that identifies with God, the part that is God in us. God is there within every one of us, if we can only open ourselves to the presence. It is the experience of non-dual or unitive consciousness. Therein lies the mystery, that within each of us is both the personal "I am" and the Divine "I AM." Goldsmith crystallizes it in saying that every truth spoken about Jesus Christ or any of the saints or sages of the past or present is the truth to be realized about every person.[11] This is where a crucial distinction has to be made between the Word of God, the Logos (as it is in Greek), and the historical Jesus – a distinction grounded in the New Testament. In Christian theology, the Christ is the eternal Word, or Logos, of God, which was with the Father and the Holy Spirit from all eternity:

In the beginning was the Word, and the Word was with God,

and the Word was God. (John 1:1).

At Jesus' birth in Bethlehem, or at the baptism of Jesus (dependent on one's theology), the Word of God, the Logos, became incarnate in the historical Jesus. At certain points in John's gospel, Jesus refers to himself as the incarnate Logos, such as in the words, *"Before Abraham was born, I am"* (John 8:58). This was very meaningful to the Jews. "I AM" was the name that God called himself in the Old Testament. When Moses stood in front of the presence of God in the burning bush, he asked what name he should give to God:

> God said to Moses, "I AM WHO I AM." He said further, "Thus you shall say to the Israelites, 'I AM has sent me to you.'" (Exodus 3:14)

In Hebrew, the words "I AM" express unchanging and eternal Being, or Becoming. John Henson, author of a new translation of the many books of the New Testament, *"Good As New,"* made the comment that the sense in Hebrew is both present and future and means "I am what I am" and also "I will be what I will be." This indicates not only the eternal existence of God, but also the eternal progressive, developing, adventurous, evolving, surprising aspect of God. The whole point of "I AM" is that it is *not* a name or title, but an assertion that God is ultimately unknowable and ultimately unpredictable. Jesus altered that somewhat by, in both deed and word, indicating that God's essential nature is love.[12]

Throughout most English translations of the Old Testament, the word 'LORD' in capital letters is actually a representation of the four letters "YHWH" (called the tetragrammaton), meaning "I AM," or "Being." In the reading of the Old Testament during Jewish worship, "I AM" was a constant reminder to the Jews of the name of God. In most English translations, we find YHWH translated as LORD (in capital letters). Why should this be so? Bruce Metzger, in the introduction to the New Revised Standard Version of the Bible, explains that the original Hebrew had only consonants and no vowel sounds indicated. These were added by Jewish scholars called the Masoretes between the 7th and 10th centuries AD. By the time the Masoretes added vowel sounds to the text, the name of God had come to be considered too sacred to be pronounced.

So they attached vowel signs indicating that in its place should be read the Hebrew word *Adonai* meaning "Lord." Ancient Greek translators employed the word *Kyrios* ("Lord") for the name. The Vulgate likewise used the name *Dominus* ("Lord").[13]

"LORD" gives a title to God that has all sorts of overtones of power, dominance and control. However, any Jews who read Hebrew would always recognize the name of God, "I AM WHO I AM," where they saw the four letters YHWH. So when, as recorded in John's gospel, Jesus said, *"Before Abraham was born, I am,"* or *"I am the way, the truth and the life,"* it would be heard by the Jews as more like *"Before Abraham was born, I was in God"*, and *"God in me is the way, the truth and the life"*. Jesus was implying that his identity was located in the consciousness of God within him. This, from a fully human being, can be seen as way of stating that the God of all is present in everyone. "I AM" referred to the eternal Logos of God, who was with the Father before the foundation of the world, who holds everything in being, and not the human Jesus born of Mary. Because most English translations use LORD instead of YHWH or I AM, we have totally lost that association in the Western Church with the "I am" statements that Jesus made. Bringing back that association makes it much more clear that Jesus was a human being immersed in God-consciousness, awakened into the universal Logos, the Word of

God. It was through this "Word" that the compassionate consciousness of God breathed all of creation.

The Christ

In traditional Christianity we refer to Jesus as Christ or Messiah – they both mean the same: "the anointed one" in Greek and Hebrew respectively. It is a title, like Earl or Duke. If a title were conferred upon, for instance, a man called Kevin, he could be called Earl Kevin, or Kevin the Earl, but not Kevin Earl – Earl would not be his surname. So it should be either Christ Jesus, Messiah Jesus or Jesus *the* Christ, Jesus *the* Messiah. Christ is *not* a surname.

To be an "anointed one" comes from the Hebrew of the Old Testament. Persons and things were anointed to signify holiness, being set apart for God. The tabernacle (tent of meeting) of the Israelites and all its furnishings were anointed because it was there that the Israelites were to meet with God.[14] Kings, priests and prophets were anointed to indicate that they were set apart by God for the task they had to do.[15] Anointing was simply an indication, a recognition that the person or object had a special, godly role to fulfill. The fact that the disciples called Jesus "The Christ" was the recognition that this man was specially anointed by the Spirit, a prophet, a specially gifted person with a godly task – and maybe the one to lead them to freedom from the Romans. "The Christ" has come to mean much more than that, and is often identified as mentioned with the Logos, the Word of God, a sort of universal Christ-principle. That was *not* what the disciples and first followers of Jesus meant.

So how did this very human person come to the exalted position of King of kings, Exalted One, Only Begotten Son, and all the other titles attributed to him in Christian tradition? Bishop John Spong, a liberal theologian, takes the realistic view that it largely came about as orthodoxy established itself through the repression of other opinions by those in power:

As theology developed in the west, Jesus became first the divine Son of God, then the incarnation of the holy God, and finally the second person of the eternal Trinity of three persons in one God. This theistic God still ruled the world, sent the sun and the rain, and made invasions to cure a sickness here or lead an army to victory there. If any part of this tightly defined theological system was challenged, excommunications resulted; and if the offence of unbelief was severe enough, death at the stake was demanded, in flames slow enough to graciously allow time for repentance before life was terminated. In the name of security, all doubts were repressed, and all ambivalence denied.[16]

In his book *"A New Christianity,"* Spong charts a courageous course away from the theistic, anthropomorphic understanding of God. For him, the concept of God as a supernatural being that can help a nation win a war, or cure a person's sickness, or affect the weather for anyone's benefit is outmoded and irrelevant. This leads on to implications for Jesus, who can, in Spong's view, no longer be seen as an earthly incarnation of a supernatural deity, with miraculous powers. Nor does he see humanity as fallen, but rather sin and evil is seen as the side effect of our evolutionary development of selfhood, our fall away from the presence of God.

Disentangling Jesus from tradition

A perennial puzzle for theologians is to try to disentangle the layers of theology that have been added to Jesus the Christ from his actual historical life and death. The American theologian, Marcus Borg, has developed the idea of the pre-Easter Jesus and the post-Easter Christ. He sees Jesus, before his death, as an enlightened Galilean Jew, executed by the Romans around 30CE. The flesh-and-blood Jesus is dead and gone. The post-Easter Jesus is what Borg perceives that Jesus became after his death, the Jesus of Christian experience and tradition. Jesus continued to be experienced by his followers after his death, and still is today, and so the post-Easter Jesus is an experiential reality. This belief has also been developed, shaped and enclosed in the tradition of the Church. The gospels were all written out of that tradition and experience, and the theology of the Church has developed it over the last two thousand years.[17] Borg understands Jesus in this way:

> The decisive revelation of what a life full of God looks like. Radically centered in God and filled with the Spirit, he is a decisive disclosure and epiphany of what can be seen of God in a human life.[18]

Borg sees in the gospels a five-strand understanding of the pre-Easter Jesus. He describes him as a Jewish mystic, a healer, a wisdom teacher, a social prophet, and a movement initiator.[19] Each of these gives insight into an aspect of Jesus' ministry as recorded in the gospels. Combine them all in one person, and you have a very special, enlightened human being of enormous wisdom, charisma and ability. But there is no indication that Jesus intended that he himself should be worshiped in the way he has been. In the gospels, he always pointed to the divine life that he called the Father, the Creator and Sustainer of all. He tried continually to put us in touch with the Father through repentance, which is turning away from or going beyond self-centeredness and the life of the ego to God-centeredness.

Did Jesus ever make the claim that he had a fully divine nature equal to that of God? He may have said, *"I and the Father are one"* (John 10:30), but he never said he was God. He also said, *"Why do you call me good? No one is good but God alone."* (Mark 10:18), which indicates that he did not think of himself as God. And again, *"The Father is greater than I."* (John 14:28). He was fully at-one with God, and it could be said he was more God-conscious than any other person has ever been. However, what if we are all at different stages of a path that takes us ever deeper into the consciousness of God? Is it too hard to believe that Jesus was at a point far ahead of us all, but which one day we, that is, the rest of the human race, will also reach? One day we may all reach the stature of Christ, and then the words from Jesus may come true:

> Very truly, I tell you, the one who believes in me will also do the works that I do and, in fact, will do greater works than these, because I am going to the Father. (John 14:12)

The theologian, John Macquarrie, follows a train of thought along the same lines:

> It seems that we must assert that at the limit of human existence Christ manifests divine Being, so that in him humanity and deity come together... If indeed Jesus Christ is true God and true man, we seem driven to posit a kind of open place, as it were, where divine Being and human existence come together; or again, where creaturely being, which seeks to be like God, has actually attained to the level of deity.[20]

If it is possible for one "creaturely being" to attain the level of deity, then it is the potential inherent in the human race and is not exclusive to Jesus. To bring in a new scientific insight, as described in Chapter 3, Jesus will have affected the morphic field of all humanity, quickening the potential for us all to be like him and do what he has done. He not only trod the path himself, he blazed a new path for us all to follow. The New Testament letters refer to this level that Jesus attained as the "mind of Christ":

> Let the same mind be in you that was in Christ Jesus (Philippians 2:5)

Those who are spiritual discern all things, and they are themselves subject to no one else's scrutiny. "For who has known the mind of the Lord so as to instruct him?" But we have the mind of Christ. (1 Corinthians 2:15-16)

In these two quotes, the mind of Christ is almost expressed as a further stage of human evolution, something that Jesus was graced with, or had awakened into, to show the full divine potential of the human being. An additional thought is that Jesus pointed away from himself to the Father, to show how humankind could progress spiritually. As already mentioned, when he said, *"I am the way, the truth and the life,"* he was not meaning his own ego-self, but the eternal "I AM" that is God, into which his awareness had awakened. He demonstrated a way of surrender, putting down his own desires, his own "fleshly nature," or ego, and giving himself in total surrender. The material, physical world could not contain him, death could not hold him, and resurrection was maybe his way to show that this path was possible for all humanity, not just one human being.

Macquarrie, however, does not concur with the idea that Jesus may have had supernatural powers, preferring to see those as "add-ons" by the early Church:

The researches of form-criticism have made it clear that the Jesus of history has, to a much greater extent than hitherto recognized, slipped beyond the horizon of what we can know, and that the figure represented in the gospels, and the incidents concerning him are, to say the least, strongly colored by the faith and teaching of the early Church. The historical, human Jesus has, in the thought of the Church, been transformed into the supernatural Christ... The story of Jesus in the gospels is told in the light of this conception of the supernatural Christ, and the beliefs of the Church about Jesus as the Christ have been read back into the story of his life.[21]

As an example, Macquarrie gives the way in which German theologian Rudolph Bultmann and others say that Jesus did not think of himself as Christ, or Messiah, and that the gospel writers have projected the beliefs of the early Church onto him in their writings, rather than just stick to historical facts (if those could ever be truly ascertained).[22] However, given the new scientific insights from epigenetics as mentioned in Chapter 2, it would seem that humanity has the potential to heal, to channel healing energy, and all the beliefs about Jesus as a healer were probably based in reality. A human mind, operating from a center of love, the compassionate consciousness of God, has potential beyond our current understanding. What seems 'supernatural' may in fact be the natural qualities of any highly evolved and spiritually awakened human being operating from the compassionate consciousness of God within. Indeed, Bishop John Spong talks of the life of Jesus in terms of love, which expresses the idea of being at-one with God in a different way:

What human life needs is not a divine rescue. What we need is a life so open, so free, so whole, and so loving that, when we experience that life, we are called into the reality of love. We are opened to the source of love and enter the empowering presence of love. Such a life then becomes our doorway into the infinite and inexhaustible power of love. I call that love God. I see it in Jesus of Nazareth, and I find myself called into a new being, a boundary-free humanity, and made whole in its presence. So God was in Christ, I say. Jesus thus reveals the source of love, and then he calls us to enter it.[23]

Disentangling Jesus from some of the later layers of tradition, we begin to perceive a new way of looking at Jesus' life. It was not so much a sacrificial life, more an evolutionary fulfillment and demonstration of the potential of a human being who has attained the full measure of the compassionate consciousness of

God. In his life of healing and miracles, he showed the ability to change reality by the power of prayer and intention, in connection with the underlying energetic fields. In his path to the cross, he showed a full surrender of the ego, a *kenosis* or *emptying* of the lower self (more on this in the next chapter). The resurrection demonstrates that there is a beyond, and that there is the possibility of those who are fully evolved and enlightened coming back in some energetic form, consciously and with full awareness, at least for a short time. In living this life and death, Jesus changed the morphic field for all humanity, a new way of seeing that he "saved us from our sins." His level of evolution of human nature has enlarged this field, gradually enabling all of humanity to express more love and compassion in this world, helping us all to reach higher levels of compassionate consciousness, i.e. to enter into God in a new way, to be "born again." From all these considerations, I believe Jesus did not intend to be exalted, he was to be followed. He did not want to be worshiped, he was to be imitated. He had no desire to be divinized separately from the rest of humanity, but he wanted to reveal the divinity within the true nature of humanity. The human race is on an evolutionary journey, with some more advanced than others. Jesus was so far ahead of the rest of us that he was seen as god-like, but he was actually mapping out a path for us all to follow. With painfully slow steps, the level of consciousness of the human race is rising, and the dawn of the kingdom of God, compassionate consciousness, is beginning.

Resurrection

What happened at the resurrection? It is so central to the Christian belief. My thoughts in this area are still being developed fully, involving other levels and realms of reality which go beyond the scope of this book, so all I can offer here are some pointers towards further consideration. His resurrection body, as recorded in the gospels, was certainly not a normal human body. He could appear and disappear through locked doors (John 20:19). He could function perfectly well with a deep wound in the side and pierced and torn hands and feet, not to mention the severe lashings and beating he received before the crucifixion (John 20:26-28). And on the road to Emmaus, he could prevent people from recognizing him until he wanted them to, and could then vanish from their sight (Luke 24:13-31). How could the bruised, battered, pierced body of Jesus do this? Following on from the thought that Jesus was a human being who fulfilled the human potential, with an element of control over the quantum physics of the world around him, we can conjecture that his energy field kept the pattern of his being at an unseen level, a higher plane, another level of vibration. His resurrection was to show humanity what we are capable of, and his resurrection body was somehow re-materialized from that energy field. At the Ascension, he dematerialized and went on to a higher dimension of being.

That last sentence might sound like new-age mumbo-jumbo to some, but it is actually expressing the Christ-event in contemporary terms. It may sound far-fetched, but to the contemporary spiritual seeker outside of Christianity, the traditional Christian version sounds much *more* far-fetched. It says that when Jesus died he overcame death for all of us, that in dying he took the sins of humanity throughout all history on himself and defeated them, and that he broke the power of Satan and evil. To many today, these statements are literally incredible and unbelievable. They have been helpful in the past when humanity in general had a pre-scientific, pre-rational worldview and to those who still hold that worldview today. They are familiar words to the Christian, but are they more believable than ideas that emerge from theories about quantum physics, energy fields and morphic resonance? It very much depends on your worldview or paradigm, which is how you make sense of the world. In the Western world, the traditional Christian worldview no longer works for most.

Christianity has always adapted its message to the prevailing worldview, which often brings new insights and understanding, and this is the task facing the Church in this present day. We live in a very rational world, in many ways dominated by the language of science, technology and the internet. You only have to think of the number of new words that have come into the vocabulary in recent years. We can now "google" information, write "blogs," we "twitter" or go for some form of "quantum" therapy. We can "download" films to entertain us with "brain candy," or listen to "mp3s" that give us an "earworm." We are "appraised" at work, we "brainstorm," we take part in "blue sky thinking." Language changes, and in order to connect, the language of religion has to move on. To convey a message, it has to be in the culture of those who are to receive it – it has to be "enculturized." Scientists face the same problem in trying to convey their perception on the world – finding the right language to convey difficult concepts is often tricky.

These ideas on the resurrection link together with the idea of morphic resonance and the atonement in Chapter 3. Jesus, in living a life of self-emptying and surrender to the divine impulse that lead to his death, changed the morphic field for all humanity. This change in the human morphic field has made it possible for us all to approach the divine through that same self-emptying. The morphic field now contains a path to overcome the selfish nature and in this way we can make the link to Jesus living and dying for our sins. When this is combined with a fuller understanding of the nature of reality – that we are all composed of seething, interacting, fields of energy that go beyond our space-time continuum – then the view espoused above about the resurrection begins to make some sense. Consciousness is prime; everything emerges from it and our bodies are held in it. Our consciousness is capable of amazing things. Jesus had not just human consciousness, but God-consciousness as well. Is it too much to consider that his level of evolved consciousness brought control over the matter that is formed from the energetic reality of our beings, and could thus come back after death in an apparently solid form?

Christ Consciousness

Over the last fifty years, the term 'Christ consciousness' has slowly crept into common use. Its history goes back much further. I first came across it in the writings of Alice Bailey, who, between 1919 and 1949, wrote, or channeled, a series of books from a theosophical perspective, espousing what she called the "Ageless Wisdom." I believe it may even go back to the writings of theologian Friedrich Schleiermacher in the 19th century. Since the 1960s, it has been used in various ways to indicate a level of access to the divine that distinguishes between the person of Jesus of Nazareth and the Christ-principle in the universe. In *"Field of Compassion,"* Judy Cannato makes this distinction between Jesus and the Christ. If God is seen as the compassionate consciousness that has brought everything into being – and holds it there – then Christ consciousness is the ultimate in human spiritual development.

> While Jesus was the evolutionary first, those who follow after him must enter into the process of accepting as fully as they can the divine self-communication that is at the heart of evolutionary history and human life. In this sense, "The Christ" is not a reference to a person, but to a kind of consciousness that is resonant with the Spirit and expresses itself in freedom and love.[24]

In Christian tradition, the Christ is the anointing, the special touch of God, uniting that person with the mind of God – hence Jesus of Nazareth became the Christ. But "Christing," or becoming like Christ, is open to all. Jesus himself is recorded as saying *"The one who believes in me will also do the works that I do and, in fact, will do greater works than these."* (John 14:12) This has been a puzzle for Christian theology – how can we be greater than the only begotten Son? In this case, it is traditional theology that is causing the problem. In defining Jesus Christ not just as Son of God, but also as the *only begotten* Son, it implies that no one can be quite like him. However, if the anointing, or "Christing," is seen as an indication of a more evolved consciousness, and even as a principle of creation, then there is a loving Christ-principle drawing us towards the consciousness of God. (I have used the term "Christing" rather than "christening," as the latter is associated with babies, entry into the church, and a formal church ceremony, rather than being recognized as the special touch of God.)

Ken Wilber, a leading writer on theories of spiritual development, speaks of love as an evolutionary force, the central driver in the universe, a force fundamentally woven in to the fabric of the cosmos. Love is the driver that brings all things into relationship, from elementary particles, atoms and molecules to sentient beings. Its purpose is to bring the cosmos to awareness and back to the divine presence that started it in the first place.[25] This is a huge concept, and fits well with Christian theology of the God of love.

The destiny of the human species is to grow towards full Christ consciousness, which can be seen as the state of being that happens when we are awakened to our existence as part of the consciousness of God. When the divine and human come together as one, then we have become Christ-conscious. This has been experienced temporarily by the mystics down through the ages – the mystical or numinous experience of the oneness of all with God, the ultimate reality. The sixteenth century mystic, Teresa of Avila described such an experience:

When the Lord so wills, it may happen that the soul will be at prayer, and in possession of all its senses, and that then there will suddenly come to it a suspension in which the Lord communicates most secret things to it, which it seems to see within God Himself... in which is revealed to the soul how all things are seen in God, and how within Himself He contains them all. Such a vision is highly profitable because, although it passes in a moment, it remains engraven upon the soul.[26]

William James, in his classic work on religious experience, identifies this experience in all religious traditions:

This overcoming of all the usual barriers between the individual and the Absolute is the great mystic achievement. In mystic states we both become one with the Absolute and we become aware of our oneness. This is the everlasting and triumphant mystical tradition, hardly altered by differences of clime or creed. In Hinduism, in Neoplatonism, in Sufism, in Christian mysticism, we find the same recurring note.[27].

This state of mystical union happened in Jesus, but not just for a moment – he remained constantly in this state of oneness with God, totally identified with the compassionate consciousness of God. Being fully "Christed" is when self-consciousness fades away and our awareness is purely of the consciousness of God holding everything in being. Thus Jesus became the divine-human God-man. He was able to go beyond self-consciousness and enter fully into God-consciousness.

This is the story of the human race that we find in the creation story of Adam and Eve (Genesis 2:15 – 3:24) and in Jesus' parable of the prodigal son (Luke 15:11-32). As already mentioned in Chapter 1, we can see these as the metaphorical story of the formation of ego and self-consciousness. Self-consciousness emerges through separation out from God-consciousness and the emergence of ego. The ego develops to bring us to the point of God-awareness. From that point, we are on the long journey back to God. We struggle to lose the separateness and duality and merge our consciousness back with God, i.e. become Christed, human and divine nature coming together again. (This is a central concept in the Greek and Russian Orthodox tradition, called "deification.") All the time, the compassionate consciousness of God is urging, encouraging and leading us back, if we can only access it within us.

The point of being a Christian is to follow the way of Jesus, to become "Christed" or become like Jesus. In these new terms, that means having our level of spiritual consciousness raised to the level at which we can transcend the ego, go beyond the individual "I am," and become one with God, the greater "I AM". This is attaining the state of unitive consciousness, or Christ consciousness. It is entering the realm of universal love, opening the heart fully to God. Jesus encapsulated it in the great commandments:

"Teacher, which is the greatest commandment in the Law?"

Jesus replied: "'Love the Lord your God with all your heart and with all your soul and with all your mind." This is the first and greatest commandment. And the second is like it: "Love your neighbor as yourself." (Matthew 22:36-39)

One website, "Ask the Real Jesus," puts it in a way that ties in with the scientific theory of primacy of consciousness mentioned in the first chapter:

The Christ consciousness can see that anything in the world of form (matter) is simply an expression of the deeper reality of God. The Christ consciousness can see beyond any outer appearance. It can even see beyond the world of form and perceive the state of pure being. The Christ consciousness is a universal state of consciousness. By that I mean that it is not individualized. It is individualized only when a spiritual being (a son or daughter of God) makes a free-will decision to unite with that Christ mind and thereby come to a full recognition of its spiritual identity and origin.[28]

This is quite reminiscent of a scene in the film, "The Matrix," when the hero, Neo, (also called "The One" with strong overtones of the story of Jesus) has a breakthrough and is able to perceive the reality behind the world of matter in which he lives. He begins to see the computer code from which the reality he is experiencing is created. It is all one big computer program, and once he can see the computer code, he is able to alter this reality to help human consciousness to escape from it. (In the film, computers have taken over the world and hold human beings in stasis in pods, whilst their consciousness experiences the computer world.) The central idea is that one human being becomes aware of the true nature of reality by extending his consciousness, and thus is able to go beyond it and use the intuitive knowledge gained to overcome the evil forces and release the rest of humanity. Basically, it seems to be an analogy to the story of Jesus the Christ.

So many words! We can read and learn and study, but until the learning is lived out, we are paddling in the shallows. The spiritual path is about living it out, entering into that compassionate consciousness that is God. In Chapter 8, we shall look at Christian practice – how we live it out – but there are some further implications to be considered first, particularly Jesus' teaching on the kingdom in the next chapter.

Chapter 6

Revisiting the Kingdom

~

Here we consider what Jesus meant in his teaching about the kingdom, touching on the true meaning of repentance and how we need awakening. It is a movement from head to heart and into compassion. We consider how the key messages of Jesus have been filtered.

~

The Kingdom

We have looked at the nature of Jesus in the light of four new scientific insights, and now we consider the dominant theme in Jesus' teaching as we have it in the gospels: the kingdom of God or the kingdom of heaven (both terms refer to the same concept). There is no indication in the gospels that he intended to start a new religion, but rather to bring a message that would help people on their spiritual path within the Jewish tradition into the awareness of the God of love. His disciples were instructed to take his message out into the world and make more disciples, in the same manner that a rabbi might want to spread his teaching. The theme of the kingdom occurs some 70 times in the gospels, and the word itself is used over 100 times, mostly in Matthew and Luke. No other word used by Jesus has been subject to so much speculation. Much of that speculation has centered on whether the kingdom he had in mind was to be earthly or heavenly. Did he intend to set up a select group of devotees who would receive their reward later? Was he advocating a political revolution? Was he predicting the imminent end of the world? Did he change his mind about whether the kingdom was here and now, or later and somewhere else? His message was *"Repent, for the kingdom of heaven is near."* His followers were told to *"Seek first his kingdom"* and *"Become like little children."* Peter was told he held the keys to the kingdom of heaven, and Jesus said they already had been given the relevant knowledge:

The knowledge of the secrets of the kingdom of heaven has been given to you. (Matthew 13:11)

The kingdom was near, among them and within them:

Once, having been asked by the Pharisees when the kingdom of God would come, Jesus replied, "The kingdom of God does not come with your careful observation, nor will people say, 'Here it is," or 'There it is," because the kingdom of God is within you." (Luke 17:20-21)

The Greek word for kingdom, *basileia*, could equally be translated as *realm* or *reign*. The usual characteristics of a realm, reign or kingdom were authority, obedience, law, compulsion, taxes to a central state, shared defense, common language etc. Jesus used many parables to describe the realm of God to his followers, to convey the radical notion of the way God wanted to see it happening. These parables were to be chewed over, to extract the nourishment like a cow chewing the cud. According to the parables of Jesus, the kingdom of heaven or realm of God is like:

A mustard seed – tiny seed that grows to become a very large plant, a veritable tree. (Matthew 13:31-32)

Yeast – a tiny bit of which works throughout a whole batch of dough. (Matthew 13:33)

Treasure in a field – so go out and buy the whole field. (Matthew 13:44)

A precious pearl – so spend all your money to buy it. (Matthew 13:45-46)

A net that pulls in all sorts of fish, some to be thrown away, some to be kept. (Matthew 13:47-49)

A man who sows good seed, only to find weeds growing up amongst them – they will be separated at harvest. (Matthew 13:24-30)

A banquet, a feast, to which all are invited. (Matthew 22:2-14)

A king who wanted to settle accounts with his servants, and the king is merciful and just. (Matthew 18:23-35)

A vineyard owner who hired men at different times during the day to work in his vineyard and all were paid equally, some with great generosity. (Matthew 20:1-16)

The ten virgins who took their lamps and went out to meet the bridegroom – some were unprepared and so missed the bridegroom. (Matthew 25:1-13)

His teaching invites two elementary questions. Is the kingdom for now or is it "pie in the sky when you die," i.e. is it a state of heaven to come, or have we somehow got it already? Secondly, is it something within us, or is it something between and amongst us? Luke's gospel implies it is both among and within us (Luke 17:21). The understanding of God as compassionate consciousness can help us with these questions. God's consciousness is panentheistic, i.e. God is both within and among us, sustaining us – the concept is that rather than God being 'in us', we are 'in God'. God is the one in whom "we live and move and have our being" (Acts 17:28). The idea that God is "among us" is the concept of a corporately shared experience of God, a unity that we can enter into. Being "in the kingdom" is akin to the state of unitive consciousness that we have been speaking about earlier, an experience in which we have the potential to share. It is the awareness of the pantheistic presence of God. The kingdom then lies both within and among us, it is "both-and" rather than "either-or." It is also both now and not-yet, as we have the potential to live the kingdom way, but not yet the level of enlightenment needed. The potential to be gained is to remain in the state of unitive consciousness, operating from a place of compassion, rather than just experiencing it in moments of enlightenment. The hope is that we can stabilize this kingdom state of oneness, so that the moments become longer, and the gap between them shorter. We have been given, in Jesus, the example of the kingdom way of living now, and we are given a hope for its fullness in the future.

Jesus demonstrated this kingdom in action, to make people think about what it really means to live God's way. Sadly, in the Church, we have lost some of the impact of that message. It is, more than anything, a way of being that leads to a way of doing. The way of being has to be firmly established first, the way of compassion, for if we do not operate from the place of compassion, our doing can become very egotistical.

Repentance and Renewal

The kingdom and repentance are linked – the gospels reveal that Jesus came to tell us to repent, because of the proximity of the kingdom. It was a call to "get yourselves sorted out now" because the reign of God was close.

"Repent, for the kingdom of heaven is near"(Matthew 4:17).

"The kingdom of God is near. Repent and believe the good news." (Mark 1:15).

Repentance is commonly taken to mean, "Say you are sorry." The act of penitence is at the heart of the Anglican and Roman liturgies, confession followed by absolution. Or, in evangelical circles, it has been expressed as "turn around and turn back to God," or even, in the harshest and hard-hearted interpretation, "turn or burn."

However, the meaning of the Greek word, *metanoia*, contains a surprise. It does not mean feeling sorrowful for doing or thinking bad things. It does not even mean, "to turn around." It is not just about starting out again with God. The word can be broken down into two parts, *meta* and *noia*. *Meta* can mean "beyond", "after", "beside", "among", or "with", and *noia* is from *nous*, which means "mind" or "thought". So it is really saying "go beyond the mind" or "go with or beside the mind". In New Testament Greek, the common meaning of metanoia was to change one's mind or heart about someone or something. The repentance that Jesus is talking about is to go beyond ourselves, to enter into the Great Mind, the consciousness of God, to change to a new level of awareness, or, as St Paul put it *"to be transformed by the renewing of your mind"* (Romans 12:2). Jesus linked repentance with the closeness of the kingdom of God, the rule of God. He was talking about a new way of being; ascending to a new level of awareness, going beyond our egos, getting out of our self-centered minds and entering the large mind, the "I AM", the compassionate consciousness of God – the kingdom.

Awakening into the Kingdom

Cynthia Bourgeault expresses the kingdom as something more subtle to be awoken into:

It's not later, but lighter – some more subtle quality or

dimension of experience accessible to you right at this moment. You don't die into it; you awaken into it.[1]

That puts a different perspective on it. It says that we are awakening or spiritually ascending to our true nature as those who live in the kingdom of God, or, to use a more contemporary phrase, as those who are in tune with the flow of God's consciousness. Bourgeault makes the point that the kingdom can be seen as a metaphor for a state of consciousness – not a place that you go to, but a state you come from, a transformed awareness that turns reality inside-out. We come from this state of oneness with God, the place where all is seen as interconnected, where there is no separateness between God and humans, or between humans and humans, or between humanity and all creation. The spiritual path is the journey we undertake to get back to that state of being. Everything is interconnected – as particle physics is now showing in the entangled nature of all particles in this physical reality, through the zero-point and Akashic fields of energy discussed in Chapter 4. Six hundred years ago, this was recognized by the mystics and expressed by Hildegaard of Bingen:

> Everything that is in the heavens, in the earth, and under the earth is penetrated with connectedness, penetrated with relatedness.

The modern name for this 'rewiring' of the brain to a state of oneness is non-dual consciousness, or unitive consciousness. Once attained only by the greatest of mystics, unitive consciousness is being sought after and found for brief moments by many today. The difficulty is in staying there, so that the consciousness is properly transformed, as we so easily revert back to being centered in the ego-mind, where we find comfort in our self-centered nature. As we continue to practice meditation, instead of having to go to or retreat to this state after we are triggered by a stressful situation, we increasingly abide in unitive consciousness and therefore meet the word from this place and can act with greater clarity and compassion

Increasingly, people are taking up forms of meditation in an effort to change themselves and the world they live in. This would correspond to the idea of morphic resonance outlined in Chapter 3. As more people experience this unitive consciousness, so more people are enabled to experience it, because the morphic field for humanity is changed. It is a new way of thinking – a new-old way. Unitive consciousness had an ancient name, the name it was called by Jesus – the kingdom of God. It was the core of his teaching and his world vision. This kingdom was not a political utopia, nor a place you go when you die. It is a different viewpoint on the world that gives a perspective of generosity, abundance and compassion. It is living to experience the fruit of the Spirit that St Paul talks about:

The fruit of the Spirit is love, joy, peace, patience, kindness, generosity, faithfulness, gentleness, and self-control. There is no law against such things. (Galatians 5:22-23)

The idea that the kingdom is for now, and that we awaken into it has had little emphasis in Christian tradition. It has largely been seen as a reward, the place we go to when we die, not something for now. This is possibly because humanity has not, on the whole, had the perceptual framework, or evolved consciousness to take the full message of Jesus on board. Entering the kingdom is about seeing reality in the same way as Jesus did, which means awakening into the state of unitive consciousness. To put on the mind of Christ is not primarily about behaving with more moral earnestness, but about 'rewiring' our basic perceptual field so that we see the world in the same way as Jesus did. In Chapter 8, we shall look in some depth at the practice of meditation and silent prayer, which has been shown to be a way to 'rewire the brain' so that a state of altered consciousness can be reached that allows us access to the divine consciousness. The silence of meditation is used to entrain us to let go of our busy thoughts, with the aim to transcend our ego-mind, and enter into the flow of God's consciousness in the silence.

The Kingdom Operating System

In a talk recorded in London in 2008, Cynthia Bourgeault uses an interesting analogy with computer systems.[2] She labels the usual mind, the normal way we think, as the "egoic operating system" (EOS), but uses the analogy of having an upgrade. Early computers struggled to get onto the internet and World Wide Web, because they did not have enough capacity in their operating systems (OS), which were fully occupied with the mundane tasks of running the everyday programs. This is the same as our ordinary mind. Our egoic OS cannot access the kingdom consciousness, because it is too taken up with life and living, getting and having, organizing and sorting, but the unitive consciousness OS can, and does. It gives us access to kingdom consciousness.

The egoic OS is a way of organizing reality for us to make sense of it. Like the binary system in a computer it divides the world into one thing or another, into subject and object. "I love God" turns God into an object, separate from us. Our egoic OS proceeds by breaking things up into little pieces, rationalizing them, and we then identify them by how they are different. We compare and contrast, them and us. This is the way the egoic OS works.

But there is another operating system within us, which we can access. We need to use the egoic OS first to make sense of the world around us, to develop a sense of self, but there is a further, higher way. Mystical tradition identifies it with the heart, the center of our being, the heart operating system, or unitive consciousness. This view perceives holographically, as a whole. It sees the whole from the parts. It sees the connections, and realizes the interconnectedness of everything. Unitive consciousness allows us to see where we are in the whole. It connects us with our fragile planet, of which we are a part, one micro-organism in the macro-organism that is the Earth, and with the divine source that is throughout the universe and also in us. The whole universe is held in that divine source, emanates from it, and is energized by it.

The Kingdom as Unitive Consciousness

In this understanding, being "in the kingdom" means being *aware* of being held in the consciousness of God, connected to the ground of being. Some of the words from John's gospel begin to make much more sense in the light of understanding the kingdom as unitive consciousness.

I and the Father are one (John 10:30)

You will know that I am in my father, and you in me and I in you. (John 14:20)

I am the vine, you are the branches. He who abides in me, and I in him, will bear much fruit. (John 15:5)

They may be one as we are one. I in them and you in me. May they be brought to complete unity. (John 17:22-23)

These, and many more, all point to Jesus' understanding and experience of unitive consciousness. He knew that he was fulfilling the human potential to be one with God, to operate from a more evolved center than the rest of humanity at the time.

This kingdom is not just within, as it is worked out in the world as well. It has both individual and social dimensions. Jesus lived in a culture dominated by "kingship" or "emperorship." All the trappings of power and glory went with the role. Royal power was exclusive, oppressive and class-distinctive. Jesus turned his back on this world of power and privilege, and often sought to undermine its meaning. He offered a counter-cultural view: a new world order marked by relationships of equality, justice, love, peace and liberation. This is what the kingdom of God is about, but it stems from seeing everything as an intercon-nected whole, working from the unitive consciousness operating system. That is the "upgrade" we need to begin to bring in the kingdom.

This new way of looking at things was to bring a sense of inclusiveness to a society where class distinction and exclusive privilege seem to have been quite common. Jesus openly challenged the religious authorities over their nit-picking laws, ignored prevailing taboos, disregarded solemn religious regula-tions, and included everyone in his offer of life. This new way, the kingdom of God, was for all. The same attitude seems to have prevailed in the early Christian communities, with mutual service and support, sharing of property, diversity of gifts, inclusion of the marginalized and oppressed, with room for many different shades of opinion and ways of being Christian. For instance, we hear of the fledgling Church in the Acts of the Apostles:

Now the whole group of those who believed were of one heart and soul, and no one claimed private ownership of any possessions, but everything they owned was held in common. With great power the apostles gave their testimony to the resurrection of the Lord Jesus, and great grace was upon them all. There was not a needy person among them, for as many as owned lands or houses sold them and brought the proceeds of what was sold. (Acts 4:32-34)

As Christianity grew and expanded, priorities became blurred. The rise of the Church as an institution, after its acceptance by the Roman Empire as the state religion, brought rules and regulations, power struggles, male dominance, and creeds and councils to decide who was in and who was out. Oppression and suppression was for those who were not "in," bringing accusations of heresy, trials, burnings, corruption, division, denominations and everything that is wrong with the Church. This was a long way from the prophetic, mystical, Galilean wisdom teacher who took pride in washing road-worn feet, who shared bread with tax-collectors and sinners, who cherished the company and giftedness of women and who denounced the religious leaders of the day as white-washed tombs, clean on the outside, rotten on the inside (Matthew 23:27).

Many Christians today yearn afresh for Jesus' radical view of the kingdom of God. Christendom established a sacred tradition, but one which has become out of step with our culture and, as many believe, has become parted from the original teachings of Jesus and is in decline and disintegration in the West.[3] This confronts the Christian community with some vital questions, some fundamental questions of meaning. As a Christian priest taking services of worship in traditional churches, I find myself dressed in a form of clothing evolved from a Roman formal toga, in the middle of a building whose style evolved a thousand years ago, conducting a service based on a pattern which developed in the fourth century, conveying concepts which have their worldview firmly set in the middle ages, singing songs which have mostly come from one to three hundred years ago and are based on those medieval concepts. I have to ask, "What relevance do all these cultural trappings have for the spiritual seeker?" The teachings of Jesus, the heart message of the Bible, the core values of love, mercy, and justice are all highly relevant, but they can get lost in the middle of all the "churchiness" of church.

Today's seekers may be interested in some spiritual things,

having done some yoga, or read about meditation. They may wonder what life is about, and whether there is more to it than having a job, a partner, two kids, mortgage and holidays. But they would not think of coming through the doors of a church for a service. Contemporary seekers do not understand all the church tradition, as it seems to have no relevance to them. They just want to feel that there is a God of love, and to live a life that is of value and worth. They might come and sit in the quiet and peace of an open church to reflect and even pray, but the liturgical straightjacket of the words and hymns is not for them. Perhaps existing congregations would be revitalized if the simple message of Jesus was taught more comprehensively. Whilst many appreciate the fine words and music of a church or cathedral service, the point of Jesus' teaching was for humanity to be transformed by love, not to enjoy a church performance, which worship can sometimes become. The best of Christian liturgy and symbolism can aid spiritual searching and enrich our corporate experience of God. However, the liturgy and symbolism often become an end in themselves, rather than a means to an end. Transformation is the goal, not to put on a comfort blanket.

Repent, Love, Forgive: Kingdom

Jesus' teaching was to love God, and love your neighbor as yourself. His central message was quite simple and can be summed up with four words: "Repent," "Love," "Forgive," and "Kingdom." Firstly, repent, as already mentioned, means going beyond the mind and entering the consciousness of God by surrendering or transforming the ego, letting go of the selfish nature. This is a life-long process, involving quite a disciplined spiritual approach. It involves coming to a new level of awareness, where the compassionate consciousness of God is allowed to embrace and form a union with our consciousness.

Secondly, love is absolutely central to his teaching. Love is the key factor, the hallmark of Christianity. Like the words in a stick of seaside rock, it runs through the whole of Christianity. The gospels record his commands to love God, neighbor and oneself, and to love one another as he has loved us. Compassionate love is utterly central to the teaching of Jesus. It is the core value of the life of faithfulness to God, as we see it modeled in Jesus. He sums it up in a very short saying *"Therefore be compassionate as God is compassionate."* [4] The word is often translated as merciful, but compassionate gives a better rendition in current day usage. Having mercy on someone implies a position of superiority to one of inferiority; whereas compassion implies feeling someone else's suffering as though your own. The word for compassion in both Hebrew and Aramaic is related to the word for bowels or womb. Thus, to be compassionate is to be moved in the guts, or to be womb-like. "God is womb-like," Jesus says, "therefore, you are to be womb-like too." Marcus Borg goes into this in some detail.[5] Being compassionate can mean feeling fiercely the protective nature of mother to child and is not to be confused with a softness. It has strength and perseverance. Being womb-like means to be life-giving and nourishing. In the Western Christian tradition, there is a Pauline emphasis that Jesus is the Savior, rescuing us from our sins. However, the Syriac tradition, which resisted the Roman influence, emphasizes Jesus as life-giver, the Single One, giving life abundantly. The Single One is not to do with celibacy, but is one who achieves the state of non-dual consciousness, going beyond the duality of God being experienced as separate from self, and entering into oneness with God. Jesus came to call us to a state of wholeness, oneness with God, to unitive consciousness, a single, unitive whole.

Having compassion as the central virtue of Christianity gives a different emphasis, moving it away from a religion for the righteous towards a way of compassionate action and heart-opening. Marcus Borg elucidates:

Contrast it for a moment to what some Christians have thought the Christian life is most centrally about, that it is really about righteousness – keeping your moral shirt-tails clean, avoiding being stained by the world – in that sense, the Christian life is profoundly different from compassion. In many ways, compassion is almost the opposite of right-eousness in that sense. If righteousness calls us to keep our moral shirt-tails clean, compassion calls us to get stuck in, get dirty in the muck and mire. Jesus, as a person, was filled with compassion, and he calls us to compassion. He didn't stay in the temple debating fine points with the Pharisees, he got stuck in with the sinners and less desirables of the world.[6]

Borg is a little heavy handed in his concept of righteousness here, as it has aspects of *doing* right as well as *being in the* right. Good works were always part of Christian righteousness. Compassion also leads into a concern for justice. The opposite of justice is injustice, which works out at both a personal level and a social level. At its most basic it is the playground cry, "That's not fair!" At higher levels of society, injustice can become endemic in the way social, political, and economic structures have grown. In the last 200 years, the West has tackled one form of endemic injustice after another, often at the instigation of Christians. Slavery, child employment, education, mental verbal and sexual abuse, racism, gender equality, and so on, have all been addressed. We are currently in a stage of discussion and change in relation to world economics, the banking crisis, and international debt. Jesus had a passion to see social justice in society, and his passion stemmed from his compassionate consciousness. He particularly aimed his criticism at the religiously righteous of the day, the scribes and Pharisees, those who had the teaching and knowledge, but failed to live out the path of love.[7] This set him against the political power structures of the time, leading eventually to his death.

Thirdly, Jesus called us to "Forgive". When someone has hurt us, we may harbor feelings of resentment, anger and hurt. If we hold on to those, they can slowly poison us, affecting not only our minds, but our bodies as well (a reminder of epigenetics in Chapter 2 and how our feelings, thoughts and intentions affect the behavior of our cells). The emotional turmoil of holding on to those feelings can lead to all sorts of physical problems. The call to forgive is a call to healing and wholeness of being. Jesus was absolutely clear in his instruction that we must forgive:

Forgive us our sins, as we have forgiven those who sin against us. (Matthew 6:12)

Then Peter came to Jesus and asked, "Lord, how many times shall I forgive my brother when he sins against me? Up to seven times?" Jesus answered, "I tell you, not seven times, but seventy-seven times." (Matthew 18:21-2)
(In Hebrew numerology, seven equals perfection)

And when you stand praying, if you hold anything against anyone, forgive him, so that your Father in heaven may forgive you your sins. (Mark 11:25)

Do not judge, and you will not be judged. Do not condemn, and you will not be condemned. Forgive, and you will be forgiven. (Luke 6:37)

The key to unlocking forgiveness lies in growing a heart of compassion. When one can see how another person has come to be the way they are and can understand what has led them to the actions they have taken, then forgiveness becomes an option, or even a necessity. It is an evolutionary step to be able to see that what is in others is also in me. We experience empathy and are moved by the compassionate consciousness of God to offer forgiveness from our heart. Our inspiration for this is the life of

Jesus, who had a core of loving forgiveness at his center.

Repent, Love, Forgive – and Kingdom, the last core part of his message. The kingdom of God was really Jesus' shorthand for the whole message. The kingdom of God is near, is within you. There are many different ways of expressing it. You are beginning to enter the kingdom when:

- you transform your mind;
- you come close to God;
- you enter the consciousness of God;
- you love your neighbor;
- you feel compassion for the world;
- you can forgive those who hurt you.

Then you are entering God's kingdom, which means:

- you are being changed, transformed, refined, purified;
- you are moving up onto God's resonant frequency;
- you are beginning to fulfill the God-given potential that you have as a human being;
- you are aligning yourself with Christ, becoming 'Christed';
- you are becoming God's child;
- you are recognizing the Christ within you.

We can get lost in doctrinal arguments about these things, as many do over baptism, or ordination of women, or homosexuality, but the main message of Jesus was not to talk about it, but to live it out – to live out a life motivated by compassionate consciousness. His message was not about being moral upstanding people living a good life, but to be compassionate people, full of life and light, giving energy and life to others. Morality should emerge from compassion; on its own it can become judgmentalism.

Filtering the message

One of the biggest problems of Christianity is that we only have records of its early development through filters. We have the filters of Paul and Peter, and the filters of Mark, Matthew, Luke and John (to put them in the most accepted order of writing). All the writings of the New Testament have come through people, who filter what they write through their own personality, culture and context. Basically, they put their own spin on the gospel stories. We do not get an unbiased or unadulterated view of Jesus. Christianity has grown to become a bit of a beast, the rolling stone that has accumulated so much moss that it has become unrecognizable at times. Hence the call from many corners to go back to the central teachings of Jesus as outlined above: *repent and unite with the mind of God, show compassionate love, and forgive*. Do these things and we are being transformed and entering the kingdom. At one level, it is so very simple. The Church has, in working out its theology over two millennia, made it very complicated. Jesus' message was about a way of life that leads us into a kingdom way of living, which helps us to progress spiritually.

I say this as a Christian priest, invested with the responsibility of guarding the faith as described in the Book of Common Prayer, the 39 Articles and the Canons of the Anglican Church. However, I came into the ministry because I was inspired by Jesus' message of the kingdom of God, about life in all its fullness in relationship with God, and because I had a desire to help others to find this treasure. The core message of Jesus the Christ is exactly right, but often too many things get in the way in trying to communicate and experience it. With a few exceptions, the Anglican and Roman Catholic Church still uses liturgy and hymnody that presents concepts which have little connection with 21st century living. Despite the fact that many people see beyond this and reach for presence of God, we are still frequently serving up pretty indigestible lumps of sacred stodge on a Sunday morning, rather than giving people some tasty aperitifs that draw them in to the main meal. The indigestibility lies in both the language that is used and the concepts that are reinforced which stem from a previous worldview. We have to get back to the simplicity of the message of Jesus.

The Wisdom Way

Jesus never intended to start a new religion, but neither was he happy with Judaism of the time. He was a Jew, firmly rooted in the tradition, but enlightened by the experience of unitive consciousness. He was working from a new place of being within himself, an awareness of God that he called the kingdom. What he wanted, above all, was to see more people entering into this way of being. He wanted "Kingdom of God" people, those who are able to enter into the compassionate consciousness of God, which sustains our very being. Cynthia Bourgeault calls it the "Wisdom" way, and summarizes it nicely:

In the Wisdom way of knowing, this gamut of subtle energy becomes directly perceivable to the awakened heart. And there, truly, it reveals a vast inner kingdom to be discovered and fulfilled. This realm has been endlessly described by mystics, theologians and visionaries of all the great spiritual traditions. The Greek fathers called it the "intelligible world," the world of pure idea preceding form. To the ancient Hebrews, it was "chesed" or the Mercy of God: a fierce, covenantal field that held divine and human energies together. In the Sufi and theosophical traditions, it's the "imaginal world"; in the Celtic, it's "faerie" – in both cases, an inward and more subtle intelligence illuminating the outward form. The name by which it is more familiar to Christians is the name by which Jesus called it: the "Kingdom of Heaven" – although the usual Christian interpretation put on this phrase, as that place of endless bliss attained after death as a reward for good behavior, is a tragic distortion of what he was actually teaching.[8]

When Jesus talked of the kingdom of God, he was talking, in the Jewish terms of the day, of a higher or deeper plane of consciousness from which we need to operate if we are to bring about a world of love, peace and harmony. This unitive consciousness is an awareness of the interconnectedness of all, sustained in the ground of being, the consciousness of God.

The transition to this is the global shift that the world is currently going through. The impact of the technological revolution connecting us all around the planet has contributed to the "Arab Spring," and is bringing other countries into play in the world scene. The world order is changing, the 'West' is no longer dominating, and change is happening at an ever-increasing rate as the vibrational level of the consciousness of humanity slowly rises. Global warming and the awareness of humanity's impact on the environment is awakening us all to the need to change the way of life that has brought us the civilization in which we live. Although this time is full of predictions of impending doom for the planet (predictions that the media is making the most of), there is another path that is emerging. It is a path of transition, where old ways are dying and a new way is being anchored in the consciousness of humanity. It is the way of compassion, cooperation and coexistence with all living creatures. It is a way of living in harmony with the planet. It is an evolutionary way of moving to a new level of consciousness for the human race. It is the kingdom or wisdom way, the way of Christ.

Chapter 7

Salvation Evolved

~

Salvation has many different shades of meaning, and in this chapter we look at its predominant meaning in connection with wholeness and healing. We consider root meanings of the word in all the biblical languages, some effects on mind, body and spirit, and what it means to be "Christed."

~

Healing and Salvation

Heal me, O LORD, and I shall be healed; save me and I shall be saved, for you are the one I praise.
(Jeremiah 17:14)

Healing and salvation are very closely linked. We especially see that when we look into the root meaning of salvation, the etymology of the word itself. Many assume salvation is simply about "saving" or being "saved" so that we can go to heaven, rather than lost to hell. It is linked with the understanding of the atonement in that Jesus is the advocate who pleads for us and sacrifices himself in our stead – Jesus died for our sins. But being "saved" is not its full meaning. In English, "salvation" traces its lineage to the Sanskrit word *sarva*, which means "all," "whole," "complete" – it is a reference to wholeness, completeness and totality. The root is *sar*, which came into Latin as *sal*, and then into English in words related to health or wholeness, such as "salutary", "salubrious" and "salute" (as in to wish someone good health). Sal is also seen in the Latin word *salvare*, meaning to save, to make safe – as in save from illness or death. In English, that root is seen in the word "salve" – an ointment that heals.

In the Old Testament, the Hebrew word most often translated as "salvation" is *yesha*, or *yeshua*, both of which come from the root *yasha*, meaning to be free, in a wide or roomy space, carrying the sense of being freed from confinement, constriction and limitation. Being brought into a spacious environment is actually the root meaning of the name Jesus, Joshua, or Yeshua. We also find healing associated with listening to the words of Wisdom personified, in the Book of Proverbs.

My child, be attentive to my words; incline your ear to my sayings. Do not let them escape from your sight; keep them within your heart. For they are life to those who find them, and healing to all their flesh. (Proverbs 4:20-22)

In the New Testament, the Greek word translated as "salvation" is *soterion*. Its root is from the word *sozo*, meaning literally "healthy." In the Phoenician system of writing, which was originally pictorial and from which the Greek and Roman alphabets were derived, the symbol that came into Greek as the word *soterion* is a picture of a broken pot or vessel – *soterion* is the process of being made whole, of re-integration. This presents us with a very different picture of salvation – about being made whole from brokenness. So the ancient meanings of salvation all relate to wholeness and health, not about being saved from eternal damnation. "Salaam" in Arabic and "Shalom" in Hebrew come from the same roots of wishing health, wholeness and peace on a person.

All humans experience brokenness in some form, in their relation to self, others and the universe. Brokenness or imperfection is a human universal. We are all on a journey to wholeness, and this is an ongoing process – everyone, no matter at what age, has the chance for growth into greater wholeness and healing, although in our human imperfections the process is never truly complete. This growth has to do with the evolution of our consciousness. As outlined in Chapter 2, the way we think about ourselves has huge effects on our bodies, and holding on to negative feelings of guilt, anger, hurt, worthlessness, etc., do long term damage, affecting the immune system and leaving us open to chronic disease and degeneration. If we operate from the kingdom mind of compassion, we become aware of our sub-conscious emotional drivers, so we are released into forgiveness for others and for ourselves. We grow into wholeness and healing – and that is our salvation.

Eternal Life?

Salvation in the Bible has other overtones of eternal life, although the word eternal ought to be changed, because, as we saw in Chapter 4, modern physics says that both space and time are part of the order of the universe. To go beyond the created order at death and to return to the Creator would mean leaving time as well as space. A more appropriate phrase would be *timeless life*, some form of existence outside of time in another realm. If we go beyond the physical bounds of the material universe, then we go beyond the bounds of time and space, into a boundless, timeless, spaceless existence, which is virtually impossible for the human brain to comprehend except, for some, in the language of higher mathematics. So to be "with God in heaven," outside the physical universe, means being in a timeless existence. Eternity, eternal and everlasting are all words in time, no longer quite fitting for the concept of God that we are trying to convey.

However, the teachings of Jesus are not primarily about being saved so that we can go to heaven or some state of eternal or timeless bliss. They are about how we find wholeness in our lives, about the ways in which we seek to become whole and complete in our relations with ourselves, others and the rest of creation. They encompass physical, mental and spiritual health. The Christian way is about entering what Jesus called "the kingdom of God," entering the spacious silence that is the compassionate consciousness of God, the ground of being. Jesus' teaching was not about what we have to do to get to heaven. In the gospel of John, Jesus said, *"I came that they may have life, and have it abundantly"* (John 10:10). Salvation is about that abundant life, which saves us from falling apart or spiraling downwards and brings us into the spacious, healthy environment that makes us whole. Salvation brings us into the stream of God's consciousness, to be reintegrated, restored. It is something, therefore, that is on offer to every single human being. To express a more complete meaning for the word salvation, Cynthia Bourgeault favors the term "restoration to fullness of being":

Stripped of the egoic self and exposed to the light, one is restored to "fullness of being," that is, to one's True Self…The perspective of self has now shifted from duality to partici-pation in God, and the final transformation into non-dual consciousness is now possible.[1]

In the gospel stories, this is exactly what Jesus went about doing, restoring people to fullness of being. His initial call to repent was a call for restoration to the Kingdom way, as we saw in the previous chapter. He told stories of restoration – the parables of the lost sheep and the prodigal son. But more than that, Jesus healed, he prayed, he preached and he healed some more. He did more than heal sick bodies and minds; he changed relationships, lifted up those who were struggling with life, he forgave sins. He made things whole. Many of Jesus' healings in the gospel stories seem to me to have an obvious psychological root, which then resulted in a physical symptom being relieved. The story of the woman who had been bent over for eighteen years is an example

(Luke 13:10-17). It seems that her illness was more of a psychological thing, and the healing was a restoration to wholeness. Her damaged mind had been affecting her physical body for years. Maybe she had been crippled with guilt, bitterness, or lack of self worth, or maybe she had been abused in some way and was carrying the mental scars that, over time, affected the balance of her energy fields and thus her physical body. As discussed in Chapter 2, the new science of epigenetics would say that Jesus was able to rebalance her subtle energy fields and thus affected the sensor proteins on the cell membranes. This was then relayed to the proteins surrounding the genes, and so her genetic pattern was reprogrammed to allow her to straighten up. She was restored to fullness of being. She was healed. The Bible records Jesus as saying, "You are set free from your infirmity," then laying hands on her, and she straightened up.

Healing the Whole

Healing in the Christian tradition and in most complementary therapies goes beyond the physical, and seeks to integrate body, mind and spirit. Healing is for the whole person; relationships, attitudes and emotions are involved as well as physical ills. We are complex human beings – our mental state will affect our physical state. Our emotions can wreak havoc with our bodies, and the science of epigenetics discussed in Chapter 2 gives an explanation for the mechanism by which that can happen through affecting which genes in our cells are "unwrapped." We have to look at the whole of who we are, body, mind and spirit. There is a social dimension to it as well – alongside the healing of broken bodies, hurt minds and wounded hearts is the healing of relationships and divisions amongst ourselves, and the healing of divided communities and nations. So too our prayers, our focused intentions, are proven to be complementary to the work of medical and other forms of healing, which are also channels of the loving and transforming purpose of the compassionate consciousness that holds us in being.

Medical knowledge has progressed – the more we know, the more we realize we do not know. Instead of seeing the body as a mechanism, medical science is moving in the direction of considering the body in a more holistic and organic way, looking at the whole person, not just the symptoms. Many complementary therapies have always done that. Complementary therapy practitioners have been using their skills for years because they believe they work, despite the ridicule of conventional medical science. Epigenetics is now providing a scientific basis to begin to explain how those complementary therapies work, which shows the wisdom of St Augustine in his statement:

"Miracles do not happen in contradiction to nature, but only in contradiction to that which is known in nature."
St Augustine, 1600 years ago

Growth into wholeness is also the concern of the Christian gospel, and the Jewish tradition from which it emerged – we are, as Psalm 139 puts it, "fearfully and wonderfully made." The gospels record many healings that Jesus of Nazareth did, and the healing ministry has been part of Christianity since its origins. Alongside this are many other claims made by a host of different complementary therapies, most of which have as good a claim to effectiveness as prayers for healing. There is often suspicion from within the Church about complementary therapies, but with an understanding of epigenetics and subtle energies, we can begin to see that what "prayer for healing" does is much the same as many other complementary, subtle energy therapies such as Reiki or Therapeutic Touch. The compassionate consciousness in which we exist has built into the cosmos the energies that are necessary for healing and wholeness, and human beings are capable of using and directing these energies to bring about healing. I believe Jesus was able to do this in a highly competent way.

First Principles

There are some first principles to consider in thinking about healing. Firstly, the human body is self-healing. Its natural state is to be self-healing, self-regulating, well and vital, and to fully express each individual's inherent strengths and gifts. It has an immune system that acts to restore us to a fully functioning state. Science calls this principle homeostasis, being in a state of balance. But various factors can affect that homeostasis and cause things to go wrong. The way we think about ourselves, the environment we subject ourselves to (both physical and emotional), the foods we eat, the people we associate with, the things we read – all these will affect the environment that our body cells exist in, and thus the genes of our DNA. With no scientific knowledge of genetics at all, St Paul urged his fellow Christians to think positively:

"Finally, beloved, whatever is true, whatever is honorable, whatever is just, whatever is pure, whatever is pleasing, whatever is commendable, if there is any excellence and if there is anything worthy of praise, think about these things." (Philippians 4:8)

Secondly, there is the maxim "Resolve the cause to restore the function." To get well and stay well we have to treat the cause of a symptom or dysfunction. Treating just the symptoms can be useful in the short run, but is not getting to the root of the matter. Once the underlying cause for a health problem is addressed, the symptoms associated with it will tend to resolve spontaneously. We may say we have a bug, a virus – but our bodies will naturally fight off viruses, so why has this one overcome the body's defenses? Is it a new strain, or are the defenses weaker for some reason? Is the immune system not working properly? Are we under some stress that is compromising us? Is there some deep-rooted problem in our lives that has not been dealt with? If the cause can be found, and the function can be restored, then it follows that the symptoms should fade away.

The cause of illnesses may be a lot deeper than just the symptoms we see on the surface. If we resolve the deep cause, we may restore the impaired function. Many of Jesus' healing miracles involve a deep forgiveness, which takes away the crippling power of guilt and the physical symptoms that can follow. His touch often seemed to impart a balancing subtle energy to the one touched – he brought about homeostasis. He also perceived that 'power' had left him.

> Immediately aware that power had gone forth from him, Jesus turned about in the crowd and said, "Who touched my clothes?"
> (Mark 5:30)

The study of epigenetics shows that the capacity for healing, developed fully in Jesus, is there in all humanity, built in for the common good. Our thoughts and emotions affect the energy field around us, and with a developed awareness of how that can be generated, the healthy energy field of the healer can balance the energies of the person seeking healing and bring about real physical change. Perhaps this is the 'power' that left Jesus when he healed.

Thirdly, and obviously, the body, mind and spirit exist in an intricate balance. We know that the human body is a delicate balance of interconnected energies and any number of factors can affect its working. Outside agents can affect us and infect us; the body can be abused in many ways by what we take into it or by what others do to it; our own thought processes can affect us deeply. We are body, mind and spirit – that is to say we are an interconnected whole. What affects one aspect of the whole will affect the other two. For example, we know that certain things in life cause us to be overstressed. In some people, that stress shows up in the mind, causing unhealthy ways of thinking, anxiety, panic attacks, depression; in others it shows up in the body, in various ailments and conditions. In some, it happens in both. The stress reaction is designed for 'fight or flight,' when a fast response is needed. If our system is flooded with stress hormones like adrenaline and cortisone for a few minutes, in response to an emergency or sudden fright, then our body soon settles back to its normal hormone levels. However, if stress hormone levels are maintained, they can lead to damage to the delicate balance of the body. Long-term exposure to cortisol and other stress hormones has bad effects. It suppresses immune response, reduces bone formation, decreases muscle mass, and damages cells in the brain that can result in impaired memory and learning.[2]

Our bodies are designed to cope with illness, to fight it, with an amazing immune system that leaps into action at the first sign of a problem. But our stressed minds can wreak havoc with that immune system, causing it to malfunction, and allowing disease to get a hold. Our minds can cripple our bodies – holding on for years to bitterness, grudges, anger and hate can bring on all sorts of physical complaints. Lack of self-worth, self-loathing, can slowly damage us physically. Our attitude to physical ailments and disabilities can cripple our spirit over time. We all know the scenario of ageing – various bits of us cease to work as well as they used to, we gradually begin to creak, what once was easy becomes progressively harder. How we cope with that, our attitude towards it can make a huge difference to our spirit and probably our physical state as well. To restate the obvious, we are one interconnected whole – body, mind and spirit – and each one affects the other two.

This interconnectedness is extremely complex and several factors – environmental, emotional, physical and spiritual – can affect our energy fields. The depth of how the human body works is still a mystery, but one that is gradually unfolding, and we now recognize a strong connection between illness and emotional stress. Many of the long-term chronic diseases are to do with the nervous system, the blood stream, the muscles and joints of our bodies – all of which are affected by energy fields and electrochemical reactions that go on in our brains. What causes these electrochemical reactions? Our thoughts and emotions; our consciousness. The state of health of our body and the way in which we think and feel are closely connected. Feelings like guilt, sadness, lack of worth, anger and helplessness can all affect our body – maybe in our posture, or our skin condition, or our musculature, or other more internal ways. Over years of affecting us in this way, we can develop serious health problems. Of course, some health problems simply come with the ageing process, as yet not understood, and others come for no reason that we know of yet – but others are a result of us carrying around a burden or an attitude to life for many years.

The paralytic on the mat (Mark 2:1-10) may have been one such person. Maybe in his case, he had done something about which he felt very guilty, and his psychological response, for whatever reason, was to shut down. He became paralyzed through guilt and fear. Then along came Jesus, this man who he has heard so much about, this Messiah-like figure – and the first words he spoke to him, looking into his heart, are *"Your sins are forgiven."* In saying that, Jesus lifted the psychological burden of guilt that had been crippling this man for years – and set him free. At the same time, coming into the presence of one whose energy fields are all in perfect balance has an effect on the paralytic, restoring harmony and balance in his physical body – and he got up and walked.

Being Set Free

Part of being human is that many people suffer from feelings of guilt, or anger, or lack of self-worth for some reason. Over years, these sorts of feelings can cripple us – sometimes literally, physically, and sometimes psychologically. We too can be forgiven and set free and we may need to find the way to let go of hurt done to us in order to offer forgiveness to another. But it is not always as easy as it was for the man in the gospel story. Sometimes it takes years to unlearn what we have been telling ourselves all our life. The tape has been stuck on continuous play and needs changing, or, to use a more modern analogy, the DVD has got stuck in a freeze frame. Part of the Christian journey is to allow God to gradually heal us from these powerful but often stuck emotions. As this happens, we are truly set free into wholeness of life, the fullness of life that Jesus talked of. This is salvation.

Sometimes we need the help of others to free ourselves, maybe through prayerful insight, or counseling, or psychotherapy, or at other times it can happen suddenly, wonderfully, miraculously as divine healing energy flows and our energies are rebalanced. When that happens, we can stand up straight and tall, knowing the sacred, healing energy in our lives in a new way. We become aligned with the compassionate consciousness of God, no longer held back, but free and aware.

However, it often doesn't happen that a person is physically healed. Being restored to fullness of life is not the same as being made physically whole. We can be set free in our spirits whatever our physical condition may be. I have known physically healthy people who are bound up in their spirit and unhappy, whilst others suffering from crippling physical ailments are free spirits, coping with their lot, giving love and joy to others. I was once honored to know a young mother with a brain tumour who was open and honest, warm and loving right to the end as she left her two daughters and husband behind. I was left thinking "What a way to go"! The ultimate freedom might be death, and is eventually for us all.

Prayers for healing are not simply requests that God does something; these are prayers of our intention, in which we align our being, body, mind and spirit, with the unitive consciousness of God, so that we ourselves, or others we know and love, may be able to draw on the divine healing energy that we see in Jesus the Christ. As Jesus has gone before us into that timeless existence, then he too is always and ever present in some way, a "now" presence whose being and essence we can draw on. In the very formation of an intention in our own minds with thought and feeling, we are affecting the subtle energy fields that govern physical health. We do not know all the elements that are in the way of that healing. We do not know the intricate web of connections between our body, mind and spirit and the barriers to health that lie there. But if we align ourselves with God, with the Source, and enter into that compassionate consciousness that undergirds the whole of existence, then maybe we can begin to bring more shalom, more peace, more health and more wholeness into this world. This is the salvation that the Bible talks of. It is a growth into wholeness and a better way of life. We are saved, liberated, and set free from 'sin', which is the separateness from God that has come about due to our egoic human nature. Through awakening to the divine energies, we can come to know that compassionate consciousness that undergirds everything, bringing us into wholeness and communion with the Source of all.

Becoming "Christed"

If salvation is truly about growth into wholeness, being set free from past hurts, wounds and wrong ways of thinking, then this effectively means that salvation is for all – we all have opportunities to grow into the wholeness on offer through awakening to the divine consciousness within. It is a form of universalism and becomes a concept common to all religions and spiritualities. If we take the idea from Chapter 5 that the Christ is the anointing, the special touch of God, uniting each person with the mind of God, then people of any religion and spiritual tradition, or none, can be "Christed" as well. I use the word "Christed" to distinguish it from becoming simply "like Jesus." Jesus was "Christed" as well, and, whilst the aim is to become like him, the anointing or "Christing" of God is the way in which we bring our consciousness to be aware of and in the compassionate consciousness that is God, as Jesus did. It is a subtle distinction, but an important one.

A passage of scripture sometimes taken to show that we must *exclusively* believe in Jesus Christ to be "saved" is the story of the jailor and his family in Acts of the Apostles. Paul and Silas are locked in jail when an earthquake came, chains fell off and the cell doors broke down. The jailor was distraught and about to kill himself when Paul called to him. The jailor fell down trembling before Paul and Silas and said:

"Sirs, what must I do to be saved?" They answered, "Believe on the Lord Jesus, and you will be saved, you and your household."
(Acts 16:30-31)

"Believe" means "put your trust in," and we have to remember that "saved" has other overtones of being delivered, protected, healed, and being made whole. Author and translator John Henson, in his gospel translation, *"Good As New,"* expresses it as *"Put your trust in Jesus and you will know true health and happiness in your life."* [3] The jailor, in asking the question, would *not* mean, "How do I avoid going to hell?" What he asked was a standard question of the Greek philosophers – "What must I do to attain a truly satisfying life?" And "believe on the Lord Jesus Christ" does not mean believing what it says about Jesus in the Apostles' Creed or any of the other creeds and statements of faith that came in later years. It is about a relationship of trust with Jesus the person, in which the character of Jesus inspires the one who is trusting, bringing them closer to God.[4] In fact, the final line in that little story is that the jailor came to believe in God (Acts

16:34), not in Jesus. The jailor was taken out of himself by the experience, went beyond his own selfish nature, surrendered himself to the divine, and was set on the path of restoration to fullness of being.

In the Acts of the Apostles is another passage that is used to support the exclusive need for belief in Jesus in order to be saved. This time it is Peter's words:

> This Jesus is "the stone that was rejected by you, the builders; it has become the cornerstone." There is salvation in no one else, for there is no other name under heaven given among mortals by which we must be saved." (Act 4:11-12)

Again, this is traditionally taken to mean that it is *only* those who confess a belief in Jesus Christ as Lord and Savior who can be saved. However, it can be expressed equally well to mean that salvation, or growth into wholeness of being, is gained by becoming as Jesus was. The "name" of a person represented their character, their way of being. Substituting that for name in the above quote, it would read, *"There is no other way of being... by which we must be saved."* So if we become the same as Jesus, having his character, knowing God as he did, we are saved from a life of not being in communion with God. We are saved, atoned, at one with God by being "Christed," as Jesus was. What Jesus did, in changing the morphic field of humanity as outlined in Chapter 3, was to make a path for everyone.

This way of looking at the passage avoids the claims of the Christian faith to exclusivity and opens up a whole new under-standing. It avoids the pitfalls of "my faith is the only way" because it looks for the way of Christ in all religions and spiritual paths. The way is one of *kenosis*, or self-emptying, so that we can be filled with the compassionate consciousness of God. It is following that way, the way to the kingdom that Jesus spoke of, that leads to 'salvation'. We can then live our lives from that transformed place rather than the competitive, defensive, judgmental, ego-based life that we struggle with.

We see this idea of salvation extended to all people in some places in the Bible. It is expressed in in ways relevant to the culture and language in which they emerged. In the Old Testament, we have the story of Naaman, the commander of the army of the king of Aram (2Kings 5:1-14), in which a non-Israelite is healed, or *made clean* of leprosy by eventually taking heed of the words of the prophet Elisha to wash himself in the river Jordan. The word used for *clean* in Hebrew was to do with ritual and spiritual cleanliness, not just being washed. This implies that it was Nathan's surrender to God that made him whole, rather than the act of washing in the river. So a person outside the Israelite race was made whole by surrender to God. Salvation was not just for the Israelites. The prophet Malachi speaks for God, saying that healing is the result of living God's way.

But for you who revere my name, the sun of righteousness shall rise with healing in its wings. You shall go out leaping like calves from the stall. (Malachi 4:2)

In the New Testament, Peter addressed the followers of Jesus in the Acts of the Apostles, implying that salvation is for all religions.

Peter began to speak to them: "I truly understand that God shows no partiality, but in every nation anyone who fears him and does what is right is acceptable to him. (Acts 10:34-35)

"Every nation" meant those of other faiths, those outside of Israel, the Jewish nation. "Fear" has more the meaning of "revere" or "be in awe of." Doing "what is right" can incorporate right practice of coming close to God or growing in awareness of divine consciousness. In other words, those of other faiths who practice their faith so that they grow in compassionate consciousness are "saved," or made whole. (This, of course, applies also to those who do not follow a faith tradition, but who are on a path of compassionate growth.) The apostle Paul thought along similar lines:

> All who have sinned apart from the law will also perish apart from the law, and all who have sinned under the law will be judged by the law. For it is not the hearers of the law who are righteous in God's sight, but the doers of the law who will be justified. When Gentiles, who do not possess the law, do instinctively what the law requires, these, though not having the law, are a law to themselves. They show that what the law requires is written on their hearts, to which their own conscience also bears witness. (Romans 2:12-15)

The "law" is not just the Ten Commandments but includes many other writings in the Old Testament, the Talmud and other documents that set out how the Israelites were to behave. Paul, in his rather roundabout way, is saying that if people respond to the highest way of living they know, they will be saved. If people respond to their conscience, to the level of their knowledge of right and wrong, if they work for the good of others, then they will experience salvation, they will grow in wholeness of being.

This way of thinking has a long history. Justin Martyr, famous Christian from the 2nd century (100-165 AD) said:

> It is our belief that those men who strive to do good have a share in God. According to our traditional belief, they will by God's grace, share his dwelling. And it is our conviction that this holds good in principle for all people... Christ is the divine word in whom the whole human race share and those who live according to the light of their knowledge are

Christians, even if they are considered as being godless.[5]

John Wesley, the founder of Methodism, argued in his sermon "On Faith," for the need for faith in God in order to be saved, but even he affirmed that this faith did not need to be explicitly Christian.

But what is the faith which is properly saving; which brings eternal salvation to all those that keep it to the end? It is such a divine conviction of God, and the things of God, as, even in its infant state, enables everyone that possesses it to fear God and work righteousness. And whosoever, in every nation, believes thus far, the Apostle declares is accepted.[6]

Even the Roman Catholic Church has relaxed its attitude towards other world religions in the words of the Vatican II declaration:

The Catholic Church rejects nothing that is true and holy in these religions. She regards with sincere reverence those ways of conduct and of life, those precepts and teachings which, though differing in many aspects from the ones she holds and sets forth, nonetheless often reflect a ray of that Truth which enlightens all men.[7]

Salvation for Everyone

Salvation is for everyone and has many overtones, but the root meaning is about restoration to fullness of being, to wholeness. This encompasses healing in physical, psychological and spiritual terms, and also restoration to relationship with God. In the evolved understanding that is being worked out in this book, we have seen how awakening to the divine compassionate consciousness within can restore an energetic balance through epigenetic action on the genes of the cell, and that a more healthy balance of thought and feeling in the energy fields we generate has an effect beyond the individual, and can be used in healing others as well. Taking this a little further, it also means that each of us, through our actions, affects the morphic field for the whole of humanity, so what you and I do in order to be restored to fullness of being (by living a compassionate life in surrender to the divine consciousness) makes it easier for others to find the same path. In actual fact, it places a responsibility on each of us to contribute to the salvation of humanity. If we accept that the way in which we think, feel and live our lives affects the morphic field of humanity, then it has far-reaching consequences for the human race. Our corporate responsibility becomes an imperative – to live a greener lifestyle which is sustainable for future generations, to build communities with compassion at the core, to send prayer intentions for the healing of not just individuals, but families, towns, nations, and even ecosystems. The agenda of salvation becomes all embracing, the redemption of the world.

Chapter 8

Spiritual Evolution

~

How do we become aware of the divine consciousness within? Here we look at a spiritual practice to help us on the journey towards the opening of the heart, that of meditation and contemplative prayer. This enables the path of self-emptying, or kenosis, that Jesus followed.

~

"The human being is an animal who has received the vocation to become God"
   - Basil the Great of Caesarea[1]

"The glory of God is humanity fully alive" – Ireneaus[2]

What makes you you? Just what is being alive all about? From the moment we are born, to the moment we die, it is a roller-coaster of experience. But physical birth is only the start – the rest of *being* alive is about *coming* alive – coming alive to the spirit within us, a voyage into the unknown. It is about getting in touch with our deepest selves, a journey into the compassionate consciousness of God. Jesus has undergone this journey ahead of us, and blazed a path, effecting a change in the morphic field of all humanity. Jesus created a new path, but it was a costly process. He had to suffer by going through the nettles, thistles and thorns. But once cleared, the path is open for us all to walk on, if we can find that timeless, narrow way, the way of unitive consciousness. Thus we are enabled to come alive.

The Opening of the Heart

The teaching of Jesus says that it is the inward state of the heart that is crucial in our spiritual development. *'Blessed are the pure in heart, for they shall see God'*. The Bible is full of phrases about the heart:

Incline your hearts to the Lord. (Joshua 24:23)

Trust in the Lord with all your heart. (Proverbs 3:5)

Your law is within my heart. (Psalm 40:8)

I will give them a heart to know that I am the LORD; and they shall be my people and I will be their God, for they shall return to me with their whole heart. (Jeremiah 24:7)

Where your treasure is, there your heart will be also. (Matthew 6:21)
God searches the heart. (Romans 8:27)

God, who said 'Let light shine in the darkness', has shone in our hearts. (2 Corinthians 4:6)

There are many, many more. In the Bible, the heart is the image for the self at a deep level, deeper than our thoughts, intellect and emotions. It has more to do with ultimate motivation and is the spiritual center of our total self, affecting our whole being. When we turn or surrender to God, we enter the divine consciousness within us that is our very being.

Marcus Borg says the spiritual path is to do with having an open heart, not a closed heart. A closed heart is turned away from God. The Bible speaks of this condition with a rich selection of metaphors. Our hearts can be 'shut' or 'hard', they can be 'fat', as if encrusted with a thick layer, they can be 'proud' or 'puffed up' and enlarged. They can be 'made of stone', rather than made of flesh. The close-hearted person is blind to the spiritual side of life. The open-hearted person is the opposite, seeing God's hand in all sorts of places and situations, alive to wonder and awe. An open heart is full of gratitude, full of compassion. An open heart feels the pain and suffering of the world and wants to respond to it, sees injustice and wants to bring change. The spiritual path is about developing an open heart, a heart of flesh, a heart of compassion.[3] It is about becoming God-conscious, living out of the God-presence within us rather than just the ego alone, so that we contribute towards changing the world to be a better place, bringing in the kingdom way of being amongst us.

John O'Donohue wrote a number of devotional books and he describes, in poetic terms, this process of change that is central to Christianity and all genuine spiritual paths. Love is the way of the heart, and living the path of transformative love changes us and remakes us in, or awakens in us, the image of Christ.

When love awakens in your life,
in the night of your heart,
it is like the dawn breaking within you.
Where before there was anonymity,
now there is intimacy;
where before there was fear,
now there is courage;
where before in your life there was awkwardness,
now there is a rhythm of grace and gracefulness;
where before you were jagged,
now you are elegant and in rhythm with yourself.
When love awakens in your life,
it is like a rebirth, a new beginning.
Though the human body is born complete in one moment,
the human heart is never completely born.
It is being birthed in every experience of your life.

Everything that happens to you
has the potential to deepen you.
It brings to birth within you new territories of the heart.[4]

The central factor about the Christian faith is not observance of the correct ritual, nor outward acts and observances; it is about what is going on in our hearts. Jesus was absolutely emphatic about this.

> But what comes out of the mouth proceeds from the heart, and this is what defiles. (Matthew 15:18)
> The good person out of the good treasure of the heart produces good, and the evil person out of evil treasure produces evil; for it is out of the abundance of the heart that the mouth speaks. (Luke 6:45)

It concerns the change that can be brought about in each and every one of us, the transformation from having a closed heart to having an open heart, open to give, open to receive, open to love, to have compassion for every other human being. That is the heart of Christianity. That is what takes us into higher spiritual vibrations and returns us to the compassionate consciousness of God.

Heart Experience
Words can be very cerebral, keeping us centered in the brain and cognitive thinking, when what is really needed is the heart experience, something that opens another channel of awareness. The heart can be opened in a variety of ways. For some, it can be sudden, an outpouring of God-awareness that is like the download of a new program showing the world in a different light. This is often followed by rather steadier growth in understanding of the experience and fitting it into a framework of religious belief. For some, it happens gradually through a disci-

plined practice over years. It can happen in a quiet moment of prayer, or a noisy praise service. Sometimes an experience of grief or loss, despair or illness can break open the heart. Maybe it happens with ageing as well, but not always. Spiritual practices vary hugely: ecstatic dancing and singing, inducing altered states of consciousness through drugs (natural or manufactured), ascetic practices of self-denial, verbal prayer, silence, communal worship, rituals and rites. Some are more effective than others, but the aim has to be for a growth in love and compassion, and the fruits of any practice should be visible in the person. Julian of Norwich, the English mystic of the 14th-15th century, describes how heart knowledge came to her through contemplation of something the size of a hazelnut:

> And the Lord showed me more, a little thing the size of a hazelnut, on the palm of my hand, round like a ball. I looked at it thoughtfully and wondered, 'What is this?' And the answer came, 'It is all that is made'. I marveled that it continued to exist and did not suddenly disintegrate; it was so small. And again my mind supplied the answer, 'It exists both now and for ever because God loves it.' In short, every-thing owes its existence to the love of God. In this little thing, I saw three truths. The first is that God made it; the second is that God loves it; and the third is that God sustains it. But what he is who is in truth Maker, Keeper and Lover I cannot tell, for until I am so essentially united with him, I can never have full rest or happiness; in other words, until I am so joined to him that there is absolutely nothing between God and me.[5]

In my own life, I can identify a number of these experiences. In my twenties, I was faced with a family situation that brought me to despair as my wife was hospitalized on and off over a period of two years with severe depression. During that time, I came to the total end of my own resources and I cried out "If there is a God, help!" Three years later, now as a conscious seeker, I experienced an outpouring of God's love like waves washing over me, and the next morning I saw the world with new eyes, as everything seemed more alive and vibrant than ever before. It was as if my senses were heightened and illuminated, as if a veil had been taken away. I have also experienced the spine-tingling presence of God many times in walking on coast-paths, hills and mountains and other natural places. Music, singing and chanting can take me to deep places, outside my normal state of mind. In recent years, it has been the practice of silent prayer and meditation that has brought me to a new depth of experience of God. And I have inevitably grown older and, hopefully, wiser!

Meditation and Contemplative Prayer

There has been a submerged tradition within the Church, but one that goes back right to its beginnings, that of meditation or contemplative prayer. There is some debate as to which term should be used, and different distinctions are drawn between them by different people. (For experienced practitioners, there are subtle nuances between different teachings, but those will not be looked into here.) Essentially, it is about the use of intentional silence to still the mind from its constant chatter and to allow our awareness of divine compassionate consciousness to grow, bringing about healing and transformation. It is a method of spiritual growth that leads to developing an open heart. The recovery of this practice into mainstream Christian teaching is essential for the Christian path. It is part of the path of restoration to fullness of being, part of salvation. We have to be aware of ourselves and the problems, hurts, and various damaged parts within us that need healing, and to sense the divine healing presence, both at the same time. Contemplative prayer is the shortest route to this, bringing us into the presence of the healing compassionate consciousness that is God. Prayer, in all its forms, is about building a relationship with the divine.

If we go right back to Jesus, who took himself off to the hills on numerous occasions to pray early in the morning or even overnight, do we imagine he talked with God all that time, or was he still and quiet? We cannot know for sure, but it seems more than likely that he engaged in contemplative prayer. His advice on how to pray was to go within, to close the door, to find God in the hidden place (Matthew 6:6). We do know about the Desert Fathers, the monks who went off into the deserts of Egypt and Syria to find time for God, and spent hours, days and years in meditation. It was out of these desert communities that the first monasteries formed, with their emphasis on the discipline of prayer. In today's society in the UK, we find that retreat houses are full and find it difficult to meet the level of demand for silence and guidance on silent prayer.

John Cassian, one of the Desert Fathers in the fifth century, recommended that anyone who wanted to learn how to pray, and to pray continually, should just take a single short verse or word and repeat it, over and over again. His idea of prayer was based on the verse in the gospel of Matthew:

When you are praying, do not heap up empty phrases as the Gentiles do; for they think that they will be heard because of their many words. (Matthew 6:7)

Prayer in the contemplative or meditative style becomes more a resting in God, being aware of the divine presence within, rather than projecting God to be somewhere else and externally talking to him and asking for things. To rest, we must become quiet and still – and repeating a short verse or word is one way to do that. It provides a much needed anchor that we can return to when we become aware of our distracting thoughts.

In the Orthodox Church, this was developed in the Jesus Prayer – *"Lord Jesus Christ, Son of God, have mercy on me, a sinner."*

This was sometimes shortened and was repeated continually in all prayer times, until it became a constant prayer happening at a subliminal level. It is a strong tradition still today in the East, often using prayer beads to count off the repetitions of the prayer. In the Catholic tradition, the rosary fulfilled a similar function.

Other people recommended the same practice. A thousand years after Cassian, the anonymous mystic English author of a very influential book, *The Cloud of Unknowing*, said:

We must pray in the height, depth, length and breadth of the spirit, not in many words, but in a little word of one syllable.[6]

In the Western Church, this teaching has not been readily accessible or taught in the churches since the reformation, as it has been largely the interest of certain contemplative monastic orders and mystics, but a number of teachers of contemplative prayer and meditation have emerged in recent years. Thomas Merton, a Trappist monk, wrote many books and constantly encouraged the contemplative life. John Main, an English Benedictine monk, developed the idea, drawing on the teaching of John Cassian and the earliest traditions of the Church. His teaching has been the essence of simplicity. Regrettably, he died in his fifties in 1982, but left many books and talks on this method of prayer using a short prayer phrase or mantra, as he called it. He was a keen proponent of using meditation as a means to discover the life of God within.

The view of meditation that many people are encouraged to take is as a means of relaxation, of retaining inner peacefulness throughout the pressures of modern life. This is not essentially wrong in itself. But if this is all it is seen as being, the view is very limited because, as we become more relaxed in ourselves, and the longer we meditate, the more we become aware that the source of our new-found calm in our daily lives is precisely the life of God within us.[7]

In meditation... we do not seek to think about God, but to be with God, to experience him as the ground of our being.[8]

The followers of John Main's teaching formed what is now the "World Community for Christian Meditation", led by Lawrence Freeman OSB. Another method of meditation is called "*Centering Prayer.*" It originated in North America, from Fr Thomas Keating, a Cistercian monk, and was developed from the teaching in the medieval text, *The Cloud of Unknowing*. The term "Centering Prayer" came from Thomas Merton as a method to facilitate going into the center of one's being in order to be present to the presence of God. The organization founded by Keating, "Contemplative Outreach," provides a support system for those on the contemplative path through a wide variety of resources, workshops, and retreats. Thomas Keating, currently in his late eighties, has developed the teachings of Centering Prayer to include many psychological insights as well, and has linked up with other leading spiritual teachers to explore connections and share ideas, such as Ken Wilber and his "Integral Life" organization. There are numerous other organizations that use silent prayer, such as "The Fellowship of Contemplative Prayer", founded by Robert Coulson, an Anglican priest, and "Julian" meetings who follow the belief of Mother Julian of Norwich that the highest form of prayer consists in simply waiting on God. They all practice one form or other of silent prayer.

Whatever form is used, it is clear that it is a very early Christian practice. Benedicta Ward identifies it in the life of the early Desert Fathers.

The aim was hesychia, quiet, the calm through the whole man that is like a still pool of water, capable of reflecting the sun. To be in true relationship with God, standing before him in every situation – that was the angelic life, the spiritual life, the monastic life, and the aim and the way of the monk. It was life orientated towards God.[9]

Interestingly, the Hebrew word for prayer, *tefilah,* is related to the verb *tofel,* to "attach," or "join," or "bind together," as two pieces of a broken vessel are pieced together to make it whole again. Contemplative prayer is about joining together human and divine consciousness in oneness.

Meditation has also been shown to have many medical benefits, with numerous well-documented studies. It has been shown to lower blood pressure, reduce the incidence of strokes, heart disease and cancer, diminish chronic pain, reduce anxiety and depression, and has various other medical benefits.[10] As Dawson Church puts it, *"If meditation were a drug, it would be considered medical malpractice for a physician to fail to prescribe it."*[11]

Almost all religions have this discipline in common – meditation or contemplative prayer. They may use different words to talk about the process, they may have different under-standings of what is going on, but the point is that there is something healing and balancing about coming before the divine presence in quiet and stillness. Many who use a meditation technique would say that little happens in a felt, experiential way during the period of meditation, but it is the effect in the rest of their life that makes a difference. Most teachings do, in fact, caution against majoring on phenomenal experiences during the prayer period, which is essentially a disciplined approach to one's inner awareness. The aim is to let go of any experience in order open into non-dual awareness and not to expect any particular experience of bliss or other feeling. The inner stillness seems to carry over into everyday life, reducing stress and bringing the ability to be more centered in the midst of hectic lifestyles. Meditation stills the endless chatter of the mind and allows access to the inner being, the hidden self. This inner self is the dwelling place of compassionate consciousness, which is where we find the unitive reality that is God. This is part of our fundamental reality, as Martin Laird, in *The Silent Land,* explains:

> People who have traveled far along the contemplative path are often aware that the sense of separation from God is itself pasted up out of a mass of thoughts and feelings. When the mind comes into its own stillness and enters the silent land, the sense of separation goes. Union is seen to be the fundamental reality, and separation a highly filtered mental perception.... 'For God alone my soul in silence waits.' (Psalm 62:1,6)[12]

Moving into this place of stillness is a discipline to be learnt, one very simple in concept, but quite tricky in practice, as our thoughts refuse to be quiet. This is what blocks our awareness of the presence of God, of the compassionate consciousness in which we exist. We cannot be separated from it, and Martin Laird makes it clear that God does not know *how* to be absent. Any sense of absence from God that we may feel is the great illusion we are caught up in, the human perception of separateness.[13] The great illusion we are caught in is self-consciousness. We are so aware of ourselves that we have lost the awareness of God-consciousness in which we exist. Our egos are too strong. We perceive God as separate from us and so we picture him as a Being that is "out there" rather than having a sense of God "in here." The spiritual path through meditation is to go beyond the ego-self, to transcend the illusory self, and to attain a sense of unitive consciousness, finding God within our own awareness of greater self. It is the way of transformative love.

Kenosis

Self-emptying, or *kenosis* (from the Greek), is what is referred to in the Bible as dying to self, or "losing your life that you may find it" (Matthew 16:25). Kenosis is about setting our egoic mind aside, letting it go. As already mentioned, the ego can be seen as a by-product of evolution. Over eons, we have evolved as beings to the stage where we are self-conscious, aware of ourselves, and hence we see ourselves as separate from God. The story of Adam and Eve and the tree of the knowledge of good and evil is about exactly this – coming to self-consciousness and hence separating from the God-consciousness that actually holds us all in being. But we are still evolving in consciousness and the human race is on a journey back to God, to unitive consciousness – and that way is to go beyond our egoic self, to self-empty.

Cynthia Bourgeault, in *The Wisdom Jesus*, points out that this is precisely what Jesus did. It was his core gesture, this *kenosis*, or self-emptying.[14] In the letter to the Philippians, Paul sets it out in the hymn to Jesus, saying:

> Let the same mind be in you that was in Christ Jesus, who, though he was in the form of God, did not regard equality with God as something to be exploited, but emptied himself, taking the form of a slave, being born in human likeness. And being found in human form, he humbled himself and became obedient to the point of death—even death on a cross. (Philippians 2:5-8)

There are two key words in this inspired passage, which is considered by many to be a very early Christian hymn. The key words are 'emptied' and 'humbled'. Emptying oneself is the kenotic action of surrender to the divine, and humility can be considered as the moral word for the action of letting go. Being humble means letting go of pride and arrogance, greed and desire. Jesus' journey to the heart of reality was by giving himself away, by letting go of his egoic nature. Bourgeault calls it the 'throwing it away' school, and contrasts it with the way of spiritual ascent characterized by a concentration of spiritual energy using genuine ascetic disciplines of prayer, fasting and other practices. Whilst this concentrative path can lead to attaining unitive consciousness, there is another way:

There's another route to center: a more reckless path and extravagant path, which is attained not through storing up that energy or concentrating the life force, but through throwing it all away – or giving it all away. The unitive point is reached not through the concentration of being but through the free squandering of it; not through acquisition or attainment but through self-emptying; not through "up" but through "down." This is the way of kenosis, the revolutionary path that Jesus introduced into the consciousness of the West.[15]

The Heart Download
Coming back to the idea outlined in Chapter 6, which Cynthia Bourgeault borrowed from computer terminology, we need an update from the Egoic Operating System to the Kingdom or Heart Operating System in order to follow this extravagant path of self-emptying, letting go of and going beyond the egoic self that sees us as separate from God.

In a conference in Norwich UK in 2011, she explained her analogy that the Egoic Operating System (EOS) is "installed" at birth as part of our normal brain function. What is needed is to download an upgrade to the EOS – the Heart Operating System (HOS). We cannot find our true divine self in the EOS, as the egoic mind only sees things in duality – we will simply move from one duality to another, swap one picture for another. The EOS does a good job of keeping track of life along the horizontal axis of time and space, but the HOS is needed to take us deeper than that, to develop the vertical axis of our relationship with God. We tend to identify selfhood with mind and cognitive thinking, which is how the EOS works. As Descartes said, "I think, therefore I am." There is an exclusive reliance on the EOS to give us our identity.

Mystical writings, such as the medieval text *The Cloud of Unknowing*, tell us that we cannot reach God by knowledge or intellect. It outlines what is called the *apophatic* path, reaching out to God with the heart rather than the intellect.

What I am saying is this: love succeeds where the intellect fails. All rational creatures, angels and men, possess two distinct powers: that of knowing and loving. To the first, the creator God is forever incomprehensible. But to the second, to the power of love, God is totally knowable.[16]

The higher part of contemplation is shrouded in darkness and this cloud of unknowing. There, in great love and blind outreach, the soul seeks for the naked being of God alone.[17]

Our intellect functions using the EOS, so in order to go beyond the EOS, we have to put, as Bourgeault expresses it, "a stick in the spokes of the mind." In other words, to deconstruct the reliance on the mind, to go beyond it, we need to find a way to still it, or negate its constant influence. In Chapter 6, we looked at the word *metanoia*, traditionally translated as "repent" and saw that its real meaning is "to go beyond the mind." This was the first recorded call of Jesus, to go beyond the mind and enter the kingdom of heaven, or unitive consciousness.

One Wisdom technique for going beyond the mind is to give stories or problems that push us beyond the mind, for example, the koan in Buddhist practice. A typical koan is "What is the sound of one hand clapping?" We cannot make sense of it with our EOS, so it pushes us into a different place to receive, a place deeper than the mind. As Bourgeault says, "It fries the mind!"

A parable or pithy saying has the same effect, and Jesus used dramatic teaching examples and situational teaching stories that left people seeking understanding beyond the EOS mind. An instance of this type of parable is the laborers in the vineyard (Matthew 20:1-16) who all get the same full daily pay regardless of what time they were engaged to work, even the ones who only worked for one hour. Those who had worked all day grumbled and complained. The playground cry would be 'That's not fair!' The response of the landowner was:

'Friend, I am doing you no wrong; did you not agree with me for the usual daily wage? Take what belongs to you and go; I choose to give to this last the same as I give to you. Am I not allowed to do what I choose with what belongs to me? Or are you envious because I am generous?' (Mat 20:13-15)

We can see this effect of making one puzzle over the meaning particularly in some of the parables about the kingdom.

He put before them another parable: "The kingdom of heaven is like a mustard seed that someone took and sowed in his field; it is the smallest of all the seeds, but when it has grown it is the greatest of shrubs and becomes a tree, so that the birds of the air come and make nests in its branches." (Mat 13:31-32)

Is this saying that the kingdom will grow to be huge (and some may have taken it as an intention to dominate the Romans), or that it has great potential, or that to enter the kingdom is to grow into wholeness, completeness? What do the birds of the air represent? Are they higher thoughts that can settle in the kingdom-orientated mind, but obviously cannot settle on a mustard seed? A similar parable follows this one:

He told them another parable: "The kingdom of heaven is like yeast that a woman took and mixed in with three measures of flour until all of it was leavened." (Matthew 13:33)

Here the yeast not only spreads through the whole but makes it bigger as well. Does that mean that there is an insidious, secret way in which the rule of the Romans can be overthrown and a Jewish king re-established, or is it about bringing everything together into oneness so that it may grow? Or maybe it is saying that living with light and love is catching – it spreads slowly through humanity. Parables can be understood differently at different levels, and Jesus often ended a parable with the exhortation "Let anyone with ears, listen!" meaning think hard about this, let it take you to a deeper place, and help you to wake up to a wider perspective than your EOS. There was often an outer, exoteric, obvious meaning and an inner, esoteric, hidden meaning to these parables.

As well as the parables, Jesus used many pithy sayings, things to chew over, such as *"the first shall be last and the last shall be first"*[18] or *"The eye is the lamp of the body. So, if your eye is healthy, your whole body will be full of light."*[19] These tricky little phrases wind their way beyond the cognitive egoic mind and stimulate the intuition, reaching the heart-mind. Trying to wrestle with what Jesus was getting at pushes us out of dualistic thinking, which is the basis of the EOS. Contrary to what some may say, we do not need to stamp on the ego, but to transcend it. This does not mean that you abandon it altogether. The egoic mind is still a part of you, but your center of consciousness has moved beyond it. Jesus realized intuitively that the difficulties we get into are due to the egoic hard-wiring of the mind, the EOS. We live within a rational, reductionist mindset, where everything is subject to our egoic, cognitive way of thinking. The upgrade needed is to the Heart Operating System, to the way of being that is centered in the heart, as seen long ago by the prophet Ezekiel.

A new heart I will give you, and a new spirit I will put within you; and I will remove from your body the heart of stone and give you a heart of flesh. (Ezekiel 36:26)

The Heart OS is referred to in many traditions as 'the mind in the heart'. Heart perception is there in all the traditions of the West – Judaism, Christianity and Sufism. The latter is widely assumed to be the inner, mystical dimension of Islam, but some would say that the Sufi philosophy is universal in nature, its roots predating the rise of Islam. Indeed, some Muslims consider Sufism outside the sphere of Islam. As Western Christianity became more concerned with defining its doctrine, it lost this vital emphasis of putting the mind in the heart. The heart is seen as the organ of perception, keeping track of the vertical axis, the subtle, causal, non-dual realms, things that are invisible to the senses, stimuli that are invisible to the EOS. It keeps track of intuition, which goes beyond the EOS. Kabir Helminski, a contemporary Sufi teacher, expresses it in similar terms:

We have subtle subconscious faculties we are not using. Beyond the limited analytic intellect is a vast realm of mind that includes psychic and extrasensory abilities; intuition; wisdom; a sense of unity; aesthetic, qualitative and creative faculties; and image-forming and symbolic capacities. Though these faculties are many, we give them a single name with some justification, because they are operating best when they are in concert. They comprise a mind, moreover, in spontaneous connecting with the cosmic mind, the total mind we call "heart".[20]

We use the heart as metaphor, separate from the physical, pumping heart, but the Institute of HeartMath shows we cannot separate the two. This new school of thinking says that the heart does much more than just pump the blood around the body. It is an electro-magnetic field generator and sends electrical and chemical signals to the brain. The field generated by the heart is the strongest in the human body and acts as a field of coherence for the body. Brain and heart are intimately connected, with the heart having much greater influence over the brain than the other way round. For over twenty years, the HeartMath Institute has been carrying out research and has found the heart to be far more complex than was ever dreamt of in medical circles.

> The answers to many of our original questions now provide a scientific basis to explain how and why the heart affects mental clarity, creativity, emotional balance and personal effectiveness. Our research and that of others indicate that the heart is far more than a simple pump. The heart is, in fact, a highly complex, self-organized information-processing center with its own functional "brain" that communicates with and influences the cranial brain via the nervous system, hormonal system and other pathways. These influences profoundly affect brain function and most of the body's major organs, and ultimately determine the quality of life.[21]

Putting the mind in the heart may well be more literal than we have ever thought. The heart as the seat of intuition and non-dual thinking seems to have some credibility. Moving from the egoic operating system to the heart operating system is more than a mental concept; it has some form of energetic reality. An established path to connecting with that energetic reality is through meditation and contemplative prayer, the path of silence. Martin Laird again sees that stillness is the way to finding that deep presence of God:

> When the mind is brought to stillness... a deeper truth presents itself: we are and always have been one with God and we are all one in God.[22]

The Cage

Laird gives a powerful story about the cage that the ego-self keeps us in, and the potential that awaits us if we can free ourselves from it. He describes how he would sometimes go on a long walk and often see a man walking his four Kerry Blue terriers:

These were amazing dogs. Bounding energy, elastic grace and electric speed, they coursed and leapt through open fields. It was invigorating just to watch these muscular stretches of freedom race along. Three of the four dogs did this, I should say. The fourth stayed behind and, off to the side of its owner, ran in tight circles. I could never understand why it did this; it had all the room in the world to leap and bound. One day I was bold enough to ask the owner, "Why does your dog do that? Why does it run in little circles instead of running with the others?" He explained that before he acquired the dog, it had lived practically all its life in a cage and could only exercise by running in circles. For this dog, to run meant to run in tight circles. So instead of bounding through the open fields that surrounded it, it ran in circles.[23]

Laird likens this running in circles to the human condition. We are free, but we limit ourselves to the cage that we live in, limited by our own perception of reality. Like the dog wagging its tail, we can be happy in our cage mentality, but it makes us believe we are separate from God. That separateness leads to us seeing God as somewhere else, and thinking that we are alone, afraid, unlovable even. We come to believe the lie, to live in the cage that is not a cage. Meditation is then a way to escape from the cage mentality, to put the ego-cage aside, to self-empty and discover true freedom in unity with God. Meditation or contemplative prayer is a practice that helps us to awaken to the awareness that we are one with God, part of his compassionate consciousness. I believe it should be taught in theological colleges, seminaries and in every church community in the land – it is vital that the church recovers this treasure.

To use another analogy, I sometimes think that traditional Christianity is rather like a fish farm. The only world the fish know is what is inside the net. They swim all day inside the net, they are fed their daily ration there, and they live out their life quite happily in that restricted environment. But the water, the medium of life for a fish, is part of the vast ocean of which they are unaware. If only the fish could escape the net, they would be free to explore the ocean's heights and depths and find a more rich and varied diet than the standardized food they are given. The form of Christianity that has been so central in the West is restrictive in the same benign way, but there are riches to be found in strands that have escaped the net, as well as in other traditions.

When a man dwells in the solitude of silence, and meditation and contemplation are ever with him...and his thoughts and words and body are in peace... then this man has risen on the mountain of the highest: he is worthy to be one with Brahman, with God.[24]

Once that quiet place is found, it is where we want to be, with God, in the stillness, allowing our spirits to grow quietly and surely – as one of the Desert Fathers, Abba Sisoes found:

A brother asked Abba Sisoes, 'Why did you leave Scetis, where you lived with Abba Orr and come to live here?' The old man said, 'At the time that Scetis became crowded, I heard that Anthony was dead and I got up and came here to the mountain. Finding the place peaceful, I have settled here for a little while.' The brother said to him, 'How long have you been here?' The old man said to him, 'Seventy-two years.'[25]

Cynthia Bourgeault grounds the idea of going beyond the egoic operating system in an attitude to everyday life, which she terms "yieldedness," as opposed to the egoic way of "bracing." She calls this the "Welcoming Practice."

> Although there are any number of spiritual practices both ancient and universal to bring a person to a state of permanent inner "yieldedness," the most direct and effective one I know is simply this: in any situation in life, confronted by an outer threat or opportunity, you can notice yourself responding inwardly in one of two ways. Either you will brace, harden, and resist, or you will soften, open, and yield. If you go with the former gesture, you will be catapulted immediately into your smaller self, with its animal instincts and survival responses. If you stay with the latter regardless of the outer conditions, you will remain in alignment with your innermost being, and through it, divine being can reach you. Spiritual practice at its no frills simplest is a moment-by-moment learning not to do anything in a state of internal brace. Bracing is never worth the cost.[26]

It is in the stillness and solitude that we can truly get in touch with the Ultimate Reality, the One who is the ground of our being. Through stilling our minds, we begin to put the mind in the heart, the deeper place of intuitive wisdom, of communication with the divine. Fr. John Main, the founder of the World Community for Christian Meditation, clearly saw this as the place we become one with God.

> In this wonderful process of coming into the full light of Reality... a great silence emerges from the center. We feel ourselves engulfed in the eternal silence of God. We are no longer talking to God, or worse, talking to ourselves. We are learning to be – to be with God, to be in God.[27]

Once our center is located in the consciousness of God, we can flourish, we can be inspired, we can emerge into "the silent music and the sounding solitude"[28] and know our destiny. This has been seen both in the Christian mystical tradition and in other traditions of theosophical and mystical thought, often represented by the symbol of a rose coming into bloom, in the same way as a lotus is used in Eastern thought for the awakening soul. Alice Bailey, writing in the theosophical tradition, used the symbolism of the rose to indicate the awakening of the soul.

> In solitude the rose of the soul flourishes; in solitude the divine self can speak; in solitude the faculties and graces of the higher self can take root and blossom in the personality.[29]

The rose symbolizes the opening of the heart, the blooming of the non-dual mind in the heart and the journey back to oneness with the compassionate consciousness of God. Mary, the mother of Jesus, is sometimes referred to as the mystic rose, and the rose is sometimes used as a symbol of Christ as well, as we see in the German Christmas song from a poem by Goethe, *Es Ist Ein 'Ros' Entsprungen (A rose has sprung up)*.[30] We also find the expression of heart-opening occasionally in the hymns sung in churches. Charles Wesley, brother of the founder of Methodism, John Wesley, was a prolific hymn writer, and his well-know hymn "And Can It Be" describes the opening of the heart in different terms:

> Long my imprisoned spirit lay
> Fast bound in sin and nature's night;
> Thine eye diffused a quickening ray –
> I woke, the dungeon flamed with light;
> My chains fell off, my heart was free.
> I rose, went forth and followed thee
> Charles Wesley

Poetic expressions of the opening of the heart are many. A rose opening, chains falling off, veils being lifted. However much we may try to *think* our way into the non-duality of the heart, it is only accessible through a different perception, the perception of the heart – the "quickening ray." Our egoic mind cannot escape from dualistic thinking in opposites; it is the way we are conditioned to think. Going beyond the mind (*metanoia*, repentance) is entering the kingdom of the heart, the compassionate consciousness that is God. Living from there is living in the kingdom of heaven, an altogether different vibrational level of being.

Spiritual Change

In summary, an emerging, evolving spiritual change is beginning to happen within the Western Christian Church. Rather than teaching doctrine and conformity, true spiritual practice is teaching the way of the heart, and this is slowly being redis-covered as the essence of Christianity. It is the way Jesus taught in his exhortations to love. He was a wisdom master teaching the path of transformative love. The opening of the heart is enabled greatly by the practice of meditation and contemplative prayer, which takes us out of the dualistic way of thinking and puts the mind in the heart. In following the way of the heart, we discover the Spirit-consciousness within, and also a connection with other spiritual traditions. For instance, Hindu scriptures contain many insights that resonate with Christianity. Here is one from the Chandogya Upanishad, which, in a few poetic lines, brings the concept of the immanence and transcendence of God to life.

There is a Spirit that is mind and life, light and truth and vast spaces. He contains all works and desires and all perfumes and tastes. He enfolds the whole universe, and in silence is loving to all.

This is the Spirit that is in my heart, smaller than a grain of rice, or a grain of barley, or a grain of canary-seed, or the kernel of a grain of canary-seed. This is the Spirit that is in my heart, greater than the earth, greater than the sky, greater than all these worlds.[31]

The recovery of the practice of meditation and contemplative prayer is essential if Christianity is to evolve into a form more suitable for the Western culture we now live in. Many people in this restless, fast-paced world are searching for coping mechanisms to be able to continue in our rapid-change society. There has been a resurgence of interest in spiritual practices in general, particularly in the area of holistic spirituality – the new name for what was termed "New Age" in the latter part of the twentieth century. The recovery of the heart tradition in Christianity will have an appeal far beyond the existing Church, and indeed may not appeal to many in the existing Church, as most are presumably still there because they are happy with the teaching the way it is. But the heart tradition fits in with the emerging scientific views on the nature of reality and consciousness, energetic connections and fields, and as new generations live with that reality, so the way of the heart will become part of it. It is the gift that Jesus has given to the world, submerged though it became for nearly two millennia in the West. Despite its submergence, it has been a strong current running through mystical and Orthodox thought, and is now bubbling back to the surface again. We shall look at some current indications and expressions of this emerging Christianity in the last chapter, but next we must consider the issue of the religious language that is used in the Church.

Chapter 9

The Evolution of Religious Language

~

In this chapter, we consider several problems to do with religious language, some insights from the Aramaic that Jesus spoke, and how we can introduce language in worship that has more in common with the scientific worldview in which we live.

~

The Problem of Language

Language is always a problem in trying to communicate religious concepts and ideas because we are dealing with experiences of the divine that can be seen differently by every individual. Everyone's experience is very personal. In any system of thought or cultural milieu, a vocabulary develops to communicate within that sphere, whether it is medical terminology, the world of music or religious thought. Each develops its own 'jargon'. The language of liturgical Christianity tends to come from the biblical and medieval worldview of a three-tiered universe. Humanity has its fragile existence in the middle layer of firmament, the earth, above us are the heavens, where God and the angels live, and below us is hell or the underworld. We are all aware that the universe is not like that, but much of the language reinforces it still, as in the Lord's Prayer, "Our Father, who art in heaven", which tells us that God is still "up in heaven," or, at the very least, elsewhere. Later in this chapter, we look at the underlying meanings of that first line of the most well known Christian prayer.

Words also evoke differing responses in different individuals depending on their age, culture and life experience. They can stir up memories, emotions, prejudices and attitudes. Words can also change their meanings quite rapidly, becoming age-related. For instance, within fifty years, the word 'gay' has moved from a meaning of brightness or liveliness, to referring to someone of a homosexual orientation. More recently, in England, I have heard it being used as a word to describe anyone who is being awkward or silly for no reason – "You're just gay." Wicked used to be synonymous with evil, but can now mean amazingly good, as in "That was wicked!" We process words according to the culture and experience we have been immersed in. Within Christianity, to talk about Christ is taken by most to be synonymous with Jesus of Nazareth, but within theosophy, the Christ is a universal principle that overlighted the soul of Jesus for his years on ministry. We might think we are talking about the same thing, but actually have very different, but related, understandings.

When we come to look at belief in Christianity, we are up against the problem of the words used to describe the experience when the doctrines of Christianity were formed in the centuries following the Christ event. Traditional liturgical language in Christianity does not fit well with the ideas we have been exploring of non-dual consciousness and the way of the heart. The egoic mind, which is where traditional liturgy mostly originates from, thinks in opposites – inner and outer, either or, you and me, God and human. What the emerging scientific view tells us is that there is no duality; we are all one pulsating, energetic reality, held and sustained in the consciousness that is the ground of our being. Christian terminology, coming from a pre-scientific worldview, emphasizes a separateness between God and humanity, and between the spiritual and the worldly. Writings from the mystics go beyond this into non-duality, but have had little influence on Church liturgy. Liturgical expression lies predominantly in an almighty, all-powerful person-like God to whom we pray, and ask him (he is always male in the traditional liturgy) to make miraculous interventions on our behalf. In the most recent Holy Communion services of the Church of England, God is still referred to most often as Almighty, which has the effect of reinforcing the belief that God is separate from us, existing somewhere else far off. This Almighty God is from the Old Testament beliefs, a powerful, war-like figure, who defends against enemies, who is full of wrath if we sin against him. More apt descriptions in line with the teachings of Jesus and with God as the Ground of Being would be, for example, all-loving, all-present, timeless, Creator, Beloved, and many other more suitable titles.

In the recently updated liturgies of the Church of England, God is also still referred to as merciful, or most merciful. As Marcus Borg points out, the word quite often translated from Hebrew into English as *merciful* is more accurately translated as *compassionate*[1]. But having compassion is quite different from showing mercy. Having mercy implies a power position, the position of a superior to an inferior, stemming from the rule of kings and queens, empires and lords. It also implies a situation of wrongdoing, with the superior offering forgiveness. Having compassion implies the co-suffering of someone who is alongside, caring, expressing the emotional capacities of empathy and sympathy for the suffering of others. As Borg says, *"mercy wears a human face, compassion a human heart."*[2] Or we could say mercy is an expression of passing something from one to another, whereas compassion is a way of being, aligning oneself with another. Why do we not refer to the "God of compassion," or even, in line with this book, the "God of compassionate consciousness"? Larry Dossey, a medical doctor who has written many books on the interrelationship between consciousness, spirituality and healing, writes:

Close examination of the many studies in distant healing and prayer reveal that non-local mind (*Dossey's term for consciousness*) is intimately connected with love, compassion and deep caring, just as healers throughout history have maintained.[3]

These studies show that compassion is essential for healing and prayer to have effect. Compassion is also considered in all the major religious traditions as among the greatest of virtues. It is there in the Golden Rule common to the scriptures of nearly all religions, expressed in Christianity in Jesus' words, "Do to others as you would have them do to you." To express God as compassionate rather than merciful is a more appropriate term for translation.

The Golden Rule

The compassionate way is shown in all religions, a truth common to all paths, as we see here.

Baha'i

> Lay not on any soul a load that you would not wish to be laid upon you, and desire not for anyone the things you would not desire for yourself.
> *Baha'u'llah, Gleanings*

Buddhism

> Treat not others in ways that you yourself would find hurtful.
> *The Buddha, Udana-Varga 5.18*

> A state that is not pleasing or delightful to me, how could I inflict that upon another?
> *Sayutta Nikaya v. 353*

Christianity

In everything, do to others as you would have them do to you; for this is the law and the prophets.
Jesus, Matthew 7:12

Confucianism

One word which sums up the basis of all good conduct, loving-kindness. Do not do to others what you do not want done to yourself.
Confucius, Analects 15.23

Tsi Kung asked "Is there one word that can serve as a principle of conduct for life?" Confucious replied, "it is the word 'shu' – reciprocity. Do not impose on others what you yourself do no desire."
Doctrine of the Mean, 13.3

One should not behave towards others in a way which is disagreeable to oneself.
Menclus 5:1517

Hinduism

This is the sum of duty: do not do to others what would cause pain if done to you.
Mahabharata 5:1517

Islam

Not one of you truly believes until you wish for others what you wish for yourself.
The Prophet Muhammad, Hadith

Jainism

One should treat all creatures in the world as one would like to be treated.

Mahavira, Sutrakritanga

In happiness and in suffering, in joy and grief, we should regard all creatures as we regard ourselves.

Mahavira, 24th Tirthankara

Judaism

Thou shalt love thy neighbour as thyself

Leviticus 19:18

What is hateful to you, do not do to your neighbor. This is the whole Torah; all the rest is commentary.

Hillel, Talmud, Shabbath 3 la

Shinto

Hurt not others with that which pains yourself.

Udana-Varga 5.18

Sikhism

I am a stranger to no one; and no one is a stranger to me. Indeed, I am a friend to all.

Guru Granth Sahib, pg. 1299

Sufism

"The basis of Sufism is consideration of the hearts and feelings of others. If you haven't the will to gladden someone's heart, then at least beware lest you hurt someone's heart, for on our

path, no sin exists but this."
Dr. Javad Nurbakhsh, Master of the Nimatullahi Sufi Order)

Taoism

Regard your neighbor's gain as your own gain and your neighbor's loss as your own loss.
Tai Shang Kan Ying P'ien, 213-218

Unitarianism

We affirm and promote respect for the interdependent web of all existence, of which we are a part
Unitarian principle

Zoroastrianism

Do not do unto others whatever is injurious to yourself.
Shayast-na-Shayast 13.29

This Golden Rule is known as the principle or ethic of reciprocity. We can see clearly that Jesus was expressing a common core of all spiritual paths, the way of compassion. Referring to God as compassionate is reinforcing the call of Jesus for us to love one another, to open the heart and to go beyond the mind, i.e. to operate from a different level of consciousness. It reminds us of the compassionate consciousness that is God and in which we share.

The words *almighty* and *merciful* are just two examples of how liturgy is skewed towards a dualistic notion of God. The emerging view, outlined in this book and backed up by various scientific theories, is that, for the 21st century, we must find a way of moving towards the expression of God as non-dual in Christian liturgy, God as the compassionate consciousness, the

Ground of Being. Duality is expressed as God is "up there" and we are "down here." Non-duality expresses the doctrine of God as immanent, within all of creation. God is both immanent and transcendent, but the latter does not mean "up there," it means "other," lying beyond the ordinary range of perception. God is both within and other than us. This has a name, *panentheism,* meaning that all is held in God, but it is not the same as God. The concept of God as the compassionate consciousness that holds all in being is therefore *panentheistic.* Many experimental liturgies are being devised which plough a furrow to break new ground for the future Wisdom path within Christianity of contemplative, compassionate consciousness. (In the appendices, I have written a new liturgy of prayers for healing and anointing, and a new version of the Holy Eucharist, based on the Church in Wales liturgy, using terminology described in this book).

Below is an example of a new creed or affirmation of faith, which I have written to encapsulate some of the ideas in this book.

Creed of Consciousness

I believe in the God of Creative purpose,
the compassionate consciousness
in which we live and move and have our being.
Mother and Father of us all, we are held in being by God,
who dwells in us and all creation,
and from whom we emanate and emerge.

I believe Jesus the Christ was a son of God,
a fully human being
who reached the depths of God-consciousness
to become fully divine,
and forged a path for the rest of humanity,
through the way of self-emptying and compassion.

I believe in the Spirit of God,
the divine energy working in the world
to bring all things to fullness and restoration.

I believe in the sacred nature of the Earth
and every human being,
and that the spiritual journey is to be transformed by love,
letting go of the selfish nature,
and entering into the compassionate consciousness
that is God.

Aramaic translations

A radical way of looking at the gospel texts we have inherited in the Bible is being pioneered by Dr. Neil Douglas-Klotz. In his book *"The Hidden Gospel,"* he explores the radical differences between a Middle Eastern understanding of the sayings of Jesus and the accepted Western interpretation. He looks at the words of Jesus from a different world view – that of the Middle East, the land where Jesus grew up, the area where the nation of Israel was founded amidst the other warring tribes of the area.

For his text, he uses the Bible of the Eastern Christians, called the *Peshitta*, written in Western Aramaic, called Syriac by Western scholars. The earliest manuscript copy of the Peshitta is from the 4th Century AD, and it is claimed, by Aramaic-speaking Christians of various denominations, to be the nearest to the original form of Jesus' words. Around the time of the Council of Nicaea, when Western Christianity was trying to sort itself out and squash some of the arguments about how Jesus Christ was to be understood, the Eastern areas of what are now Turkey, Syria and Iraq were controlled by the Persian Empire. Christians had established themselves there by the time of the destruction of Jerusalem in AD 70, and they were largely of Semitic extract and Aramaic-speaking. These early Christians were not repressed and persecuted as they were in the Roman Empire, and they built schools, libraries and places of worship, with Persian support. Moreover, from the earliest days, they had access to copies of early scriptures that they could study in their homes, in their natural dialect, Aramaic. This was the version of the scriptures that came to be known as the Peshitta – meaning simple, straight, true. It included the four gospels, but in a form of Aramaic close to the dialect that Jesus himself would have used. The consensus of scholarly thought is that the books of the Peshitta New Testament were translated from Greek into Aramaic, although some dispute that and claim that the gospels may well have been written in Aramaic in the first place – but there is no real evidence of this. Syriac Christians still feel that the Peshitta is a version of the original Aramaic words of Jesus, and that it is very close in spirit to his original message.

After the Council of Chalcedon in AD 451, there was a split in Christianity. What have become known as the Oriental Orthodox Churches, including these Aramaic-speaking groups, broke contact with the still united Roman and Eastern Orthodox Christianity over the increasingly complex creeds and the forceful attempt to impose a single theology on all Christians. Little was heard about them in Europe for the next 1500 years. The irony is that most Christians in Europe were not allowed to read the scriptures until well after the advent of the printing press in the Middle Ages – yet Aramaic-speaking Christians of the Syrian Orthodox Church had copies of the gospels in Aramaic in their homes for their open use a thousand years earlier. We have to ask the question, who is most likely to have something nearer the original?

Douglas-Klotz takes the Peshitta version of Jesus' words, and tries to translate them directly into English in a way that brings out some of the nuances of meaning in the Aramaic – and these are many. Because there are fewer words in the Aramaic language, each word contains more nuances of meaning. Although the gospels were first written in Greek, the words of

Jesus would have been spoken in Aramaic. When the writers of the gospels wrote them down in Greek they had to choose a word with a much more limited meaning to express the Aramaic words of Jesus. Imagine a family tree of words, with an Aramaic parent word and a large number of Greek offspring. To write in Greek means to choose only one of the words that is just a part of the meaning in Aramaic, and thus it narrows down the meaning hugely. Going back to look at the Aramaic words implies that there is not one definitive translation (as our rational, Western minds would like), but several, depending on how we hear it, what we read into it, and the resonances created in the individual. The translator has to decide which English word to use, and whatever word is used will inevitable reduce the nuances of meaning that are in the original. Andrew Harvey elucidates the difficulty of translating Aramaic into other languages:

Jesus taught mostly in Aramaic – a rich, poetic language that does not draw sharp lines between means and ends, inner quality and outer action, and whose grammar, sentence structure, and way of moving, like Arabic, in webs of constellated meanings, enshrines a fluid and holistic view of the cosmos, in which the arbitrary boundaries in Greek or Latin between body, mind and spirit fall away. In other words, the language itself that Jesus used – and used with such brilliance and spiritual beauty – emanated something of the Kingdom and involved those who listened to him naturally in an act of imaginative listening so much greater and more complex than any that can be conveyed by subsequent translations... According to Hebrew scholar Fabre D'Olivet, the tragedy of biblical translation has been that expressions that were meant to resonate on many different levels of meaning – at least intellectual, metaphorical and universal – have been "whittled down to become gross in their nature... restricted to material and particular expressions" (The Hebrew Tongue Restored, 1815).[4]

Douglas-Klotz gives numerous shades of meaning for each of his translated passages and also takes the etymological roots of the words into account, which throws a whole new dimension of profundity into the statements of Jesus.

For example, consider these expansive translations of some well-known words of Jesus:

"Blessed are those who mourn, for they will be comforted."
(Matthew 5:4)
"Blessed are those in turmoil and confusion; they shall be united inside."
"Ripe are those who feel at loose ends, coming apart at the seams; they shall be knit back together within."[5]

"In my name..." can be interpreted as:
"With my atmosphere..."
"From within my experience..."
"In rhythm with my sound..."
"With my sense of illumination..."
"With the light of my essence..."[6]

"Your eye is the lamp of your body. If your eye is healthy, your whole body is full of light; but if it is not healthy, your body is full of darkness. (Luke 11:34)
"The degree of your illumination – your understanding of all that is – shines through your eyes, your face, and all you do. When your expression is straight and expansive, without holding back, like light through a clear lens, then everything you embody shows the same flash of intelligence that helped create the world. But when your expression is veiled, the eye cloudy and darting, the action at the wrong time and place, what you embody of light

and understanding will be chaotic, swirling, obscure. Your non-understanding then participates in the primal darkness of the cosmos."[7]

"Your will be done on earth, as it is in heaven" (Matthew 6:10)
"Let your light flow through us, in wave and particle."
"Let your pleasure manifest in us, in light and form."
"Let your desire act through us as communal and individual
    purpose."[8]

The author gives numerous other examples of translations from the Peshitta that cast a whole new light on Jesus' words, and could revolutionize Christianity if they were taken on board within the mainstream. In particular, he points out the Aramaic meaning of *Alaha*, the word translated as *God* in the New Testament:

In Aramaic, the name Alaha refers to the divine, and wherever you read the word "God" in a quote from Yeshua (*Jesus*), you can insert this word. It means variously: Sacred Unity, Oneness, the All, the Ultimate Power/Potential, the One with no opposite... By contrast, the English word "God" is based on a Germanic root meaning good. No doubt, one can see goodness as one aspect of the divine, but it is not the same as unity.[9]

Here we see the link between the understanding of God as the divine consciousness that holds everything in unity and the concept emerging from science that all is one, everything is interconnected in a vast interlacing of energetic fields. The "One with no opposite" particularly reminds us of the state of non-duality, or unitive consciousness spoken of in the last chapter. In the original language spoken by Jesus, God was the sacred unity in which the All existed. We find that Jesus spoke about God in non-dual terms. Douglas-Klotz goes on to point out that in Arabic the name for God, *Allah*, comes from the same root meaning of unity and is not exclusive to Muslims:

We find it (*Allah*) simply refers to the primary concept of the divine in the Middle East for the past two to four thousand years. Even before the Jewish scriptures were composed, some people in the Middle East used a form of this word – Allat or Elat – to refer to Sacred Unity.[10]

This work of Douglas-Klotz has the potential to completely change our mind-set about the nature of God. If the understanding of the greater nuances and range of meanings of some of the words of Jesus could be taken into mainstream liturgy, it could bring radical insights to the understanding of Western Christianity, and move us from being centered on the anthropomorphic, person-like, "God made in our image" view of the divine to a view of Oneness and Sacred Unity – and compassionate consciousness.

Jesus also frequently refers to God as "Our Father." The words of first line of the Lord's Prayer, in Aramaic, is *Abwoon d'bashmaya*, translated in the King James Version as "Our Father, which art in heaven." When the Aramaic is examined a syllable at a time, various revelations appear.

The ancient Middle Eastern root *ab* refers to all fruit, all germination proceeding from the source of Unity. This root came to be used in the Aramaic word for personal father – *abba* – but still echoes its original ungendered root in sound-meaning. While *abwoon* is a derivative of this word for personal father, its original roots do not specify a gender and could be translated "divine parent"... *Bwn* shows the potential of that father/motherhood proceeding from potential to actual, here and now... a birthing, a creation, a flow of blessing, as if from the "interior" of the Oneness to us... *Oo* is the breath or spirit that carries this flow, echoing the sound of breathing... *n* is the vibration of this creative breath from Oneness as it touches and interpenetrates form.[11]

Hence, the first two words of the English version of Lord's Prayer, "Our Father" contain overtones of motherhood, of birthing, of creation, and of the flow of spirit or breath. The second phrase, *d'bashmaya*, has a number of surprises as well.

In *d'bashmaya*, the central root is found in the middle: *shm*. From this root comes the word *shem*, which may mean light, sound, vibration name, or word. The root *shm* means that which "rises or shines in space," the entire sphere of a being. In this sense, one's name included one's sound, vibration or atmosphere, and names were carefully given and received. Here the "sign" or "name" that renders *Abwoon* knowable is the entire universe... In effect, *shmaya* says that the vibration or word by which we can recognize the Oneness – God's name – is the universe. This was the Aramaic concept of "heaven"... In Greek and later in English, "heaven" became a metaphysical concept out of touch with the processes of creation.[12]

So hidden within "which art from heaven" are concepts of the recognition of the divine nature from the universe of sound and vibrational energy in which we exist – not a separate place called "heaven," but where we are here and now. When Jesus spoke of the "kingdom of heaven," it referred to the Oneness in which we exist now. Based on his reading of the subtle flavors in that first phrase of the Lord's Prayer, Douglas-Klotz gives the following poetic renditions:

O Birther! Father-Mother of the Cosmos, you create all that

moves in light.

O Thou! The Breathing Life of all, Creator of the Shimmering Sound that touches us.

Radiant One: You shine within us, outside us – even darkness shines – when we remember.

Name of names, our small identity unravels in you, you give it back as a lesson.

Wordless Action, Silent Potency – where ears and eyes awaken, there heaven comes.[13]

Without belaboring the point, Aramaic is a very poetic language, and the many shades of meaning cannot usually be expressed in an English word. The various authoritative gospel translations that we have today are taken with great accuracy from the Greek language, but they fall far short of expressing the shades of meaning that were in the Aramaic words of Jesus. Douglas-Klotz is not trying to lead a revolt against these authoritative transla- tions. He is not saying that they are wrong, just that they are limited, if the words were initially spoken in Aramaic. He uses his understanding of Aramaic to round out the reader's under- standing of Jesus' most fundamental teachings. Further on in the Lord's prayer he explains that the Aramaic word *tzevyanach*, translated as "will" in the King James Bible could also be under- stood as, "deep desire." Thus the line, "Thy will be done," puts the emphasis less on an outside force controlling our lives from above and more on a harmonization of our heart's desire with the compassionate consciousness of God. It becomes obvious that this radical way of bringing out the hidden sense of the words could transform liturgy and hymns if it were to gain acceptance as a valid expression of what Jesus said. It gives us permission to write our own version, knowing the root meanings of the words. As an example, here is a version of the Lord's Prayer I have written, based on the interpretations of Douglas-Klotz.

O Breath of Life, who flows in all creation,
May the light of your presence fill the universe,
your way of being come, your desire be done,
in this and all realms of existence.
Bring forth the nourishment we need for this day.
Forgive the failures that bind us,
as we let go of our hold on other's failures.
And let us not be satisfied with the surface of life,
but deliver us from wrong paths.
For you are abundant life, creative unity and glorious
harmony,
through all time and beyond. Amen.

The Nature of Reality

In addition to the deeper meanings that can be found in the Aramaic language, there are deeper understandings of our existence that have to be incorporated into the language of worship. We live in a world in which there is a dawning understanding amongst the general populace that the nature of reality is actually very different from the way that we have always conceived it. Slowly, there is a downward trickle from the scientific world that we inhabit an existence composed of energetic information fields, not solid matter. Neurophysiologist Dr. Mary Schmitt has expressed this well in an essay entitled *"If All is Consciousness, What Then is my Body?"*[14] In a playful way, she describes first the way the body looks under an electron microscope, in the range of a millionth of a centimeter:

In that domain, the body appears more like a vast sea,

inhabited by many types of creatures. Ocean caves (pores of the skin) seem to be inhabited by various sea creatures (bacteria): nerve cells of the inner ear look like sea anemones; and the taste buds as beautiful flower arrangements... Sea snakes piggybacking giant sea lions are actually muscle tissue with nerve fibers running along the surface – and on and on.[15]

The body at this level is still seen as solid matter, real, though strange. But going to a much greater magnification still, one hundred millionth of that size (i.e. 10^{-14} cm for the mathematically minded), we come to a domain where all solidity is gone. At this level we would see (if we could magnify this much) each atom of which the body is made. If we could enlarge the nucleus of the atom to the size of a speck of dust, the electrons are in orbit hundreds of yards away (considering them as particles and not waves for the moment). In between is nothingness, emptiness. She makes the delightful and sobering point that if we could get rid of all the emptiness within our atoms, we could fit on the head of a pin with room to spare!

Going further still, she enlarges the magnification to the subatomic level within the atomic particles. At that level, it becomes difficult to refer to our bodies as made of "matter" at all.

The hundreds of subatomic portions of the protons and neutrons of the nucleus, such as leptons, mesons, quarks, though spoken of as particles, are not so much "entities," as intelligent, vibratory patterns of interacting, communicating energies. Some of these so-called "particles" can go backward in time, go in and out of existence.[16]

This is what we are made of; this is the nature of the reality of our bodies: we are essentially interacting, communicating energies, at a more subtle level than was ever imagined only fifty years ago, where even time and space are not fixed. At this level, we begin to see connections between matter and mind, or consciousness. To continue magnifying, we get down to the unimaginably small (10^{-33} cm), the length termed Planck's constant, which seems to be as small as nature wants to go. Planck's constant reflects the size of quanta in the quantum theory. (This was discovered by Max Planck in 1899, which shows how long it takes for scientific knowledge to filter down into general terminology.) Mary Schmitt expresses the wonder of this level of reality:

At this point, we can no longer speak of space or time, or even of manifest reality. We are in "Implicate Order," as David Bohm refers to it, where nature (including ourselves) does all her creating, holds all her memories (morphogenetic fields) and where what exists is infinite potential. We are in the realm of "The Unified Field"... I am one with all that is in the timeless domain of infinite complexity but utter simplicity.[17]

In many ways, this sort of understanding of reality has become something of a backdrop to Western culture. The unimaginably small has become an everyday term. We talk of nanotechnology, extremely small technology at the nanometer scale (10^{-9} of a meter). The word "quantum" has entered the world of religious writing, films, music and social media. A brief internet search shows we now have Quantum Jumping, Quantum Touch, Quantum Healing, Quantum Retail, Quantum Media, even Quantum Mousetrap! The effect of this is to make a difficult concept seem not so strange after all, as the word is familiar. As more words and concepts come into everyday usage, so the backdrop is constructed. The challenge for religious language is whether or not to move into this new understanding of the nature of reality as interacting, communicating energetic fields and use some of the language. Do we stay with the traditional language, which stems from an earlier time, or do we take a long look at the linguistics and express our belief in the divine and the nature of the human being and all creation in modern language, symbols and metaphors? The evidence in the Western world is that many have turned away from Christianity and are embracing holistic, contemporary spiritualities which use precisely this sort of language of subtle energies, quantum processes and energetic fields, and combines them with existing concepts of auras, chakras and meridian lines. One only has to look at the "Mind, Body Spirit" section of a local library or bookshop to see this. It is my belief that Christianity would benefit from and be strengthened by new terminology stemming from our understanding of the nature of reality. We can still express the same timeless truths, but in a new way for a new generation.

A New Language

The insights from the Aramaic and Wisdom tradition and the emerging understanding of the nature of reality can be expressed in church liturgy, hymns and songs, by expressing a belief in a non-dual universe in which all is one, held in the compassionate consciousness of God. To give an example, we can use the 'collect for purity', the prayer traditionally used at the beginning of the Holy Communion service in Anglican liturgy. Here is the traditional version and a contemporary expression:

Almighty God, to whom all hearts are open, all desires known, and from whom no secrets are hidden: cleanse the thoughts of our hearts by the inspiration of your Holy Spirit, that we may perfectly love you, and worthily magnify your holy name; through Christ our Lord. Amen.

God of all compassion, whose presence within sees our heart's desires and hidden secrets: let your energy and light flow, so that we may know your breath of life in our inner beings, and show heartfelt praise in our lives, as did Jesus the Christ. Let it be so.

Another standard prayer is the confession, and, whilst there are many newer versions of it, some much improved, the traditional version is still in regular use. The two are shown in comparison, the second being a version using the type of concepts in this book.

Almighty God, our heavenly Father,
we have sinned against you and against our fellow men,
in thought and word and deed,
through negligence, through weakness,
through our own deliberate fault.
We are truly sorry,
and repent of all our sins.
For the sake of your Son Jesus Christ, who died for us,
forgive us all that is past;
and grant that we may serve you in newness of life
to the glory of your name. Amen.

God of all Creation, in whom we live and move and have
our being,
we acknowledge our separation from you within,
our self-centeredness and hardness of heart
towards others and ourselves.
We are truly sorry, and ask that you would help us to move
beyond our minds
into the heart of your loving presence.
May we be remade in the image of Jesus the Christ, the
divine human,
that we may know fullness of life in the energy of your love.
Amen. Let it be so.

In Appendix 3, I have attempted a version of the Holy Eucharist service, again embodying the concepts in this book. Hymns also will need attention. Over the last few decades, there has been an explosion of Christian hymns and songs, from different camps. The evangelical charismatic camps in America, Britain and Australia have seen a huge outpouring by a variety of writers from such organizations as the Vineyard movement from the USA, Spring Harvest from the UK and Hillsong from Australia, but the overall emphasis, as one would expect, is very evangelical and "Jesus-is-Lord-centered". They are also embedded in a dualistic understanding of the God of miracles who is Lord and Master and Mighty, rather than the Presence at the Ground of our Being. From the Iona Community in Scotland we have a large number of often socially radical songs, many based on Scottish folk tunes. From the Taizé Community in France, there are chants in a variety of languages and there are many offerings from around the world that are making it into newer hymnbooks. But there is relatively little to be found that encourages us to understand the God-human relationship in terms of consciousness or oneness or unity.

Author and translator John Henson has reworded many hymns and prayers in his book *"Wide Awake Worship,"* using fresh, simple language. Whilst it does not embrace the language of consciousness as in this book, it has a directness that is refreshing. Here is his version of the Lord's Prayer:

Loving God, here and everywhere,
help us to proclaim your values
and bring in your New World.
Supply us with our day to day needs.
Forgive us for wounding you,
while we forgive those who wound us.
Give us courage to meet life's trials and evil's power.
We celebrate your New World,
full of life and beauty, lasting forever. [18]

Henson translates the Kingdom of God as the "New World,"

which captures something of the change happening, but misses out on ideas to do with energy and the unitive consciousness that we are all journeying towards, which are there in the Aramaic offerings from Neil Douglas-Klotz. To move towards the way of understanding outlined in this book, a sea change will have to happen in language used in churches – but then the sea does change, ever so slowly, as the tide comes in. It creeps up on you, and before you know it, a wave has filled your shoes. There are new hymns, prayers and liturgy being written all the time, and as always, the best will last. Words are so important, they shape our understanding, they hold our concepts, they express our feelings. T. S. Eliot expresses the problem we have with words when attempting to convey the depth of our heart's longings:

Words strain,
Crack and sometimes break, under the burden,
Under the tension, slip, slide, perish,
Decay with imprecision, will not stay in place,
Will not stay still.[19]

Words and language are notoriously difficult to translate and convey the original meaning and, as mentioned earlier, when we have the words of Jesus in English, translated from Greek but originally spoken in Aramaic, then there is huge room for revisiting the original language and meaning. The poetic nature of that original spoken word could revitalize our liturgical language. It could bring it into line with our understanding of the nature of reality and our own beings as a sea of interacting, communication subtle energies, held in the consciousness of God.

Chapter 10

Moving Forward

~

In this final chapter, some of the current indications and expressions of the emerging way of seeing Christianity are considered.

~

A New Breed of Christian

There are a number of recent developments that support the emerging view outlined in this book. Modern scholarship has revealed much about the Bible and its origins and is gradually changing viewpoints within the Church on the nature of the gospels and of Jesus. There is the growing recovery of the practice of meditation and contemplative prayer as mentioned in Chapter 8. "Fresh Expressions of Church" is a movement in the Church of England that has been trying out some radical paths. Wisdom Schools have sprung up in the USA, conveying the Christian path in a different form, much more aligned with the concepts of this book. And there are numerous other insights and practices from both secular and spiritual sources that are available to use for the opening of the heart that is a mark of this path. We shall look at some of these in this chapter. A new breed of Christian is emerging, who is prepared to cross boundaries and use learning from outside the box, who sees benefits in embracing and integrating scientific concepts into their beliefs, and who is willing to experiment and take risks so that the true teaching of Jesus the Christ, the wisdom teacher of transformational love, can be conveyed.

Modern Scholarship

In the last hundred years, there has been a sea change in biblical scholarship, through the many different forms of textual criticism. This is a huge area of discussion, and can only be touched on here. These different critical ways of looking at the text of the Bible have asked a series of different questions, such as:

- Is the text we have a faithful rendering of the original?
- What were the sources used by the author?
- What was the historical and cultural context of the author?
- Is there evidence that the author is really the one traditionally assigned?
- What genre of literature is the writing?
- What was the intention of the author and who was he addressing?
- What did the text say to the original reader, and what does it say now?

In order to give answers to these sorts of questions, scholars have researched all kinds of early manuscripts and texts in different languages, to compare, contrast, and date. An example can be found in analysis of linguistic style, which can often show that letters are not all written by the same author. For instance, the letters accredited to Paul are not all thought to be written by him – many think that Colossians, Ephesians, Titus, and I and II Timothy were published after Paul's death, as they seem to differ in style from the authentic letters of Paul. Some scholars argue that these texts are Pauline texts reflecting Pauline thought at a later age, and so using different expressions. Others argue they were written by a secretary of Paul (he used a secretary for most of his letters). Still others argue that they were written by someone claiming to write in the spirit of Paul (it was a common practice for someone to write in the spirit of a known author and credit it to them). Dating of these letters is disputed at anywhere from 65 A.D. to 125 A.D. They contain troublesome passages about slavery and women, though they also mention women deacons and possibly women priests. These sorts of issues have been deeply researched in recent years, resulting in a huge body of knowledge that was simply not available one hundred years ago.

The gospels have been an area of intense investigation and also sharp dispute as the words and actions of Jesus came under the critical lens. Are these his words, or are they paraphrases or later insights? Did he really do all the miracles, or have some of the miracles emerged from dramatizations and glorifications of more everyday events? How much has been added to the story of a radical Jewish teacher and healer who was put to death? The Jesus Seminar is a group of about 150 critical scholars and laymen founded in 1985 by Robert Funk and John Dominic Crossan to look again at the texts and form an opinion on how authentic the quoted words of Jesus were. This resulted in his words being categorized in a color-coded version of the gospels,[1] which included the gospel of Thomas, rediscovered in the Nag Hammadi library of texts found in 1945. (This chance discovery in a remote part of Upper Egypt of fifty-two texts dating back to the early days of Christianity included many previously lost writings). The Jesus Seminar categorized the words of Jesus in four ways and in four colors:

- Red: Jesus undoubtedly said this or something like this
- Pink: Jesus probably said something like this
- Grey: Jesus did not say this, but the ideas contained in it are close to his own.
- Black: Jesus did not say this; this represents the perspective or content of a later or different tradition.

As the whole gospel of John was categorized as *not* the literal words of Jesus of Nazareth, but a later tradition, this caused some consternation and dispute. They are still truly inspired words, written in reflection on inner meanings, but they were probably not actually spoken by Jesus at the time. This type of work came under much criticism from the more conservative elements of the Church, but has actually been liberating for many.

Writers such as John Dominic Crossan and Marcus J. Borg have taken the findings of the Jesus Seminar and developed them into new paradigms of Christianity. Borg calls this new view 'emerging' Christianity as opposed to 'earlier' Christianity. Earlier Christianity emphasizes a literal way of looking at the Bible, and sees salvation in terms of believing now to attain heaven later. It has a strong strand of exclusivism, seeing Jesus as the only way and Christianity as the only true religion.

The second way of seeing Christianity, the "emerging paradigm," has been developing for over a hundred years and has recently become a major grass-roots movement within mainline denominations. Positively, it is the product of Christianity's encounter with the modern and postmodern world, including science, historical scholarship, religious pluralism, and cultural diversity. Less positively, it is the product of our awareness of how Christianity has contributed to racism, sexism, nationalism, exclusivism, and other harmful ideologies.[2]

Bishop John Shelby Spong has also been a persuasive voice in liberal theology, fundamentally rethinking a path that brings a fresh vision of Christianity. The titles of some of his many books give a flavor; *"Liberating the Gospels: Reading the Bible with Jewish Eyes"*; *"Why Christianity Must Change or Die: A Bishop Speaks to Believers In Exile"*; *"A New Christianity for a New World: Why Traditional Faith Is Dying and How a New Faith Is Being Born"*. In these books, he gives a view of the God who is not made in our image, person-like, but is the Source of Life and Love, very similar to the God of compassionate consciousness outlined in this book.

> God is the Ground of Being who is worshiped when we have the courage to be. Jesus is a God-presence, a doorway, an open channel. The fullness of his life reveals the Source of Life, the wastefulness of his love reveals the Source of Love, and the being of his life reveals the Ground of All Being. That is why Jesus continues to stand at the heart of my religious life.[3]

These views, and many others, have contributed to the growing groundswell of opinion that there is a different way of being Christian, an evolution of Christianity that draws on ancient understandings, but incorporates modern insights. It is also creating a path that is not exclusive, but speaks to and informs other spiritual paths. The world is tired of calls to exclusivity, which have led to many disputes, wars and loss of life in the name of one god or another, and more recently to fundamental terrorist organizations. The future call has to be to unity, inclusiveness, and the oneness of the whole of humanity. Only that will lead to a world of mutual, peaceful co-existence.

Fresh Expressions and Emerging Church

In Britain, the movement called "Fresh Expressions of Church" has emerged within the Anglican and Methodist traditions. A fresh expression is a form of church for our changing culture, established primarily for the benefit of people who find traditional church structures hard to cope with for one reason or another. In North America, this has had the label "emerging church," and is similarly trying to find ways of holding an integrity of believing and being in today's culture. The aim of these movements is, on the whole, not to provide a stepping stone into existing traditional church settings, but to form new Christian communities, working out their faith in the culture in which they dwell. In Britain, this has resulted in numerous different expressions, growing from the grass roots, appropriate to the context. Some of these have been in existence for years before the term "fresh expression" was used.

One strand of this Fresh Expressions movement is new monasticism, which takes some of the principles of monastic formation and reinterprets them for the 21st century. A core element is usually a form of "rule" or "rhythm of life" by which members of the community try to abide. The theology of such fresh expressions often comes from the evangelical camp, but some are quite different. There is a strong emphasis in some on contemplative formation, getting in touch with God as the Ground of Being, the compassionate consciousness that is the central tenet of this book. In Britain, "Contemplative Fire"[4] draws much more on the writings of the early Church and desert mystics to form a "dispersed sacramental community of traveling companions with a common rhythm of life of contemplative, creative and compassionate practice." Another initiative is "Still Point,"[5] which seeks to deepen spiritual practice, particularly exploring the contemplative and mystical streams of the Christian tradition, and engaging with other spiritual traditions and the arts. Yet another is "Moot"[6] in London, offering a spiritual path within the Christian contemplative tradition for those who may not relate to traditional or contemporary expressions of church. The "Norwich Contemplative Forum"[7] seeks to bring about a vision of contemplative community combined with ecological awareness, helping people to reconnect with the natural world, and with community development and collaborative decision-making. These different expressions of emerging church (and there are probably many more, especially in North America) have a freedom and creativity that crosses traditional boundaries and engages with the God outside the box, the "Blue-

Sky God."

All of these are drawing on the deep wells of the contemplative tradition to start a new stream flowing. This new stream is taking on board the necessity for Christianity to evolve to fit within the culture and context of Western society today and is crossing all sorts of traditional boundaries and borders in doing so. It seeks a path of transformation, not confined to dogma or doctrine, but drawing from deep, hidden wells of the past, and willing to take risks and experiment. Above all, it is experiential, grounded in communion with the Ground of Being, in the silence of contemplative prayer and meditation.

Wisdom Schools

One of the important tasks in developing a new path for Christianity is to find an appropriate form in which to offer a synthesis of the research and teaching that has been accumulating in recent years. In North America, a number of Contemplative Wisdom Schools have been running in various locations, guided by Revd Dr Cynthia Bourgeault. The aims of these are twofold: firstly, to make available to Christians the breadth and depth of their own, often submerged, Christian heritage, particularly looking at new resources and insights that come from the Near East, such as the Gospel of Thomas, and from the Orthodox Church heritage. In all these, the idea of divinization of the human being occurs. It goes by different words, but divinization, deification, making divine, or *theosis* is a strong tradition in the history of Christianity, particularly in the Orthodox Church. It has been largely lost to Protestantism except in the idea of being sanctified or made into the image of Christ. Sanctification is rarely seen as being made to be the *same* as Jesus, but just being changed by the Holy Spirit to be a *bit* like him. The understanding outlined in this book is that the human potential is to be the same as Jesus, capable of being everything that he was, when we can become awakened to the energetic vibration of the compassionate consciousness of God. This understanding is there in the Bible in the words of Jesus, *"the one who believes in me will also do the works that I do and, in fact, will do greater works than these"* (John 14:12). We also find it stated boldly, in the terms of the time, in many of the writings of the early Church Fathers:

- St. Irenaeus of Lyons stated that God *"became what we are in order to make us what he is himself."*[8]
- St. Clement of Alexandria says that *"he who obeys the Lord and follows the prophecy given through him . . . becomes a god while still moving about in the flesh."*[9]
- St. Athanasius wrote that *"God became man so that we might become deified."*[10]
- St. Cyril of Alexandria says that we *"are called `temples of God' and indeed `gods,' and so we are."*
- St. Basil the Great stated that *"becoming a god"* is the highest goal of all.
- St. Gregory of Nazianzus implores us to *"become gods for (God's) sake, since (God) became man for our sake."*[11]

In the Orthodox Church, which takes much inspiration from these early Fathers of the Church, divinization has always been a central doctrine. To the Orthodox Christian, salvation is not being rescued by Jesus, through the wrath of God being appeased by his death on the cross, it is working to become more like God and, with the help of divine grace, to be united with God.

Theosis ("deification," "divinization") is the process of a worshiper becoming free of *hamartía* ("missing the mark"), being united with God... For Orthodox Christians, theosis is salvation. Theosis assumes that humans from the beginning are made to share in the Life or Nature of the all-Holy Trinity... Theosis also asserts the complete restoration of all

219

people (and of the entire creation), in principle.[12]

In the Christian West, this was only really found in the teachings of some of the mystics. Meister Eckhart (c.1260-1328AD) taught a doctrine of the possible union between the human soul and God. Cyprian Smith, in an article in '*The Study of Spirituality*', says that Eckhart knew that this possibility of a God-human union depends on the grace of God, freely given; but he maintains that it also rests upon something within the soul itself, its intrinsic similarity or likeness to God. Eckhart sometimes stressed this likeness so much that he seemed to obliterate the distinction between the human being and God.[13]

In the West, there has been a slow but steady influx of these teachings over the last fifty years, conveying the idea that the human being's destiny is to attain the consciousness of God, the unitive state, or wholeness, which is salvation. That is one element of Wisdom School teaching. Underlying that is the second aim of the Wisdom Schools, the purpose of transformation of being, through development of core practices such as meditation, contemplative prayer, Lectio Divina, sacred chant, and the daily practices of mindfulness, inner observation and surrender. While these come from the Christian tradition, they are not exclusive to that tradition, as the Wisdom practices leading to inner transformation are present in all the great world religions, as Cynthia Bourgeault makes clear. She identifies the "nuts and bolts" of the transformative path as looking much the same in whatever spiritual path is followed; surrender, detachment, compassion, forgiveness. She also makes the point that the teachings of the Wisdom path are scattered around the whole family of world religions, clothed in a variety of theologies and devotional practices, and they cannot be found in just one tradition.[14]

The recovery of many of these scattered practices to form a whole body of teaching is at the heart of the idea of Christian

Wisdom Schools, bringing the teaching of Jesus as a Wisdom master of the path of transformative love into focus.

The first title given to Jesus by his immediate band of followers was a *moshel meshalim*, "master of Wisdom." In the Near Eastern culture into which he was born, the category was well known, and his methods were immediately recognizable as part of it. He taught *mashal*, parables and wisdom sayings. He came to help people awaken. But awakening is not that easy, and as a *moshel meshalim*, Jesus had mixed success. As the four Gospels all record, some people glimpsed what he was saying while others missed it altogether. Some people got it part of the time and missed it the rest. Some people woke up and others remained asleep.[15]

In Britain, there has been little so far in the development of this path of Christian Wisdom as a framework to embrace the teaching and practice of the Wisdom tradition. It is there in a piecemeal fashion in various strands of Christianity. The evangelicals place a great emphasis on a daily "quiet time" for reflection on scripture passages and intercessory prayer and some have rediscovered the practice of "Lectio Divina" from the Benedictine tradition. The contemplatives emphasize need for silence and meditation. Ignatian spirituality has seen a resurgence of interest in the Ignatian Spiritual Exercises and imaginative contemplation. The retreat movement in general often uses creative arts to access the divine. The Taizé community in France and many others have recovered the power of sacred chant. The liberal scholars have given new insights into the scriptures. These are all practices to bring transformation of the heart, the core of the Wisdom tradition, and the combination of these as a powerful teaching synthesis is wider than the emerging Christianity – it is working towards the future evolution of human consciousness. There is also much room for incorporating the new scientific discoveries into this teaching, emphasizing the concepts outlined in part one of this book:

- the unity and oneness of all creation in the consciousness from which our material reality emerges;
- the untapped potential of the human being who has access to that enlightened consciousness;
- the influence we have on each other through morpho-genetic fields and morphic resonance;
- the understanding that we are held effectively in a quantum sea of light energy, with which we are constantly interacting at the most minute and intense energetic level of being.

The other area that could be incorporated into the idea of Wisdom Schools is the green agenda, the respect and care for the whole of creation. We are a part of the biosphere of the earth and our future depends on it being in a healthy balance. Spirituality has to contain an ecological awareness. Matthew Fox has done much groundwork in his book "*Original Blessing: A Primer in Creation Spirituality.*" He and Rupert Sheldrake had a fruitful conversation in "*Natural Grace: Dialogues on Science and Spirituality*" which contains much food for thought on the idea of the soul and biological information fields, prayer, morphic resonance and ritual. The development of a theology which incorporates the concept of the Earth having consciousness of some order is an important aspect of developing a new Christian cosmology.

Spiritual/Psychological Practices

Into this heady brew of practices, which can be brought together in the term 'Wisdom tradition', we could place many of the new spiritual and psychological healing processes that have been developed in recent years, often drawing on ancient wisdom and healing traditions. A good example of this is what is known as "Meridian Tapping." Casting our minds back to Chapter 2, we saw how the meridian lines of Chinese acupuncture exist as routes in the connective tissue that surrounds every organ of the body. The structure of connective tissue is liquid crystalline, which means that it is a very good conductor of electricity, and that when stimulated it can produce a tiny electric current (the principle by which a piezo-electric spark is produced from a crystal in a firelighter). Acupuncture is thought to work by stimulating points on the meridian lines with a needle; acupressure and possibly reflexology work by applying pressure to these same points. Tapping some of the key meridian points whilst using mental affirmations has been developed in recent years to free up emotional blocks and restrictions that have brought healing and a new freedom to many. Tapping was developed as a technique called Emotional Freedom Therapy (EFT) by Gary Craig, based on Thought Field Therapy, developed by Dr Roger Callaghan. It has now taken on a life of its own. It essentially works to reduce the emotional sting of many issues by focusing on the problem, summarizing it in an affirmation and, while keeping the affirmation in mind, tapping a series of meridian points on the chest, face and hands. EFT also adds some specific eye movements, the humming of a short tune and counting 1-5. It sounds bizarre, but it has taken off in a big way because it seems to work. Somehow, the combination of an affirmation and sending minute electrical impulse via the tapping points works to remove emotional blocks. It is so easy to do that anyone can try it, and, unlike many new therapies, it is free.[16]

Another example is "The Work" by Byron Katie,[17] a process that can bring psychological and emotional healing by questioning one's thoughts and coming to a deeper realization of the way in which we can trap ourselves in fear, depression, frustration and suffering. This allows compassion for self and others to arise, and our actions, in what were previously stressful situations, become harmonized with Divine Will as opposed to reacting from our egoic mind. It is a kind of psychotherapeutic shortcut that can be easily learnt and used and is based on a central tenet of the Lord's Prayer – forgive us our trespasses as we forgive those that trespass against us. Another helpful technique that can be used in group work is "The Affinity Process", devised by Paul Ferrini.[18] This group process effectively creates a very safe, non-judgmental space for sharing of thoughts and emotions that are happening at that moment, with the opportunity to give and receive unconditional love, acceptance and support. It allows people to open their hearts and be vulnerable in a trusted environment. These and many other techniques and processes are available to use to help in the transformation of the heart that is the whole point of the spiritual journey to wholeness and oneness. They do not come from any specific religious tradition, and can be used by all – they are both faith friendly and faith neutral. Some considerable degree of discernment is needed in this sphere, as some of the practices on offer can be either rather shallow, or simply 'off the wall.'

A New-Old Beginning?

One of the hardest things to do in the Church is to instigate change, especially if it is to do with either doctrine or tradition. I speak from within the Anglican Church, whose three pillars are said to be faith, tradition and reason, although it often feels to me that the first two predominate and the latter is sidelined. I am arguing from reason that a change has to happen if the Anglican way is to be credible for future generations in the Western world. That change needs to embrace the emerging scientific worldview that everything is connected in a surging sea of interacting, nonlocal energetic fields, and that consciousness is the source from which all emerges. It has to work on its theology to bring back the submerged wisdom tradition that Jesus taught, which is about transformation of the human being through awakening to unitive compassionate consciousness. It also has to change its language to move beyond the dualistic understanding of God 'out there' to a God within. It is vital that contemplative prayer or meditation becomes part of regular worship and certainly is a discipline to be fostered for personal daily prayer. The recovery of these meditative practices would be a new beginning, drawing fresh spiritual water from old wells.

In this book, I have introduced a range of concepts and ideas, many of which are not new at all, but simply have risen again to the surface in recent years. The new ideas are those that are coming from the scientific world, as described in Part One, and they have, in my view, much to say to Christian theology. I have tried not to get too mired in the depths of theology here, but to present a coherent overall view, drawing from a wide variety of views, aiming to spark off creative thoughts and ideas from others. There exists a spiritual path that includes elements of all the world's great religions, is not exclusive, and yet has a place of centrality for Jesus the Christ as a Wisdom teacher of the path of transformational love. Through his life and death, he made changes to and advanced the morphic field of all humanity, which enables us to truly follow that path. The journey is back to the heart of God, the divine compassionate consciousness from which we have come, and in whom we exist. That journey is helped by the practice of meditation and contemplative prayer as a means to attain unitive consciousness, a state of oneness with the divine, the "Sacred Unity."

In summary, the evolved understanding that I have come to through study, conversation and spiritual and devotional practices is this:

- God is the compassionate consciousness, the Ground of Being, the Sacred Unity in which the whole universe exists, from which everything emerges and which holds everything in being;

- Jesus has shown us what humanity is capable of when a human being is fully aware and one with that compassionate consciousness. In doing so he changed the morphic field for all humanity and cleared the path back to God, making it possible for us all to walk that way;
- the Holy Spirit is the expression of the energy of that compassionate consciousness, present in all creation;
- we are all energetically interconnected in this compassionate consciousness that is God.

This understanding connects with current understandings of the way the universe functions, and also with many of the mystics and visionaries in the Christian and other religious traditions. It recaptures the essence of the teaching of Jesus and many in the early Church, yet sets it in a contemporary context for the 21st century.

There is much talk across the globe of humanity coming to a tipping point, both ecologically and spiritually. Environmental experts, social and physical scientists are all pointing to the future of the human race as being threatened by the way in which we are living, but the situation is so multifaceted, and so bound up with human nature and society, that we seem to be defeated by its very complexity. As a metaphor, the tipping point is very helpful, as its very meaning is that it can go either way, and a tipping point is a place where a small difference makes a big change. We are in that place now, and some are saying that it is a looming environmental disaster. The sensationalist doom-mongers in the media are fond of telling us that the worst is bound to happen – it sells and grabs attention, but it is the road to fear and despair.

Tipping the other way is the view that humanity is on the verge of a growth in consciousness, the next stage in evolution of the human race. That way, there is a new beginning. If, as some speculate, there is a tipping point to do with the number of human beings who are moving towards a higher stage of consciousness, then there is a hope and a mission for us to work towards that change. A small change can make a big difference at the tipping point. My view is that Christianity can contribute to the positive change by losing its claims to exclusivity and returning to the Wisdom teaching from which it emerged. This is the evolution of science and Christianity in the title of this book – the coming together of the two, united in Wisdom. If we can think outside the boxes into which we have been conditioned, we can begin to make the connections and rediscover the Blue Sky God, the Sacred Unity at the Ground of Being, the One that humanity has never been able to confine to any religious box. Aligning ourselves with this deep well of compassionate consciousness has the potential to tip us into a different way of being, a new path for humanity, one of deep compassion, oneness and harmony. To conclude, a Jewish Hasidic tale captures the essence of this dawning consciousness:

"How can we determine the hour or dawn, when the night ends and the day begins?" asked the Teacher.

"Is it when from a distance you can distinguish between a dog and a sheep" suggested one of the students.

"No" was the answer.

"Is it when you can distinguish between a fig tree and a grapevine?" asked a second student.

"No."

"Please tell us the answer then."

"It is," said the Teacher, "when you can look into the face of another human being and you have enough light to recognize, in him or her, your brother or sister. Up until then, it is night, and darkness is still with us."

My perception is that the hour of dawn is coming, in the form of a higher state of consciousness that humanity is moving into, a state of Christ consciousness, an anointing of oneness with the compassionate consciousness of God. As this level of consciousness is reached by increasing numbers of people, the human world of relationships will move on to fulfill the call of Jesus to love one another on a global scale. This will transform the approach to politics, commerce, finance, and international relationships. The hour of dawn is coming.

Appendix I

The Virgin Birth and Nativity Story

How the idea of the virgin birth arose is a bit of a jigsaw puzzle. Many people outside the Church see the nativity story as a load of nonsense, a fairy story, and turn their backs on Christianity because of that. Many Christians struggle with it. How can there be such a thing as a virgin birth? Where did it come from? It is from Luke's gospel that the developed idea of the virgin birth emerged. The story of Gabriel's appearance to Mary, her visit to Elizabeth, and the birth in the stable with angels and shepherds only occur in Luke's gospel. Matthew's gospel only touches on it, and the other two do not have any reference to it at all. So how can we understand Luke's story of the virgin birth? There are some clues we can pick up on.

Clue One: we go back to the book of Isaiah, written around 700 years before the birth of Christ. Specifically, to Isaiah 7:14, which reads *'Behold a young woman shall conceive and bear a son and shall give him the name Immanuel (NRSV)*. Note that it says 'a young woman', not 'a virgin' shall conceive. The word in Hebrew is *almah*, which literally means a young woman. The specific word for virgin, *betulah*, is not used by Isaiah. The young woman could be a virgin before she conceived, but the word virgin is not mentioned in this passage. Many Bible translations wrongly translate it as virgin (but not the New Revised Standard Version that has been used in this book). What these translators are doing is reading from the New Testament back into the Old, and translating the Old so that it agrees with the New, or so that it agrees with the doctrine of the Church. That, to my mind, gives a distortion of the original meaning and is rather deceptive.

Clue Two: now jump forward 500 years to the second century

BC. At this time, the Greek language dominates the Mediterranean world. The Hebrew Scriptures are translated into Greek, and become known as the Septuagint. The word *almah*, young woman, is mistranslated to the Greek word *parthenos*, virgin. In the Greek world, all around the Mediterranean, it becomes known, due to the mistranslation, that the Jewish scriptures say that the Messiah would be born to a virgin.

Clue Three: enter Luke the physician and writer, the doctor, a friend of Paul. He traveled with Paul on some of his later missionary journeys. He was a Gentile convert to Christianity, so he did not have the Jewish background that Paul had. He was also born in Greece, and so would have read the Hebrew Scriptures in Greek, and hence he would have read the mistranslation that the Messiah would come from a virgin. He was a very good communicator and wrote the Acts of the Apostles as well as one of the gospels, and he wrote about people – poor people, outcasts, people who had made a mess of their lives and needed to be sorted out. His gospel shows he had sympathy for anyone in trouble, especially the sick.

His writing also shows that Luke had a tidy mind and liked to get things in a sequence that made sense to him, so that the events he relates can be followed by his readers. He was writing to the Greek-speaking world, reflecting a Greek approach to life. He is excited about the Christian message and the retelling of the life of Jesus the Messiah, the Christ, the anointed one, and he wants the world to believe in him, to believe that he is the chosen one, the Son of God, and that God has broken into history through Christ. So he gathers his material about the life of Jesus very carefully.

Clue Four: if you were telling the life of a famous person in those days, the custom was to write a prologue to the life. This was to herald the importance of the facts that you were going to relate about the person, and it often focused on the events surrounding the birth. The first two chapters of Luke's gospel are that prologue. They are written in the style of a Jewish legend or poem. To herald the importance of the message that his gospel contained, it meant that the birth of Jesus had to be shown to have special meaning. Luke carefully looked into the Old Testament prophesies about the coming of the Messiah (in the Greek translation, the Septuagint), and carefully constructed his prologue to fit in with the prophecies he found, one of which was that a virgin would conceive and give birth.

Luke may have come across the Jewish belief (described in the Talmud, Niddah 31a) that there are three partners in the conception of any child – a man, a woman and the Holy Spirit of God, who breathes life into that creation. With that under-standing, it was perfectly natural for the angel to say to Mary *"The Holy Spirit will come upon you and the power of the most High will overshadow you."* That is what happened at any birth – the power of God overshadowed the moment of conception to breathe new life. Luke's other themes are there as well – God was coming to ordinary, humble circumstances, to ordinary people, not to royal finery. Also, the outcasts were there – the shepherds, the rogues, the sinners, the low-life – all given a special place of importance in the story, heralding what was to come.

So we see that Luke is building the prologue to show the significance of the rest of the story he has to tell of Jesus' life, death and resurrection. Some of the prologue may be based on what others have told him, some of it he has constructed to fit the prophecies, but all of it is full of significance for the rest of the gospel. It basically said to the reader "Listen up: this is about a very important person." Luke has constructed a prologue that contains all the pointers to indicate to the reader that this is a very significant man. But the prologue did not have to be a true account of events – people understood that. We see this again in the hagiographies of the saints, those worshipful or idealizing biographies of the Christians of old. For the best of motivations, many stories of the lives of early saints are embellished with fantastic occurrences in order to inspire the reader to listen to their message and to give it more authority. Our modern minds find this a very difficult concept, as we expect everything that is put down as a life story to be an accurate account of what happened, and we feel deceived if this is not so. But our modern concept of accurate biography did not exist then – the mindset of the day did not see it that way. If Luke had not written a great prologue, the way all the Greek legends were written, he would have been doing Jesus a disservice.

It is also helpful to ask the question, "Does it matter?" Central in Luke's story was Mary, shown to be a virgin to fit in with what was thought to be the Old Testament prophecy. And of course, over the years, Mary has gained hugely in importance in the tradition of the Church, the virgin birth being central to that. But if you take out the idea that Mary had a virginal conception, it actually makes very little difference to the story. It is not mentioned in any of the earlier letters, nor in the gospels written by Mark and John – for them the story begins with Jesus' ministry, and John the Baptist is the herald to tell of the significance of the rest of the story. The only other place it can be construed to be mentioned is in a similar prologue to Matthew's gospel. Matthew simply says, *"When Mary had been betrothed to Joseph, before they came together, she was found to be with child by the Holy Spirit."* (Matthew 1:18) In Jewish understanding, any pregnant woman was with child by the Holy Spirit – it was God's breath, God's Spirit, which gave life to any child. This was normal. What was not normal, given that Mary must have been made pregnant by intercourse with someone else, was that Joseph was being asked to remain betrothed to her, and it shows the generous nature of Joseph that he took her in.

Luke tells us of a special man, born as a baby, a man who grew up to be more god-like than any human being, full of love and compassion, wisdom and strength – so full of God that he was called the Son of God and was seen by those Jews around him as the Messiah who was prophesied in their scriptures, the one who would be their salvation. Does it matter whether God did something miraculous to conceive the child in Mary, or whether it was actually Joseph or someone else in the natural way of things, with God's presence overshadowing the moment of conception? The truth of the matter is that Jesus grew up to be specially anointed by God, the anointed one, the Christ, the Messiah.

The nativity story can be taken in two ways – either as a literally true story that Luke based on actual eyewitness accounts, or as an allegorical story that points to the significant truths of the momentous events that happen during the ministry years of Jesus the Messiah, his death and resurrection. Either way, it sets the scene and complements the rest of the gospel.

Many outside the Church see it as a fairy story. It is not. It is a story of great significance in the gospels, whether you see it a factual or allegorical. It weaves together elements of expectation, anticipation and hope from the Old Testament and joins the Old Testament to the New. It is like the old Native American story teller says as he begins his tribe's story of creation, "I don't know whether it happened this way or not, but I know this story is true." Or a priest who once said, "The Bible is true – and some of it happened."

We can get into a very sterile debate about 'whether it happened this way or not', and lose the greater truths that are there if we see it as a metaphorical story. The story of Jesus being conceived by the Spirit of God affirms that what happened in Jesus was of God. The glory of God filling the sky and the special star suggest light in the darkness, breaking into this world, a special, anointing, divine light shining into the world. The story of the Gentile magi from lands afar affirms that Jesus is the light for all, not just for the Jews (this story appears only in Matthew's gospel). The story of the shepherds shows that the good news is especially for the marginalized, the poor, the disadvantaged. The song of the angels declares Jesus as Lord and Savior – not Caesar, who used those titles for himself. These were royal titles, fit for a king.

Read metaphorically, the nativity story means all of this and more. And it means it independently of whether we see it as a factual story or not. Arguing about whether it is factual or not can actually distract from its deeper meaning and lose something of its significance. Personally, I do not see the nativity story as factual, but I see truths within it.

A Service of Prayers for Healing
With Laying on of Hands and Anointing

This could take place in a home, church or any suitable space. It may be led by one person or a number of people.

Suggested set up: a circle of chairs or cushions. Participants may be invited to bring other meaningful objects to place around the center-piece.

Resources:

In the center, a tray of sand (if burning paper during confession) with large candle in the center.

Oil for anointing

It may start with time of quiet, and maybe a chant or song

Opening

Blessed are you, loving God, ground of our being.

Blessed be God forever.

Jesus, Wisdom Teacher, the anointed one, brings healing to our brokenness and distress; he shows the way of love that transforms and takes us beyond our lower self, that we might share in his nature.

Beloved One, remember in your compassion all for whom we pray; continue your transforming work within us, that we may be restored to fullness of being, and renewed in your love.

Blessed be God forever. Amen

Holy God, in whom we live and move and have our being, we make our prayer to you saying,

Beloved One, hear us:
and open our hearts
We come before you to receive the assurance of your presence, your power and your peace.
Beloved One, hear us:
and open our hearts

We acknowledge our need of your healing grace: bring us to wholeness in body, mind and spirit.
Beloved One, hear us:
and open our hearts

Hear us, Holy One, Mother and Father of life and love:
heal us, and make us whole.

A period of silence follows.

God of all, Sacred One, as we turn to you; may your compassion flow freely within us; for you are gracious, O lover of souls, and in you we find true life and our place of rest, now and forever. **Amen.**

Confession/Admission
An opportunity for the admission of sorrow or regrets, faults and failings in word or symbol.

  (One way to do this is by giving an opportunity to write on small pieces of paper, then invite each person to say a few words before burning the paper in the sand tray – or just burn them all symbolically)

Song or Chant

The Laying on of Healing Hands.

Hands are laid on the person asking for healing. We act as channels for the divine energy to flow...

In the name of God and trusting in his loving presence deep within our being, receive the healing touch of the Holy Spirit, the energy of God, to bring you harmony and balance and make you whole in body, mind and spirit.

Allow time for healing energy to flow

May the Spirit of the living God, present within us now, bring healing for body, mind and spirit. May the love and consciousness of the Christ bring you wholeness, deliver you from harmful thoughts, feelings and past wounds, and bring you peace. May you know love in your life, that it may overflow from within you like running water. Know these three: love, joy and peace.
Amen.

The Anointing
Bible Reading: e.g. Mark 14:3-9, Luke 7:36-50, John 12:1-8

A Prayer over the Oil
God of life and love, giver of health and salvation, sanctify and bless this oil as a symbol of the healing love of Jesus, that those who are anointed with it may be freed from suffering and distress, find inward peace, and be restored to fullness of being, through your transformative love shown in Christ Jesus, and known by Mary Magdalene, who anointed Jesus.
Amen.

[The anointing can be done in the form of a cross on the forehead, or anointing the feet. Any form of these words may used as anointing with oil is administered, either by one person, or from person to person]

N, I anoint you in the name of God who gives birth to life. Be whole.

N, I anoint you. May the God of all compassion grant you the riches of his grace, his wholeness and his peace.

N, I anoint you in the name of God who gives birth to life. Know that in coming to this time and place you are forgiven, you are held in the compassionate consciousness of God, you are being restored to fullness of life and wholeness, through love and the full acceptance of who you are in God, a blessed one.

May the God of all compassion grant you the riches of his grace, his wholeness and his peace.

Amen.

We say together:
The living God, in whom we live and move and have our being, who sustains the universe, be now and evermore the source of *our* being.
May Jesus the Christ be *our* guide and inspiration.
May the Holy Spirit overflow and bring joy in *our* lives and lead us on the path to enlightenment.
May *we* become healed and whole, knowing fullness of life.
To this we give our highest assent – let it be so. Amen.

A period of silence follows.

Let us pray to the holy One for the realizing of the kingdom among and within us:
Eternal Spirit,
Earth-maker, Pain-bearer, Life-giver,
Source of all that is and that shall be,
Father and Mother of us all,

Loving God, in whom is heaven:

The hallowing of your name echo through the universe!
The way of your justice be followed by peoples of the world!
Your loving will be done by all created beings!
Your way of compassion sustain our hope and come on earth.

With the bread we need for today, feed us.
From the wounds we hold within us, free us.
In times of temptation and test, strengthen us.
Through trials and pain and hurt, hold us.
From the grip of all that is evil, free us.

For you are the glory of the power that is Love, now and forever
Amen.

May the Beloved God of all creation, the source of our being, the heart of compassion, lead us in the way of transformative love, into wholeness of living and the joy of loving, through the Christ, our Wisdom teacher, and the anointing of the divine within us.
Let it be so. Amen

The service may end with a chant or other ending.

(The Lord's Prayer adapted with permission from a version by Jim Cotter. Treating 'Eternal Spirit' as the first line, those changed are: 8, 9, 11, 13, 15

Other liturgy © Don MacGregor 2011)

Appendix 3

A Consciousness Eucharist

This liturgy is based on the Church in Wales format and wording, but altering the language to be more aligned to the concepts outlined in this book. It has no authorization for use in the Anglican Communion.

1. The Gathering

Welcome & Opening song or chant

In the name of the Triune God, Sacred Unity, Source of all. **Amen**.
Grace and peace be with us all:
and keep us in the love of Christ.

God of all compassion, whose presence within knows our heart's desires and hidden secrets: let your energy and light flow, so that we may know your breath of life in our inner beings, and show heartfelt praise in our lives, as did Jesus the Christ. Let it be so.

In the awareness that we often fail to follow the path of love shown to us in Christ, we open our heart to the divine presence within, that we may be made whole.

Lord, have mercy. **Lord, have mercy.**
Christ, have mercy. **Christ, have mercy.**
Lord, have mercy. **Lord, have mercy.**
(or chant Kyrie Eleison)

Silence, followed by prayer of confession:

God of all Creation, in whom we live and move and have our being,
we acknowledge our separation within from you,
our self-centeredness and hardness of heart towards others and ourselves.
We are truly sorry, and ask that you would help us to move beyond our minds
into the heart of your loving presence.
May we be remade in the image of Jesus the Christ, the divine human,
that we may know fullness of life in the dynamism of your love. Let it be so.

God is the compassionate consciousness in which we exist, loving and forgiving. May God strengthen us in goodness and help us grow towards wholeness, in the Way of Christ. **Amen.**

We sing a song or chant, giving praise to God

The collect – *the prayer of the day*

2. The Proclamation of the Word

One or two Bible readings, after which is said:
This is the inspired Word:
Thanks be to God.

Song or chant, appropriate to the reading

Another reading from the Christian tradition may be used here

Talk, sermon or interaction in groups

An Affirmation of Faith

We believe in the God of Creative purpose,
the compassionate consciousness in which we live and
move and have our being.
Mother and Father of us all, we are held in being by God
who dwells in us and all creation,
and from whom we have been breathed into life.

We believe Jesus the Christ was a son of God,
a fully human being who reached the depths of God-
consciousness to become fully divine,
and forged a path for the rest of humanity,
through the way of self-emptying and compassion.

We believe in the Spirit of God,
the divine energy working in the world
to bring all things to fullness and restoration.

We believe in the sacred nature of the Earth and every
human being,
and that the spiritual journey is one of becoming transformed by love,
letting go of the selfish nature,
and entering into the compassionate consciousness that is God.

3. The Intercession

*Prayers of intention are focused thought and feeling to bring about
positive change in cooperation with the divine consciousness. We
offer spoken prayers to verbalize that process.*
After spoken prayers, we keep a silence for further prayer.

Final response:
Loving God, accept our prayers, made in the consciousness
of Christ. Amen

4. The Peace

...God's peace be always with you... **and also with you**
A sign of peace may be exchanged

Song or chant during which a collection for the life of the Church is taken

5. The Thanksgiving

We stand for the prayer of thanksgiving.

Offering of the gifts:
Blessed are you, God of all creation.
Through your goodness, we have this bread to offer,
which earth has given and human hands have made.
It will become for us the bread of life.
Blessed be God for ever.

Blessed are you, God of all creation.
Through your goodness, we have this wine to offer,
fruit of the vine and work of human hands.
It will become our spiritual drink.
Blessed be God for ever.

Blessed are you, God of all creation.
Through your goodness, we have ourselves to offer,
fruit of the womb and the work of your love.
We will become, for you, whole people.
Blessed be God for ever.

God is here.
His Spirit is within us.
Open your hearts.
We open them to God.
Let us give thanks to God our Sustainer.
It is right to give our thanks and praise.

It is indeed right, it is our duty and our joy, at all times and in all places, to give you thanks and praise, holy One, Mother and Father of us all, existing before time, through Jesus the Christ, the divine human.

In him, your eternal Word dwelt: through that same Word, you breathed the universe and formed us, man and woman, in your own image. In Jesus the Christ, the anointed One, you have shown us the Way of transformative love. By his life and death, he emptied himself, embracing us in perfect love and compassion, overcoming the power of evil, suffering and death for us all. Love is stronger than death and his resurrection opened to us the gate of timeless life. Through following his path, we come to know your holy and life-giving Spirit, the divine energy within, and we become transformed into your likeness.

Therefore with angels and archangels and with all the company of heaven, we proclaim your great and glorious Unity, forever praising you and saying:

Holy, holy, holy One,
God of love and presence,
heaven and earth shine forth with your glory.
Hosanna in the highest!
Blessed is he who follows the Way of Christ.
Hosanna in the highest!

Be with us, Sacred One, as you were in Christ Jesus, the divine human. We open ourselves to praise you and offer this remembrance of the Last Supper. May these gifts of bread and wine be symbols for us of the essence of his being and the vitality of his blood;

who in the same night that he was betrayed, took a loaf of bread, and blessed it; he broke it and gave it to his disciples, saying, "Take, eat, this is my body."

Then he took a cup, and after giving thanks, he gave it to them, and all of them drank from it. He said to them, "This is my blood of the covenant, which is poured out for many."

And so, Holy Presence within us, we remember the death and resurrection of Jesus, and offer to you in thanksgiving this bread and this cup, your gifts to us, that the essence and vitality of Christ may be in us.

Fan into flame your Spirit within all of us who open our hearts to you. Strengthen our faith, make us one in you, and guide us and all your people in the Way of Christ, leading to the Kingdom of Love that is our destiny.

In union with him and the Holy Spirit, all honour and glory are yours, God of all, in and beyond all time and space. **Amen.**

We say together, from his own language, the prayer Jesus taught us:
O Breath of Life, who flows in all creation,
May the light of your presence fill the universe,
your way of being come, your desire be done,
in this and all realms of existence.
Bring forth the nourishment we need for this day.
Forgive the failures that bind us,
as we let go of our hold on other's failures.
And let us not be satisfied with the surface of life,
but deliver us from wrong paths.
For you are abundant life, creative unity and glorious harmony,
through all time and beyond. Amen.

6. The Communion

We break this bread to share in the body of Christ.
Though we are many, we are one body, for we all share in one bread.

The invitation
Come, let us receive these symbols of the body and blood of Jesus the Christ, given for us,
and take his life into our hearts by faith with thanksgiving.

The priest and people receive the communion. This may be passed from person to person with suitable words such as,
The body/blood of Christ be yours.
The life/love of Christ be in your heart
The divine life/love of Christ be yours

A time of quiet follows.

Post-Communion Prayer
Give thanks for the graciousness of God:
who is Love Everlasting, Divine Consciousness, Ground of Being.

We say together:
God of all time and space, comfort of the afflicted and healer of the broken, you have fed us at the table of life and hope: teach us the ways of gentleness and peace, that all the world may acknowledge the Way of love, shown to us in Jesus the Christ. Amen

Song or Chant

7. The Sending Out

May God be seen in your life.
And also in yours.

This blessing or another may be said (whilst making the sign of the cross, if desired):
May Christ, the light of the world,
open your hearts with the good news of his kingdom way,
and the blessing of the one Creator God
be amongst you now and remain with you always. **Amen**

Go in peace to show the love of God.
In the Way of Christ. Amen.

Notes to Chapters

Preface
1. Tompkins & Bird, 1975
2. The Findhorn Community, 1976.
3. The Great Invocation:
    From the point of Light within the Mind of God
    let light stream forth into the minds of men.
    Let Light descend on Earth.
    From the point of Love within the Heart of God
    let love stream forth into the hearts of men.
    May Christ return to Earth.
    From the center where the Will of God is known
    let purpose guide the little wills of men:
    The purpose which the Masters know and serve.
    From the center which we call the race of men
    let the Plan of Love and Light work out
    And may it seal the door where evil dwells.
    Let Light and Love and Power restore the Plan on Earth.

Introduction
1. Hans Kung, ed., 1996. *Yes to a Global Ethic.* London: SCM
2. Trevelyan, 1981, p.13
3. The Flat Earth Society, 1998. Available from www.alaska.net/~clund/e_djublonskopf/Flatearthsociety.ht m (Accessed 9.11.2010)
4. Wikipedia, (updated May 2011). *Vergilius of Salzburg.* Available at http://en.wikipedia.org/wiki/Vergilius_of_Salzburg (Accessed 1.3.2011)
5. Armstrong, 1993, p.332
6. Comby, 1989, p.39
7. De Mello, 1984

8. Albert Schweitzer, 1955. *The Mysticism of Paul the Apostle.* New York: MacMillan
9. James Bryant Conant, 1893-1978, Past President of Harvard University

Chapter 1: Quantum Reality and God as Consciousness

1. McTaggart, 2007, p.253
2. Goswami, 2001 p.13
3. Max Planck, quoted in Braden, 2000, p.110
4. Goswami, 2001, p.28
5. Ibid., p.30
6. *What the Bleep Do We Know,* 2005 (DVD), Revolver Entertainment
7. Laszlo, 2007 p.117
8. The 'double slit' experiment consists of firing electrons at a barrier containing a double slit. On the other side of the barrier is screen to show where the electrons hit it. If electrons are particles, they can go through either one slit or the other, and one would expect to see two bright lines on the screen. Instead, what is found on the screen is an interference pattern of alternating brighter and darker lines, the same as if a wave had gone through the slits, not a stream of particles. To grasp this experiment, imagine the barrier and slits in a large tank of water. You drop a pebble in at one edge, and a ripple spreads out to hit the barrier. The ripple passes through each slit at the same time, and two ripples emerge on the other side of the barrier, which interfere with each other, so that there is a pattern of peaks and troughs. This ripple pattern is exactly how electrons behave – they are a wave, not a particle.
9. McTaggart, 2007 p.39-41
10. Ibid., p.13.
11. Ibid., p.15.
12. This comes as no surprise to me, as I have long known that

my wife and eldest daughter have an effect on computers! When they are around, strange 'slowings down' happen, odd little things occur. They both hate technology, and holding this intent towards the equipment seems to generate some form of energy field that affects the electronics. Many others would corroborate this sort of effect. There are numerous stories of people who effectively send computers haywire by their presence.

13. Gregory of Nyssa, *Life of Moses*, (Patrologia Graeca 44,377), in Clement, 1993, p.27
14. McGrath 2001 p.321
15. John Climacus, *The Ladder of Divine Ascent*, 30th step, 2(6), p.167, in Clement, 1993, p.34
16. Spong, 2001 p.70-73
17. Genesis chapters 2-3
18. Clément, 1994, p.84
19. Luke 15:11-32
20. Tompkins & Bird, 1973
21. Bourgeault, 2003, p.53.
22. Church, 2007, p.313.

Chapter 2: Epigenetics, Healing & Prayer
1. Lipton, 2005, p.115
2. Ibid., p.114-5
3. Schlitz, M.J. & Braud, W., 1997, cited in McTaggart, 2001, p.133
4. Braud, W., 1991, cited in McTaggart, 2001, p.136
5. Lipton, B., 2005, p.111
6. Church, 2007, p.32
7. Ibid., p.71
8. McTaggart, 2007, p.135
9. Ibid., p.137
10. House of Lords Select Committee on Science and Technology – Sixth Report. Available at: http://www.publi

cations.parliament.uk/pa/ld199900/ldselect/ldsctech/123/12
301.htm (Accessed 25 January 2011)

11. Church, 2007, p.104
12. Ibid., p.242
13. O'Regan, B. & Hirshberg, C., 1993. *Spontaneous Remission: An Annotated Bibliography*. Petaluma CA: Institute of Noetic Sciences, cited in McTaggart, 2007, p.190
14. Church, 2007, p.256
15. McTaggart, 2007, p.131
16. Church, 2007 p.136-7
17. Ibid., p.121
18. McTaggart, 2001, p.55
19. Church, 2007, p.121
20. Rosanfeld, 2006, cited in Church, 2007, p.121
21. McTaggart, 2007, p.187
22. Ibid., p.189
23. Ibid., p.189
24. Ibid., p.190
25. Church, 2007, p.223-4
26. McTaggart, 2007, p.254

Chapter 3: Morphic Fields and the Works of Christ

1.   Sheldrake, 1988, p.113
2.   Jung, Carl. (1959). *Archetypes and the Collective Unconscious*.
3.   Sheldrake & Fox, 1996
4.   Sheldrake, 1988, pp.174-181
5.   Sheldrake, 1987
6.   Matthew 26:36-46, Mark 14:32-42
7.   Bourgeault, 2010, p.156
8.   Ephesians 1:18
9.   Romans 12:1,2
10. Macquarrie, 1965, p.284
11. Ibid., p.288
12. Borg, 2003, p.151

13. Clément, 1994, p.46

Chapter 4: The Quantum Sea of Light

1. Haisch, 2006, p.93
2. Available at http://www.thefieldonline.com/ (Accessed 6 Jun 2007)
3. "A specific experiment to tap this energy supply has been proposed by Dr. Bernard Haisch, an astrophysicist who was funded by NASA and Lockheed Martin to investigate zero-point physics, and Prof. Garret Moddel, an engineering professor at the University of Colorado."
   Gough, W.C., Foundation for Mind-Being Research, (May 2005) *Zero Point Energy*. Available at http://www. fmbr.org/editoral/edit04_05/edit8-may05.htm. (Accessed 10 May 2011)
4. McTaggart, 2001, p.26
5. Laszlo, 2007, p.70-71
6. McTaggart, 2001, p.85
7. Ibid., p.95
8. Ibid., pp.77-96
9. Ibid., p.82
10. Ibid., p.93
11. Ibid., pp.77-96
12. Ibid., p.138
13. Ibid., p.39-55
14. Cannato, 2006, pp.68-77
15. Ibid., p.71
16. Ibid., pp.74-5
17. Ibid., p.75
18. Haisch, 2006, p.93.
19. Quoted from the Haggadah in Haisch, 2006, p.99
20. Laszlo, 2007, p.76
21. Chandogya Upanishad, Part I, chapter 9.1, Spirit Mythos: *A World Beyond, Akashic and Akashic Records, References from*

Various Scholarly and Religious Sources. Available at
http://www.spiritmythos.org/TM/akashic/akashicref.html
(Accessed 10 May 2011)
22. Laszlo, 2007, p.31
23. Ibid., p.53
24. Ibid., p.50
25. Ibid., p. 76
26. Ibid., p.105

Chapter 5: Rethinking Jesus

1. Quoted in Bourgeault, 2007
2. "There is no means of tracing precisely when the trade
   route was first used. However, historical records reveal that
   in the time of Julius Caesar, Romans were already intrigued
   by the fine quality of silk from China."
   Adel Awni Dajami, 2011. *Islamic Frontiers of China.* London:
   Tauris
3. "By the first century CE the Silk Road trade had established
   connections from China to the Mediterranean Sea."
   Xiuni Liu, 2010. *The Spice Road.* New York: OU, p.47
4. Wikipedia, (updated June 2011) *Incense Route.* Available at
   http://en.wikipedia.org/wiki/Incense_Road (Accessed 22
   July 2011)
5. Bourgeault, 2008, p.25
6. The reference to angels as sons of God can be seen in a
   number of places. Job 1:6 says, *"Now there was a day when the
   sons of God came to present themselves before the LORD, and
   Satan came also among them."* This is from the Revised
   Version. The New Revised Standard Version refers to them
   as 'heavenly beings', and again in Job 38:7
7. The king of Israel is referred to as the son of God: *"I will
   announce," says the king, "what the LORD has declared. He said
   to me: 'You are my son; today I have become your father. (Psalm
   2:7)*

8. The title "son of God" was applied in the Old Testament to persons having any special relationship with God. Angels, just and pious men, the descendants of Seth, were called "sons of God" (Job 1:6; 2:1; Psalm 88:7; Wisdom 2:13; etc.). In a similar manner, it was given to Israelites (Deuteronomy 14:50); and of Israel, as a nation, we read: "And thou shalt say to him: Thus saith the Lord: Israel is my son, my firstborn. I have said to thee: Let my son go, that he may serve me" (Exodus 4:22 sq.).
The leaders of the people, kings, princes, judges, as holding authority from God, were called sons of God.
The Catholic Encyclopedia (2009). *Son of God in the Old Testament.* Available at http://www.newadvent.org/cathen/14142b.htm (Accessed 15 May 2011)
9. Ehrman, 2003, p.2
10. Goldsmith, 1972, p.17
11. Ibid., p.20
12. Personal correspondence with John Henson on the text before publication.
13. Metzger, B.M. *To The Reader.* Preface to the New Revised Standard Version of the Bible
14. See Exodus 30:22-30
15. See Judges 9:8, 2 Samuel 2:4, 1 Kings 1:34, Exodus 28:41, 1 Kings 19:16
16. Spong, 2001, p.111
17. Borg, 2003, p. 82-3
18. Ibid., p.88
19. Ibid., pp.89-91
20. Macquarrie, 1965, p.272
21. Ibid., p.252
22. Ibid., p.253
23. Spong, 2001, p.141
24. Cannato, 2010, p.56
25. Integral Life (2009). *The Loft Series: Love and Evolution.*

Available at http://integrallife.com/node/76038 (Accessed 23 May 2011)

26. Peers, E.A. (trans.), 1990. *Teresa of Avila, The Interior Castle*. New York: Bantam Doubleday Dell Publishing Group, p.193-4.

27. James, W., 2008. *The Varieties of Religious Experience: A Study in Human Nature*. Rockville MD: Arc Manor, p.307

28. Ask The Real Jesus (2009). *Discourse 7. Understanding Christ Consciousness*. Available at http://www.askrealjesus.com/as krealjesus/trueteachings/christhood/Christh7.html (Accessed 10 May 2011)

Chapter Six: Revisiting the Kingdom

1. Bourgeault 2008, p.30

2. Cynthia Bourgeault, 2008 (CD). *Putting on the Mind of Christ – Transforming your Consciousness through Centering Prayer*. Talk in the series 'Silence in the City'. Southport: Agape Ministries.

3. Christianity is a vibrant faith in Africa, South America and China, where different worldviews have sustained a non-rational outlook on life, willing to embrace the Bible as the literal word of God.

4. Luke 6:36

5. Borg, 1995, p.47

6. Marcus Borg, 2001. *Taking Jesus Seriously*. Lenten Noonday Preaching Series, Calvary Episcopal Church, Memphis, Tennessee, March 15th 2001. Available at http://www.explorefaith.org/LentenHomily03.15.01.html (Accessed May 2011)

7. The scribes and Pharisees are famously criticized by Jesus in the 'Woes' of Matthew 23 and Luke 11

8. Bourgeault, 2003, p.47-9

Chapter 7: Revisiting the Kingdom

1. Bourgeault, 2010, p.132
2. Church, 2007 p.123
3. Henson, 2004, p.274
4. I am indebted to John Henson for this example.
5. Justin Martyr, *The First Apology*, 46:1-4
6. Global Ministries (2011). *The Sermons of John Wesley: On Faith*, Sermon 106 para.10. Available at at http://new.gbgm-umc.org/umhistory/wesley/sermons/106/ (Accessed May 2011)
7. Declaration on the Relation of the Church to Non-Christian Religions, Nostra Aetate. Proclaimed By His Holiness Pope Paul VI on October 28, 1965. Available at http://www.vatican.va/archive/hist_councils/ii_vatican_council/documents/vat-ii_decl_19651028_nostra-aetate_en.html (Accessed 18 July 2011)

Chapter 8:

1. Words of Basil of Caesarea, quoted by Gregory Nazianzen, Eulogy of Basil the Great, Oration 43,48 (PG36,560) in Clement, 1993, p.76
2. Iraneaus, *Adversus Haereses (Against Heresies)*, 4.34. 5-7.
3. Borg, 1998, p.113-5
4. O'Donohue, 1997, p.26
5. Julian of Norwich, 1966. p.68
6. Backhouse, 1985. ch.35, p.64
7. Main, 1987, p.14
8. Ibid., p.17
9. Ward B. (trans.), 1975. *The Sayings of the Desert Fathers; The Alphabetical Collection*. (Kalamazoo: Cistercian Publications), p. xxi, xxvi
10. Murphy, M., Donovan S., 1988. *Contemporary Meditation Research:* A Review of Contemporary Meditation Research With a Comprehensive Bibliography, p.131 (San Francisco:

The Esalen Institute) quoted in Church, 2007, p.155

11. Church, 2007, p.155

12. Laird, 2006, p.10

13. Ibid, p.15

14. Bourgeault, 2008, pp.62-5

15. Ibid., p.66

16. Backhouse, 1985, p.25

17. Ibid., p.33

18. Found in the gospels at Matthew 19:30, 20:16, Mark 10:31, Luke 13:30

19. Matthew 6:22

20. Helminski, K., 1992. *Living Presence: A Sufi Way to Mindfulness and the Essential Self.* New York: Jeremy Tarcher, p.157. Quoted in Bourgeault, 2008, p.36

21. Institute of HeartMath, (2011), *Science of the Heart: Exploring the Role of the Heart in Human Performance.* Available at http://www.heartmath.org/research/science-of-the-heart/introduction.html (Accessed 14 June 2011.)

22. Laird, 2006, p.16

23. Ibid., p.19

24. Mascaro, J., 1962. *The Bhagavad Gita.* Harmondsworth UK: Penguin Books, chapter 18:52-53, p.119-20

25. Ward B. (trans.), 1975. *The Sayings of the Desert Fathers; The Alphabetical Collection.* Kalamazoo MN: Cistercian Publications), p.183

26. Bourgeault, 2003, p.74

27. John Main, 1987. *The Joy of Being.* London: Dartman, Longman and Todd, p.39

28. From the Spiritual Canticle of St. John of the Cross

29. Bailey, A. 1967. *A Treatise on White Magic.* London: Lucis Press, p.132

30. The first two verses of the song read, in literal translation, *"A rose has sprung up, from a tender root. As the old ones sang to us, its lineage was from Jesse. And it has brought forth a*

floweret, in the middle of the cold winter, right upon midnight. The rosebud that I mean, of which Isaiah told, is Mary, the pure, who brought us the floweret. At God's immortal word, she has borne a child remaining a pure maid." From Wikipedia, (updated 17 July 2011). Available at http://en.wikipedia.org/ wiki/Es_ist_ein_Ros_entsprungen (Accessed 5 July 2011)

31. Chandogya Upanishad III xiv 2-3

Chapter 9: Evolution of Religious Language

1. Borg, 1995, p.47. Borg refers here to the Hebrew word *rachAm*, seen in Exodus 34:6, 2 Chronicles 30:9, Nehemiah 9:17, 31, Psalms 103:8, Joel 2:13.
2. Ibid., p.48
3. Dossey, L., *Non-Local Mind: Why It Matters.* In Pfeiffer, 2007, p.5
4. Harvey, 1998, p.56
5. Douglas-Klotz, 1999, p.49
6. Ibid., p.71
7. Ibid., p.79
8. Ibid., p.103
9. Ibid., p.27
10. Ibid., p.28
11. Douglas-Klotz, 1994, p. 13
12. Ibid., p.14
13. Ibid., 1994, p.12
14. Schmitt, M., *If All is Consciousness, What Then is my Body?* In Pfeiffer, 2007, p.51
15. Ibid., p.52
16. Ibid., p.53
17. Ibid., p.54
18. Henson, 2010, p.7
19. T.S. Eliot, Four Quartets, Burnt Norton

Chapter 10: Moving Forward

1. Funk, R.W., Hoover, R.W., 1993. *The Five Gospels: The Search for the Authentic Words of Jesus.* New York: Harper Collins
2. Borg, M. 2003, p.xii
3. Spong, 2001, p.145
4. For more information, see www.contemplativefire.org
5. For more information, see www.thestillpoint.org.uk
6. For more information, see www.moot.uk.net
7. For more information, see www.contemplativeforum.org
8. St Iraneaus of Lyons, *Against Heresies*, book 5, preface
9. St. Clement of Alexandria, Stromata 7,16,101,4 (Ed. Stählin)
10. St. Athanasius, Migne, *Patrologia Graeca*, 25, 192 B De Incarnatione Verbi, 54
11. References 5, 6, 7 and others here are taken from Wikipaedia at http://en.wikipedia.org/wiki/Divinization _(Christian)#cite_note-6 (Accessed 1 July 2011)
12. Orthodox Wiki, (updated 2 May 2011), *Theosis.* Available at http://orthodoxwiki.org/Theosis (Accessed 4 July 2011)
13. Article on Meister Eckhart in Jones, C. et al, 1986 p.317
14. Bourgeault, 2003, p. xvii
15. Ibid., p.4
16. There are many websites that give tapping advice, for instance, www.tapping.com, www.tappingtherapy.co.uk, www.emotional-health.co.uk, www.thetappingsolution .com
17. For more details see www.thework.com
18. Ferrini, P., 1998 *Living in the Heart – The Affinity Process and the Path of Unconditional Love and Acceptance.* Greenfield, MA: Heartways Press.

Bibliography

Armstrong, K., 1993. *A History of God.* London: William Heinemann Ltd.

Backhouse, H., 1985. *The Cloud of Unknowing – a new paraphrase.* London: Hodder & Stoughton,

Bourgeault, C., 2003. *The Wisdom Way of Knowing – Reclaiming and Ancient Tradition to Awaken the Heart.* SanFrancisco (CA): Jossey-Bass

Bourgeault, C., 2007. *Love is Stronger than Death.* Texas: Praxis Publishing

Bourgeault, C., 2008. *The Wisdom Jesus: Transforming Heart and Mind – a New Perspective on Christ and His Message.* Boston: Shambhala Publications Inc.

Bourgeault, C., 2010. The Meaning of Mary Magdalene. Shambhala: Boston

Borg, M. & Wright, N.T., 1999. *The Meaning of Jesus.* London: SPCK

Borg, M., 1995. *Meeting Jesus Again for the First Time.* New York: HarperCollins

Borg, M., 1998. *The God We Never Knew.* New York: HarperCollins

Borg, M., 2003. *The Heart of Christianity.* New York: HarperCollins

Bladon, L., 2007. *The Science of Spirituality – Integrating Science, Psychology, Philosophy, Spirituality & Religion.* Esotericscience.org

Braden, G., 2000. *The Isaiah Effect: Decoding the Lost Science of Prayer and Prophecy.* London: Hay House UK Ltd.

Burton, U. & Dolley, J., 1984. *Christian Evolution – Moving Towards a Global Spirituality.* Wellingborough: Turnstone Press

Cannato, J., 2006. *Radical Amazement.* Notre Dame (IN): Sorin Books

Cannato, J., 2010. *Field of Compassion.* Notre Dame (IN): Sorin Books

Capra, F., 1982. *The Tao of Physics*. 3rd ed.Hammersmith: Flamingo

Cheslyn, J., Wainwright, G., Yarnold, E., 1986. *The Study Of Spirituality*. London: SPCK

Church, D., 2007. *The Genie in your Genes*. Santa Rosa: Elite Books

Clément, O.,1994. *The Roots of Christian Mysticism*. 2nd ed. London: New City

Comby, J. with MacCulloch D., 1989. *How To Read Church History: volume 2 from the Reformation to the present day*. London: SCM Press Ltd.

De Chardin, P.T., 1966. *Let Me Explain*. London: William Collins Sons & Co. Ltd.

De Mello, A., 1984. *The Song of the Bird*. New York: Doubleday.

O'Donohue, J., 1997. *Anam Cara – Spiritual Wisdom from the Celtic World*. London: Bantam

Douglas-Klotz, N.,1994. *Prayers of the Cosmos: Meditations on the Aramaic Words of Jesus*. New York: HarperCollins Publishers.

Douglas-Klotz, N., 1999. *The Hidden Gospel*. Wheaton (IL): Quest Books.

Ehrman, B. D., 2003. *Lost Christianities: The Battles for Scripture and the Faiths We Never Knew*. New York: Oxford University Press.

Fox, M., 1983. *Original Blessing: A Primer in Creation Spirituality*. Santa Fe: Bear & Co.

Fox, M., Sheldrake, R., 1996. *Natural Grace: Dialogues on Science and Spirituality*. London: Bloomsbury Publishing

Goswami, A., 1993. *The Self-Aware Universe*. New York: Penguin Puttnam.

Goswami, A., 2001. *Physics of the Soul*. Charlottesville (VA): Hampton Roads Publishing Co.

Goldsmith, J.S., 1972. *The Mystical 'I'*. London: George Allen & Unwin Ltd.

Griffiths, Bede, 1989. *A New Vision Of Reality*. Springfield (IL): Templegate Publishers.

Haisch, B., 2006. *The God Theory*. SanFrancisco: Weiser Books.

Harvey, A., 1998. *Son of Man: The Mystical Path to Christ*. New York: Penguin Putnam Inc.

Henson, J., 2004. *Good as New: A Radical Retelling of the Scriptures.* Winchester UK: O Books

Henson, J., 2010. *Wide Awake Worship: Hymns and Prayers Renewed for the 21st Century.* Winchester UK: O Books

Jones, C., Wainwright, G., Yarnold, S.J. (eds.), 1986. *The Study of Spirituality*. London: SPCK

Julian of Norwich, 1966. *Revelations of Divine Love*. London: Penguin Books

King, U., 1998. *Christian Mystics*. London: B.T.Batsford.

Laird, M., 2006. *Into the Silent Land – A Guide to the Christian Practice of Meditation*. Oxford: Oxford University Press.

Laszlo, E., 2007. *Science and the Akashic Field.* Rochester: Vermont: Bear & Company.

Lipton B. & Bhaerman S., 2009. *Spontaneous Evolution*. New York: Hay House Inc.

Lipton, B., 2005. *The Biology of Belief.* Santa Rosa: Elite Books

Macquarrie, J., 1966. *Principles of Christian Theology*. London: SCM Press Ltd.

Main, J., 1980. *Word Into Silence*. London: Dartman Longman & Todd Ltd.

Main, J., 1987. *The Inner Christ*. London: Dartman Longman & Todd Ltd.

McGinn, B., Meyendorff, J., Leclerq, J., (eds.), 1989. *Christian Spirituality, Origins to the Twelfth Century*. London: SCM Press Ltd.

McGrath, A.E., 2001. *Christian Theology, An Introduction*. 3rd ed. Oxford: Blackwel Publishing

McTaggart, L., 2001. *The Field – the Quest for the Secret Force of the Universe*. London: Harper Collins.

McTaggart, L., 2007. *The Intention Experiment*. London: Harper Collins.

Merton, T., 1997. *The Wisdom of the Desert.* London: Burns & Oates.

O'Murchu, D., 1997. *Reclaiming Spirituality.* Dublin: Gill & Macmillan.

Pfeiffer, T., Mack, J. (eds), 2007. *Mind Before Matter, Visions of a New Science of Consciousness.* Ropley UK: O Books

Robinson, J.A.T., 1950. *In The End, God...* London: James Clarke & Co. Ltd.

Russell, P., 2009. *Waking Up In Time.* Llandeilo: Cygnus Books.

Scott-Mumby, K., 1999. *Virtual Medicine.* London: Thorsons

Sheldrake, R. & Fox, M., 1996. *Natural Grace.* London: Bloomsbury

Sheldrake, R. Mind, Memory, and Archetype Morphic Resonance and the Collective Unconscious. *Psychological Perspectives* 1987

Sheldrake, R, 1988. *ThePresence of the Past: Morphic resonance and the habits of nature.* London: Collins.

Smith, A.B., 2008. *God, Energy and The Field.* Winchester UK: O Books

Spong, J.S., 1996. *Liberating the Gospels: Reading the Bible with Jewish Eyes.* New York: HarperCollins Publishers

Spong, J.S., 1999. *Why Christianity Must Change or Die: A Bishop Speaks to Believers In Exile.* New York: HarperCollins Publishers

Spong, J.S., 2001. *A New Christianity for a New World: Why Traditional Faith Is Dying and How a New Faith Is Being Born.* San Francisco: HarperCollins Publishers

Tacey, D., 2004. *The Spirituality Revolution.* Hove: Brunner-Routlege

The Findhorn Community, 1976. *The Findhorn Garden: Pioneering a New Vision of Man and Nature in Cooperation.* London: Turnstone Books & Wildwood House Ltd

Tompkins, P. & Bird, C., 1975. *The Secret Life of Plants.* Harmondsworth UK: Penguin Books Ltd

Trevelyan, G., 1981. *Operation Redemption.* Wellingborough:

TurnstonePress Ltd.

Zukav, G., 1979. *The Dancing WuLi Masters – An Overview of the New Physics.* London: Rider/Hutchinson

Index

Circle Books

Circle is a symbol of infinity and unity. It's part of a growing list of imprints, including o-books.net and zero-books.net.

Circle Books aims to publish books in Christian spirituality that are fresh, accessible, and stimulating.

Our books are available in all good English language bookstores worldwide. If you can't find the book on the shelves, then ask your bookstore to order it for you, quoting the ISBN and title. Or, you can order online—all major online retail sites carry our titles.

To see our list of titles, please view www.Circle-Books.com, growing by 80 titles per year.

Authors can learn more about our proposal process by going to our website and clicking on Your Company > Submissions.

We define Christian spirituality as the relationship between the self and its sense of the transcendent or sacred, which issues in literary and artistic expression, community, social activism, and practices. A wide range of disciplines within the field of religious studies can be called upon, including history, narrative studies, philosophy, theology, sociology, and psychology. Interfaith in approach, Circle Books fosters creative dialogue with non-Christian traditions.

And tune into MySpiritRadio.com for our book review radio show, hosted by June-Elleni Laine, where you can listen to authors discussing their books.

MySpiritRadio

Printed and bound by CPI Group (UK) Ltd, Croydon, CR0 4YY